Garfield
life in the
fat lane

BY JIM DAVIS

Ballantine Books Trade Paperbacks • New York

2014 Ballantine Books Trade Paperback Edition

Copyright © 1995, 2014 by PAWS, Inc. All rights reserved.
"GARFIELD" and the GARFIELD characters are trademarks of PAWS, Inc.

Published in the United States by Ballantine Books, an imprint of Random House,
a division of Random House LLC, a Penguin Random House Company, New York.

BALLANTINE and the HOUSE colophon are registered trademarks of Random House LLC.

Originally published in slightly different form in the United States by Ballantine Books,
an imprint of Random House, a division of Random House LLC, in 1995.

ISBN 978-0-345-52600-7
eBook ISBN 978-0-345-54994-5

Printed in the United States of America on acid-free paper

www.ballantinebooks.com

9 8 7 6 5 4 3 2 1

First Colorized Edition

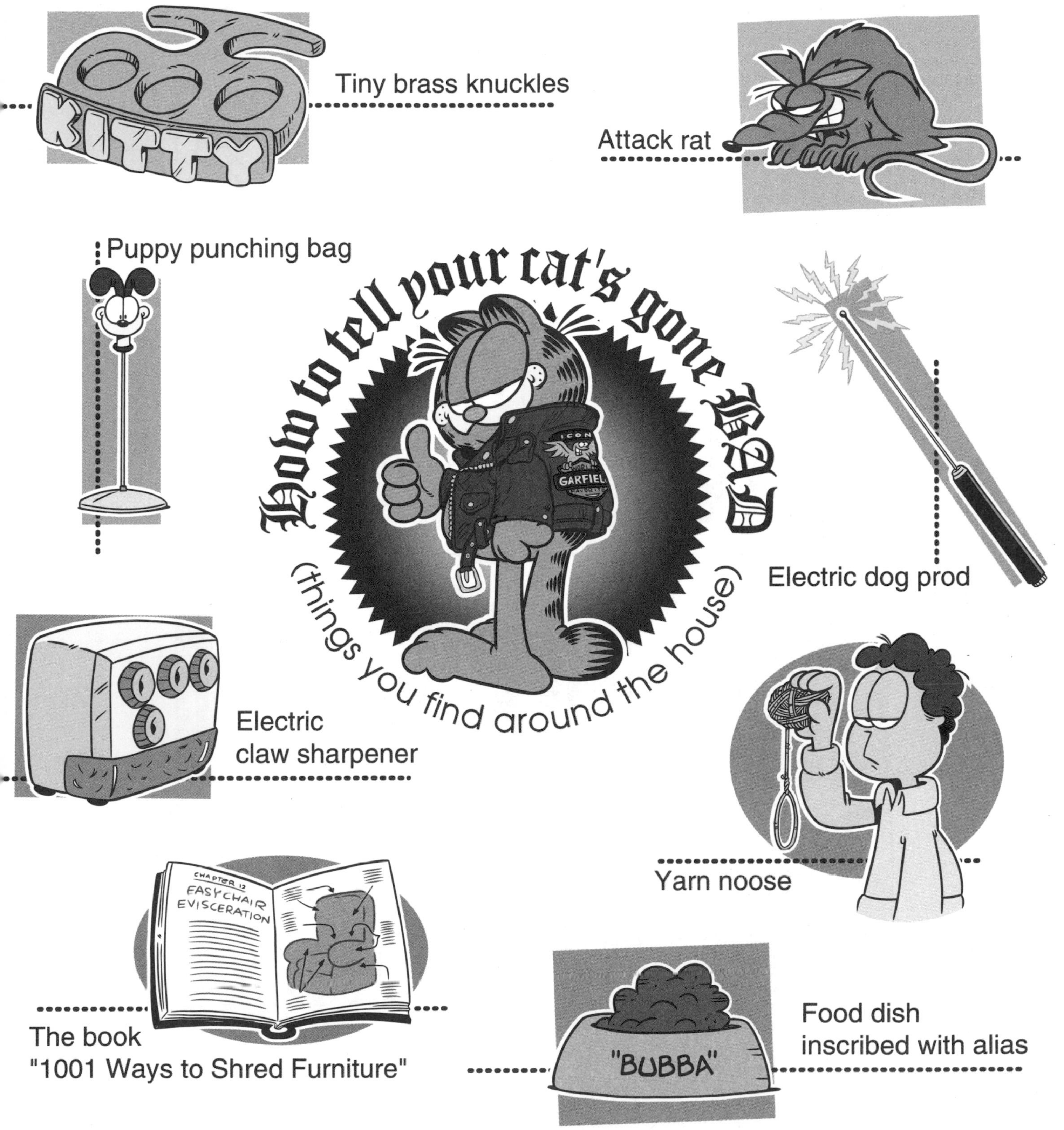
How to tell your cat's gone BAD
(things you find around the house)
KITTY
Tiny brass knuckles
Attack rat
Puppy punching bag
Electric dog prod
Electric
claw sharpener
Yarn noose
CHAPTER 12
EASY CHAIR
EVISCERATION
The book
"1001 Ways to Shred Furniture"
Food dish
inscribed with alias
"BUBBA"

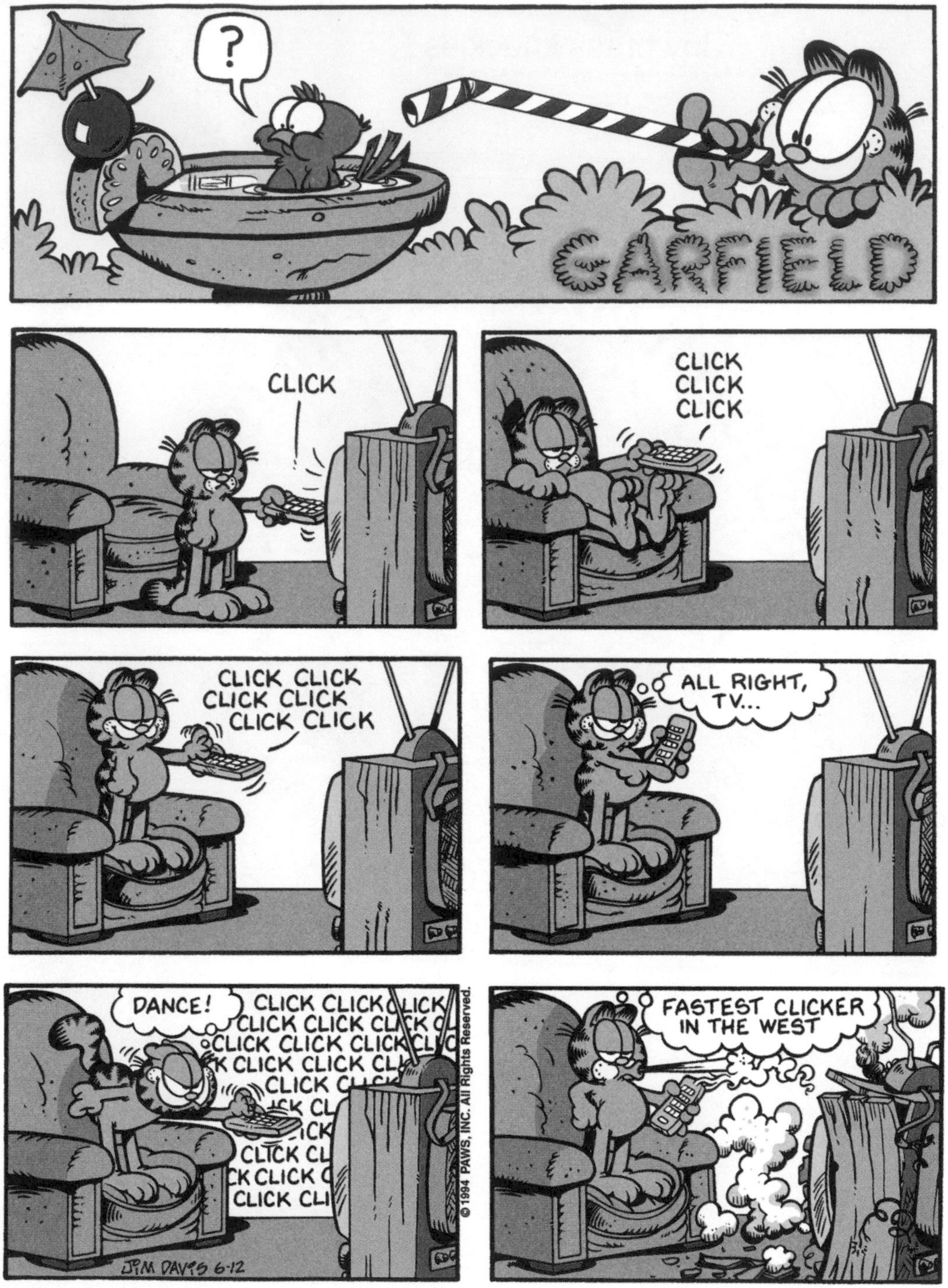
?
GARFIELD
CLICK
CLICK
CLICK
CLICK
CLICK CLICK
CLICK CLICK
CLICK CLICK
ALL RIGHT, TV...
DANCE!
CLICK CLICK CLICK
JIM DAVIS 6-12
© 1994 PAWS, INC. All Rights Reserved.
FASTEST CLICKER IN THE WEST

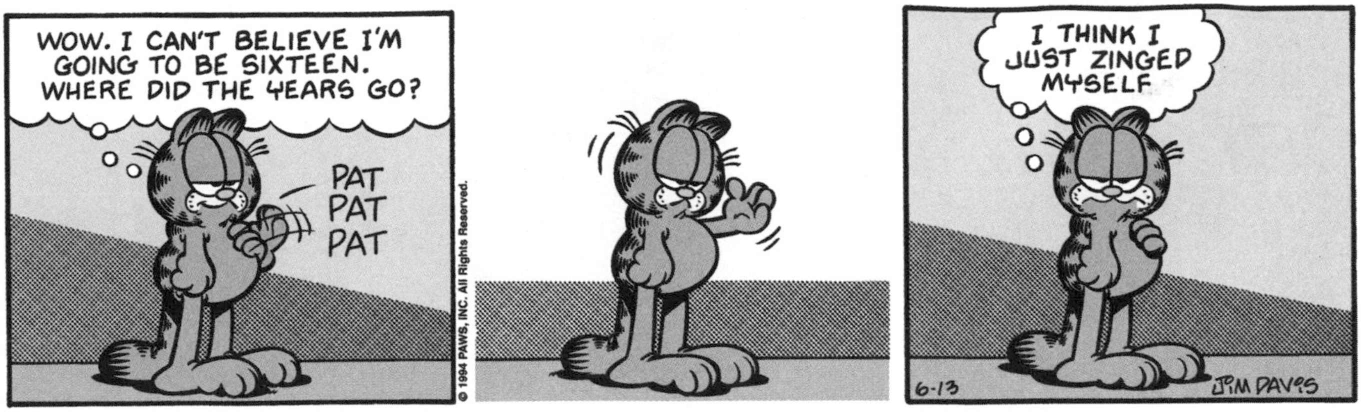
WOW. I CAN'T BELIEVE I'M GOING TO BE SIXTEEN. WHERE DID THE YEARS GO?
PAT PAT PAT
© 1994 PAWS, INC. All Rights Reserved.
I THINK I JUST ZINGED MYSELF
6-13
JIM DAVIS

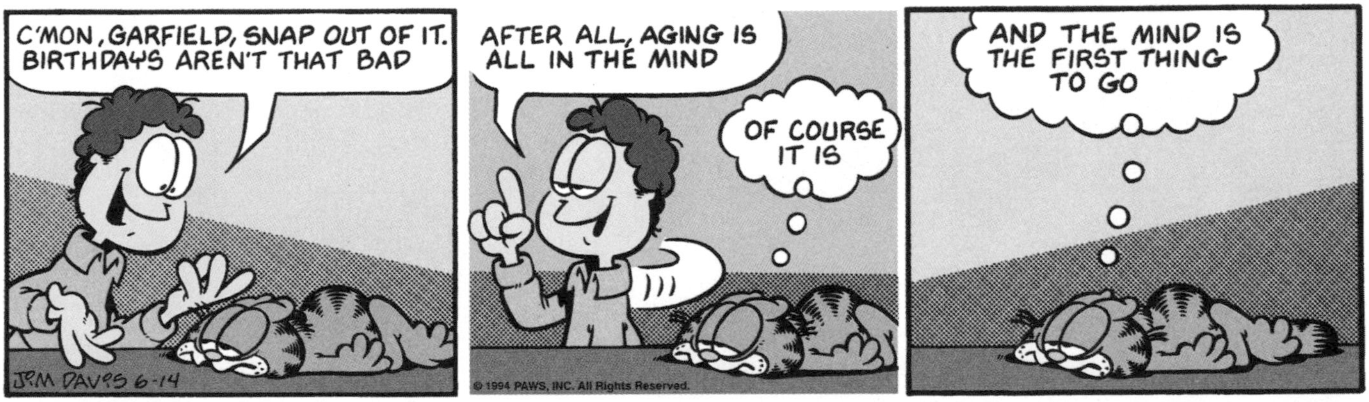
C'MON, GARFIELD, SNAP OUT OF IT. BIRTHDAYS AREN'T THAT BAD
JIM DAVIS 6-14
AFTER ALL, AGING IS ALL IN THE MIND
OF COURSE IT IS
© 1994 PAWS, INC. All Rights Reserved.
AND THE MIND IS THE FIRST THING TO GO

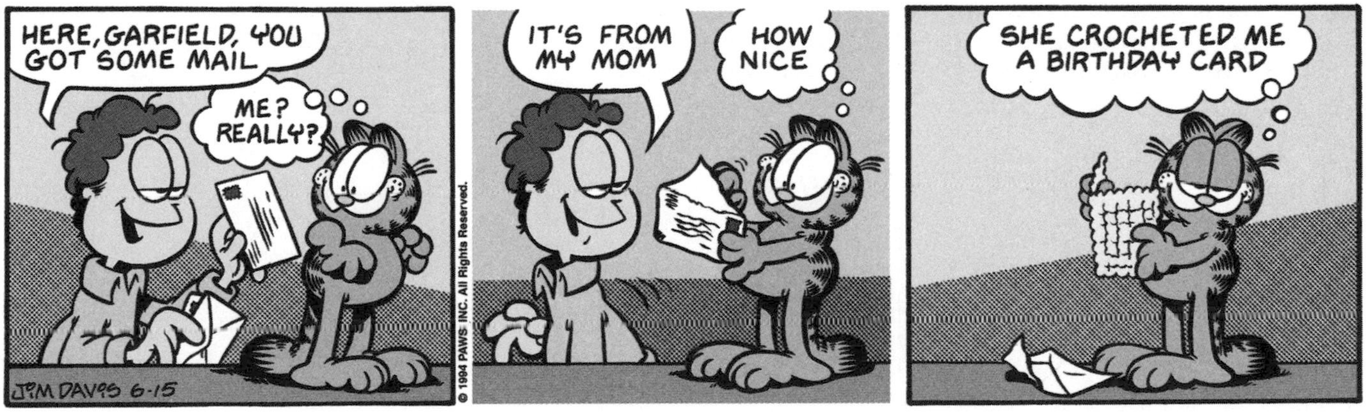
HERE, GARFIELD, YOU GOT SOME MAIL
ME? REALLY?
JIM DAVIS 6-15
© 1994 PAWS, INC. All Rights Reserved.
IT'S FROM MY MOM
HOW NICE
SHE CROCHETED ME A BIRTHDAY CARD

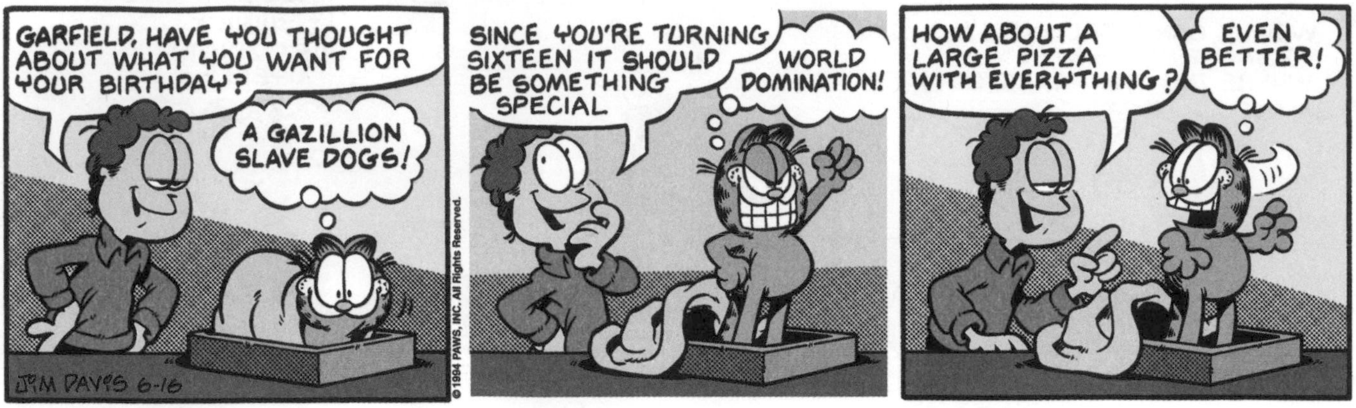
GARFIELD, HAVE YOU THOUGHT ABOUT WHAT YOU WANT FOR YOUR BIRTHDAY?
A GAZILLION SLAVE DOGS!
JIM DAVIS 6-16
© 1994 PAWS, INC. All Rights Reserved.
SINCE YOU'RE TURNING SIXTEEN IT SHOULD BE SOMETHING SPECIAL
WORLD DOMINATION!
HOW ABOUT A LARGE PIZZA WITH EVERYTHING?
EVEN BETTER!

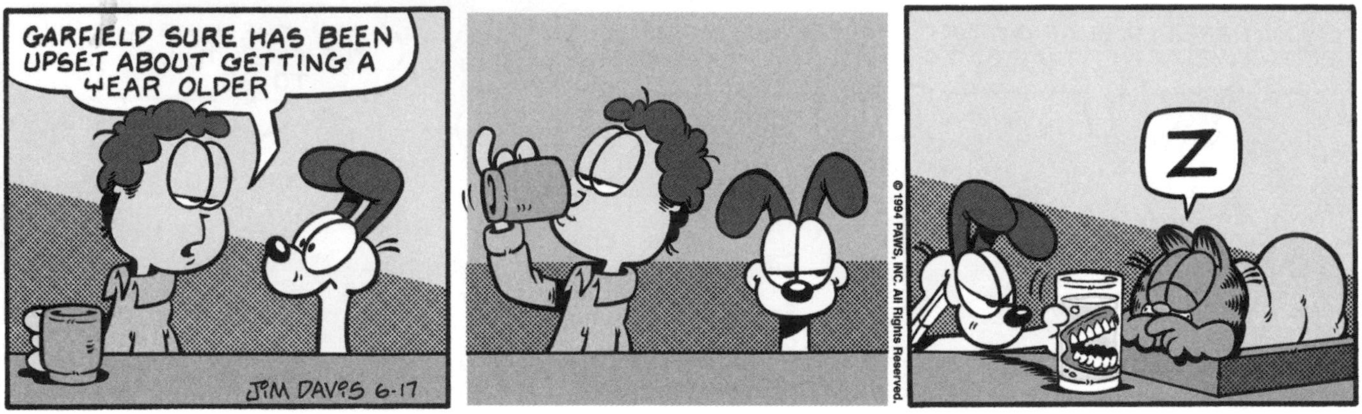
GARFIELD SURE HAS BEEN UPSET ABOUT GETTING A YEAR OLDER
JIM DAVIS 6-17
© 1994 PAWS, INC. All Rights Reserved.
Z

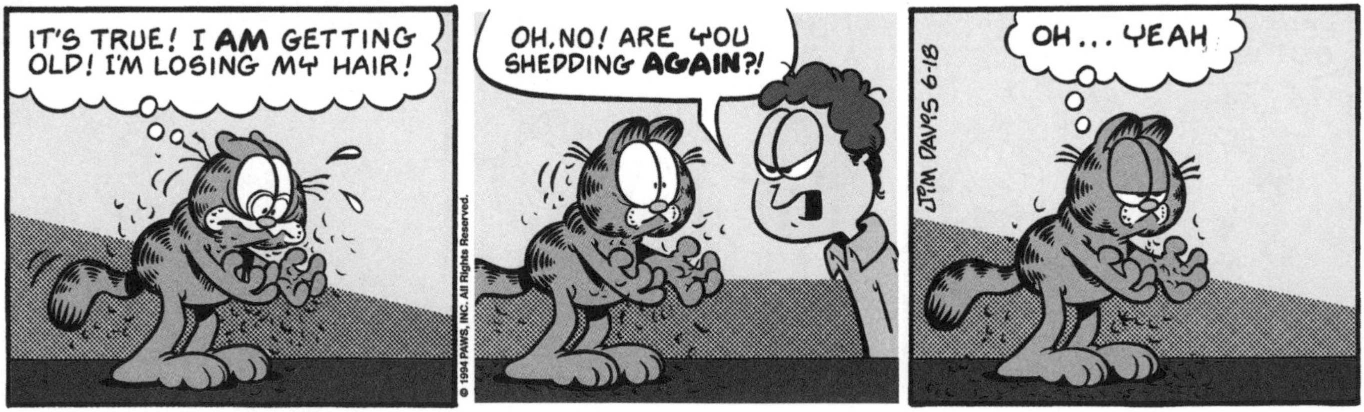
IT'S TRUE! I AM GETTING OLD! I'M LOSING MY HAIR!
© 1994 PAWS, INC. All Rights Reserved.
OH, NO! ARE YOU SHEDDING AGAIN?!
JIM DAVIS 6-18
OH... YEAH

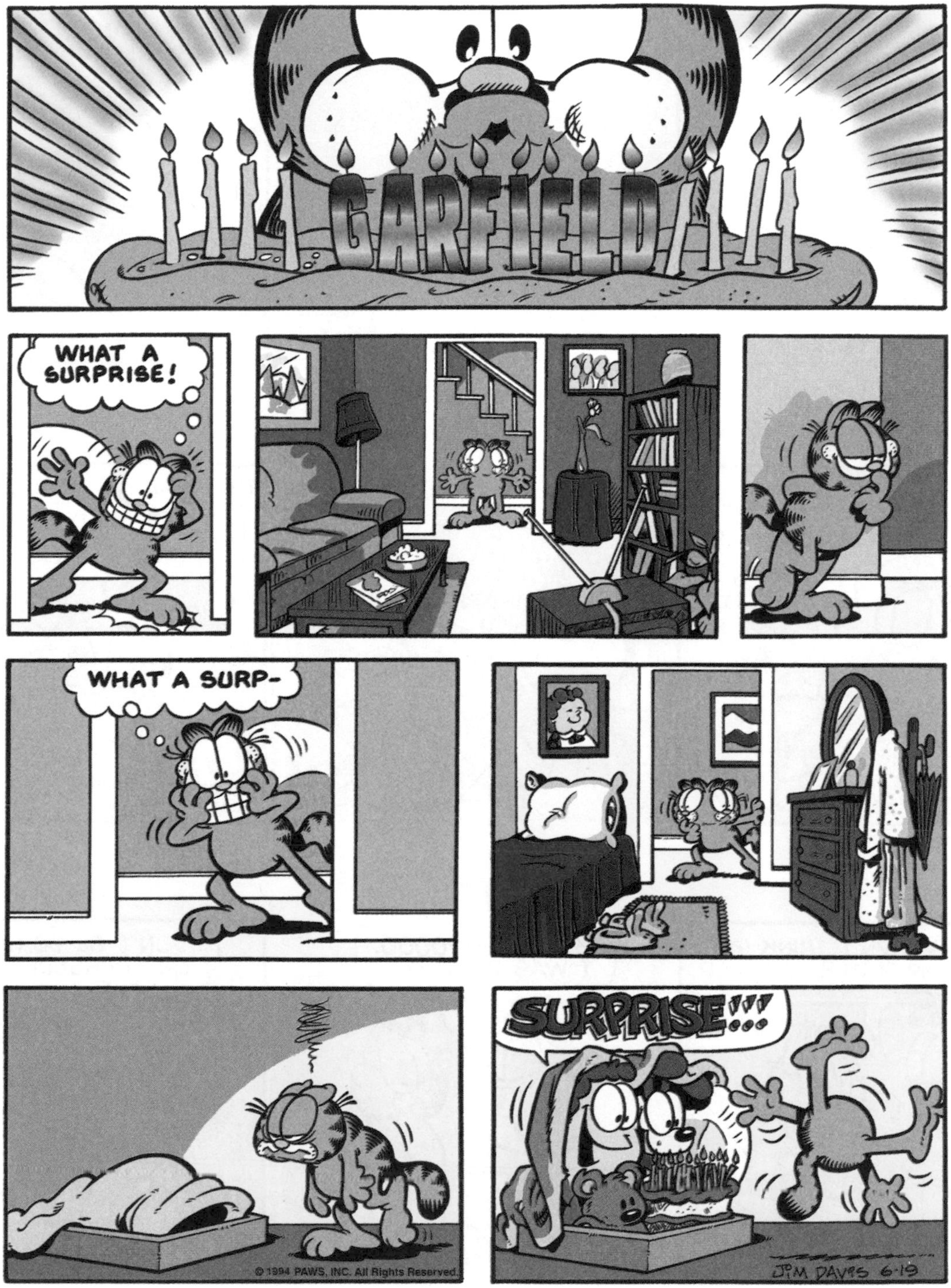
GARFIELD
WHAT A SURPRISE!
WHAT A SURP-
© 1994 PAWS, INC. All Rights Reserved.
SURPRISE!!!...
JIM DAVIS 6-19

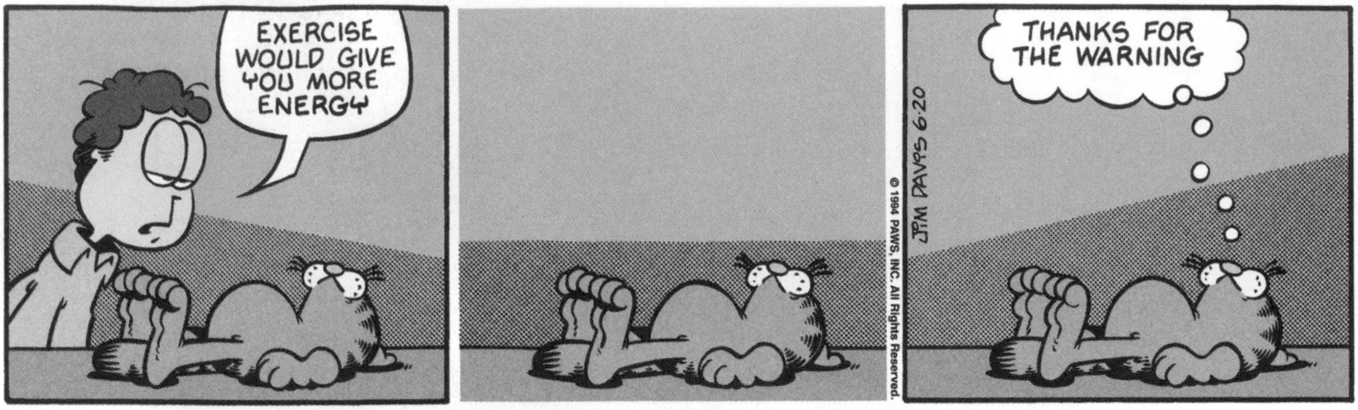
EXERCISE WOULD GIVE YOU MORE ENERGY
THANKS FOR THE WARNING
JIM DAVIS 6-20
© 1994 PAWS, INC. All Rights Reserved.

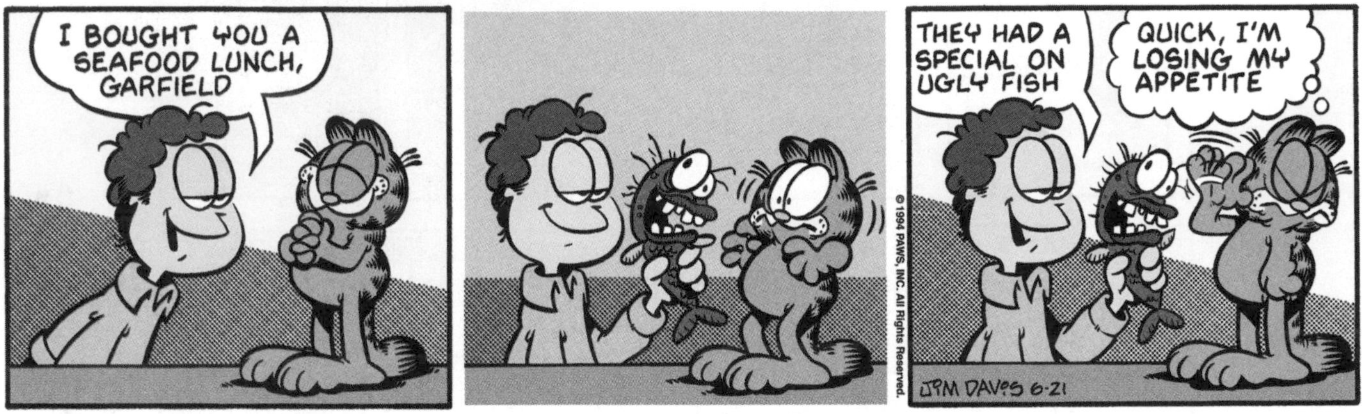
I BOUGHT YOU A SEAFOOD LUNCH, GARFIELD
THEY HAD A SPECIAL ON UGLY FISH
QUICK, I'M LOSING MY APPETITE
JIM DAVIS 6-21
© 1994 PAWS, INC. All Rights Reserved.

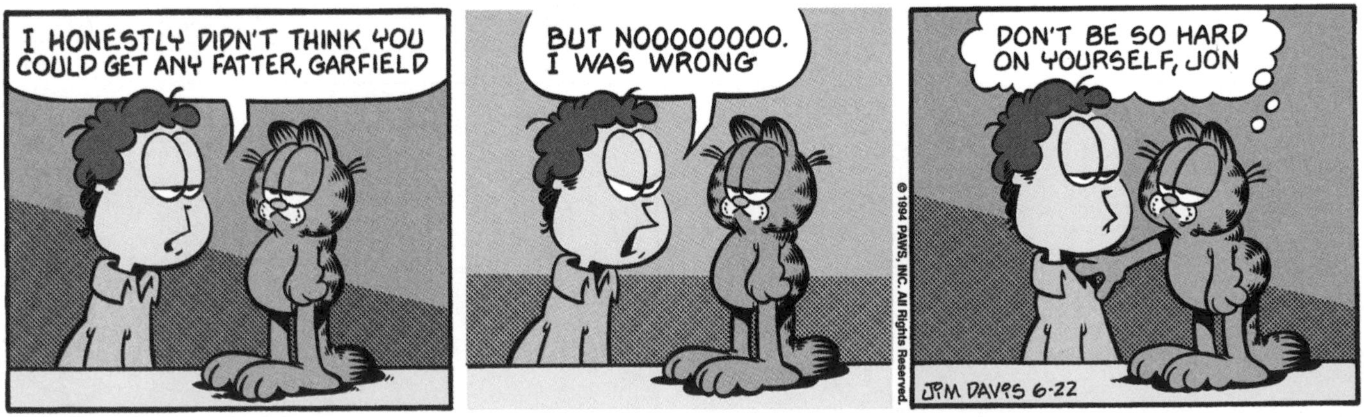
I HONESTLY DIDN'T THINK YOU COULD GET ANY FATTER, GARFIELD
BUT NOOOOOOOO. I WAS WRONG
DON'T BE SO HARD ON YOURSELF, JON
JIM DAVIS 6-22
© 1994 PAWS, INC. All Rights Reserved.

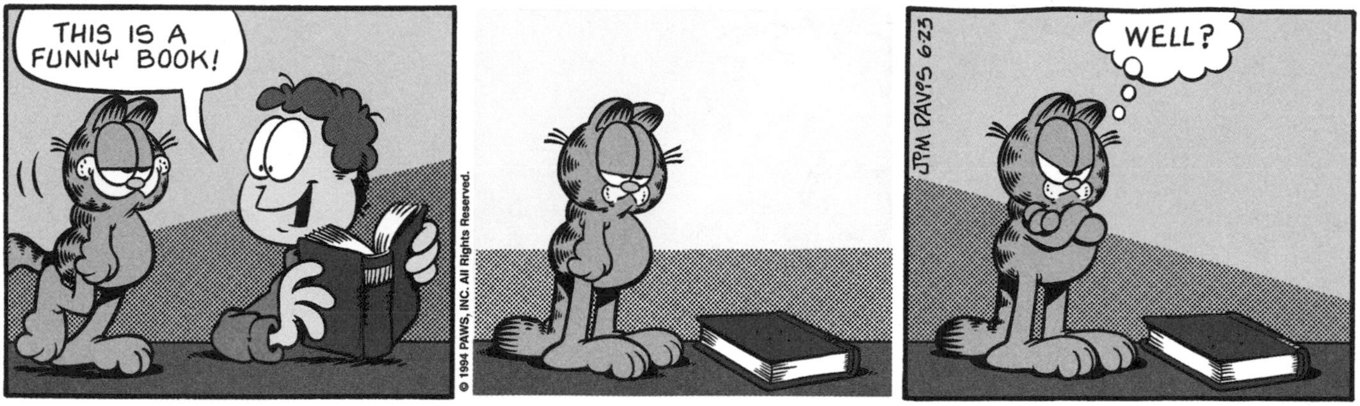
THIS IS A FUNNY BOOK!
© 1994 PAWS, INC. All Rights Reserved.
JIM DAVIS 6-23
WELL?

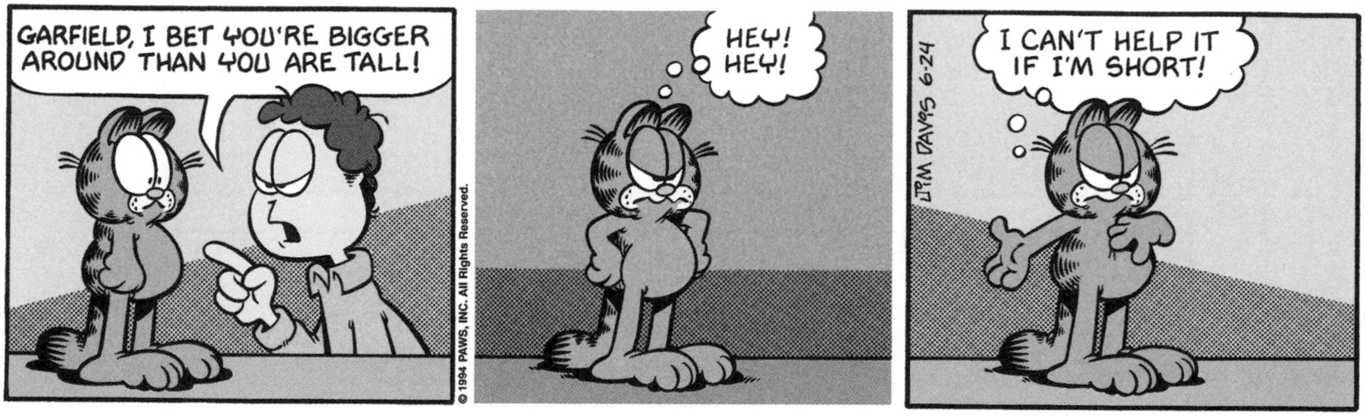
GARFIELD, I BET YOU'RE BIGGER AROUND THAN YOU ARE TALL!
© 1994 PAWS, INC. All Rights Reserved.
HEY! HEY!
JIM DAVIS 6-24
I CAN'T HELP IT IF I'M SHORT!

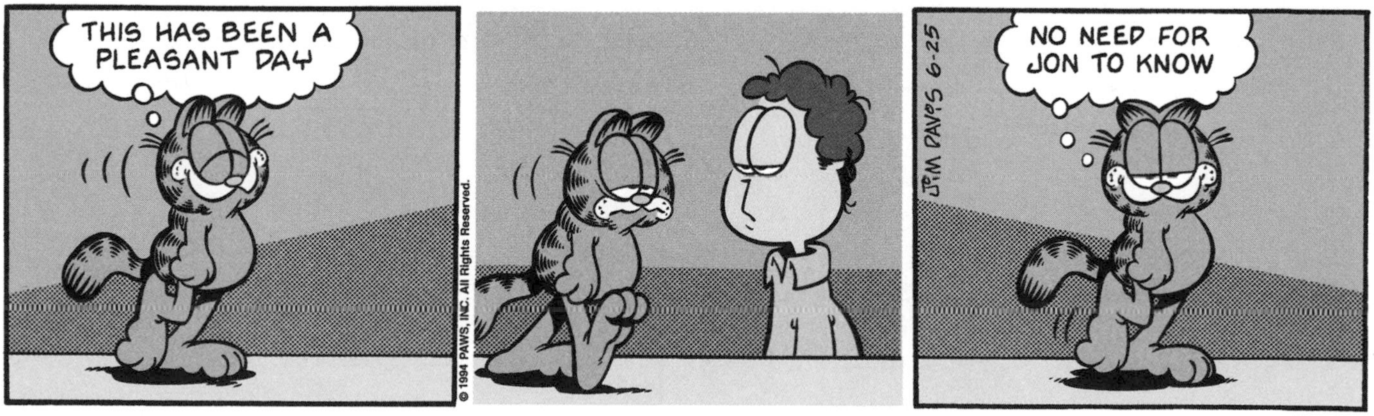
THIS HAS BEEN A PLEASANT DAY
© 1994 PAWS, INC. All Rights Reserved.
JIM DAVIS 6-25
NO NEED FOR JON TO KNOW

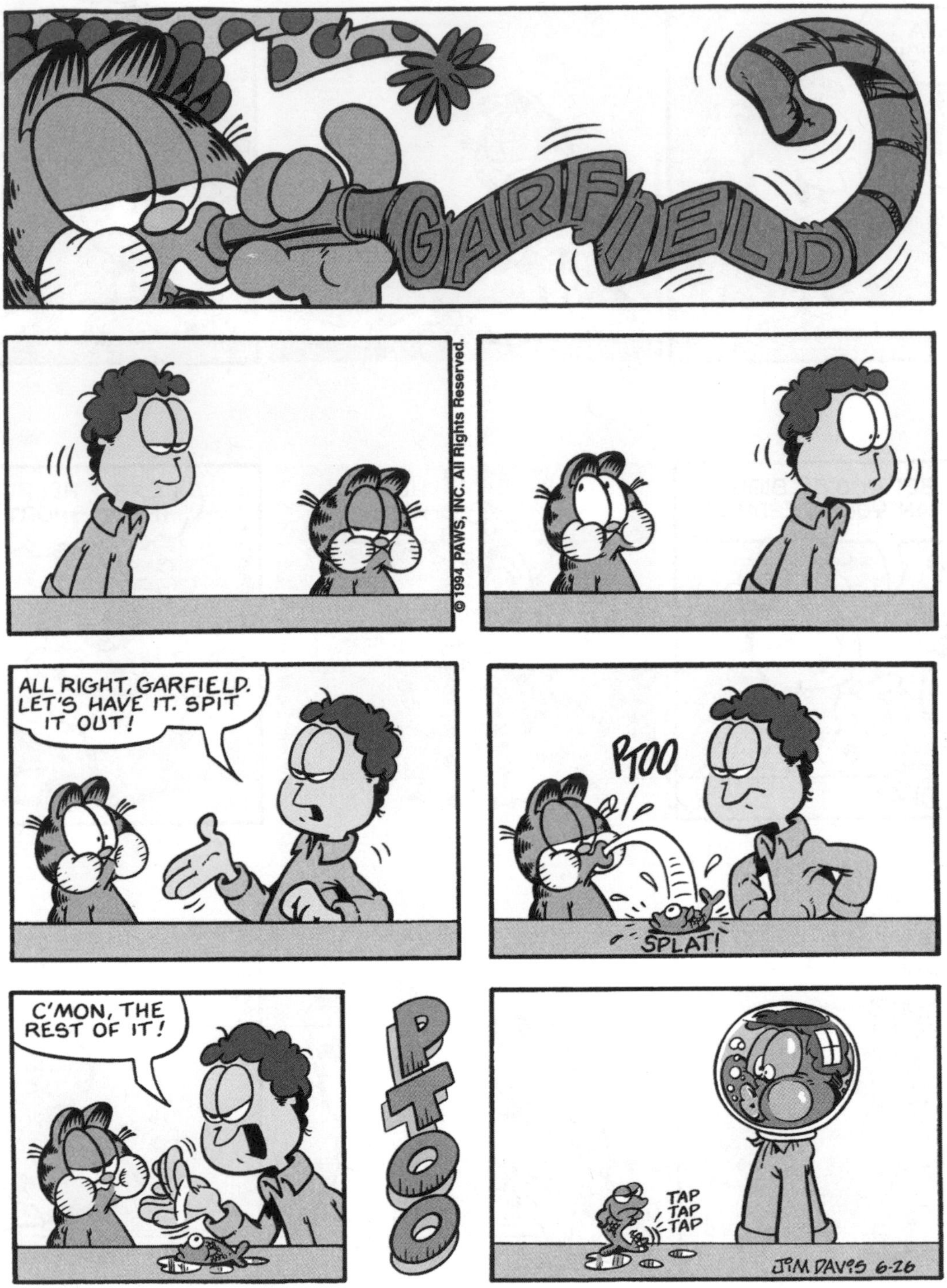
GARFIELD
© 1994 PAWS, INC. All Rights Reserved.
ALL RIGHT, GARFIELD. LET'S HAVE IT. SPIT IT OUT!
PTOO
SPLAT!
C'MON, THE REST OF IT!
PTOO
TAP TAP TAP
JIM DAVIS 6-26

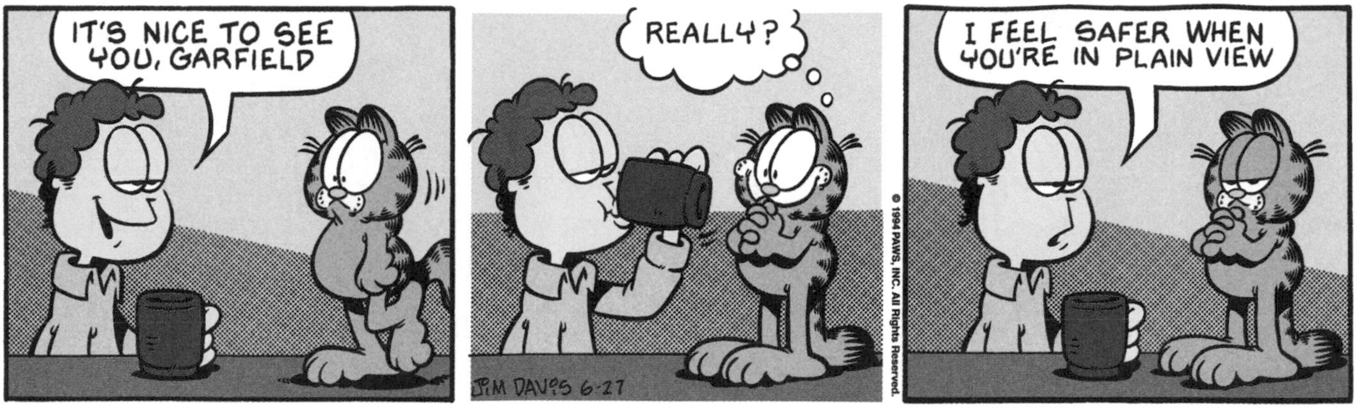
IT'S NICE TO SEE YOU, GARFIELD
REALLY?
I FEEL SAFER WHEN YOU'RE IN PLAIN VIEW
JIM DAVIS 6-27
© 1994 PAWS, INC. All Rights Reserved.

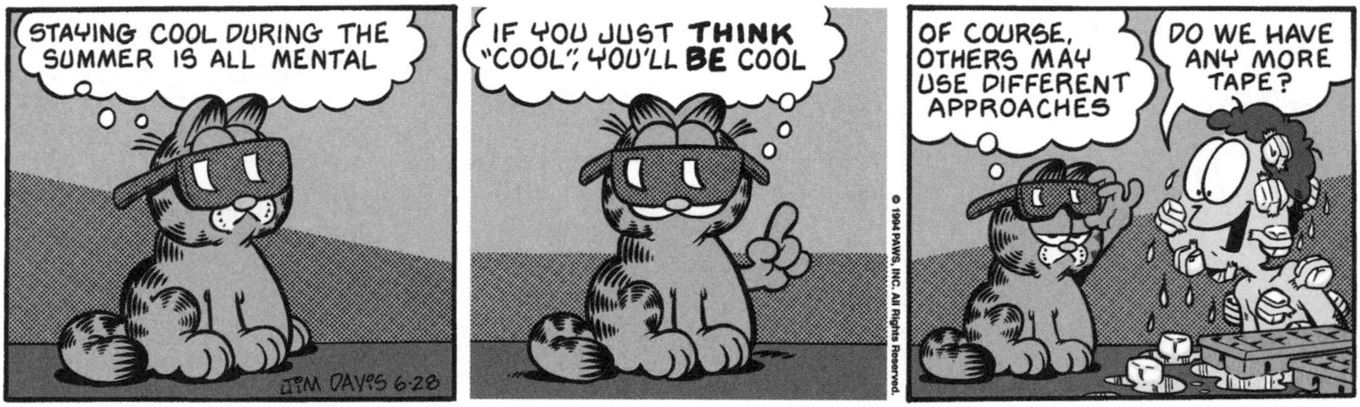
STAYING COOL DURING THE SUMMER IS ALL MENTAL
IF YOU JUST **THINK** "COOL", YOU'LL **BE** COOL
OF COURSE, OTHERS MAY USE DIFFERENT APPROACHES
DO WE HAVE ANY MORE TAPE?
JIM DAVIS 6-28
© 1994 PAWS, INC. All Rights Reserved.

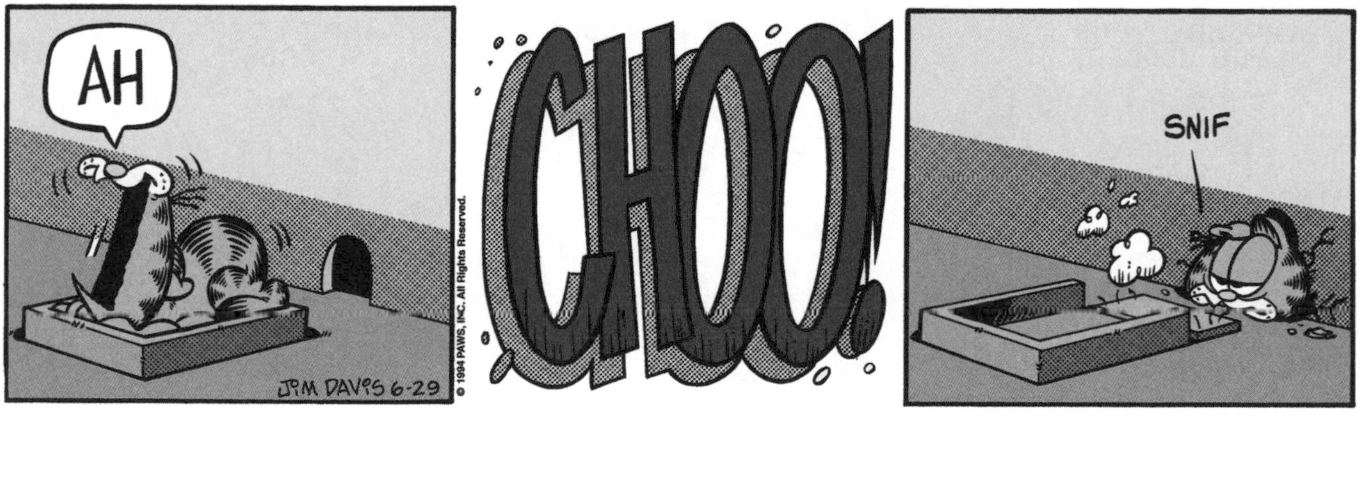
AH
CHOO!
SNIF
JIM DAVIS 6-29
© 1994 PAWS, INC. All Rights Reserved.

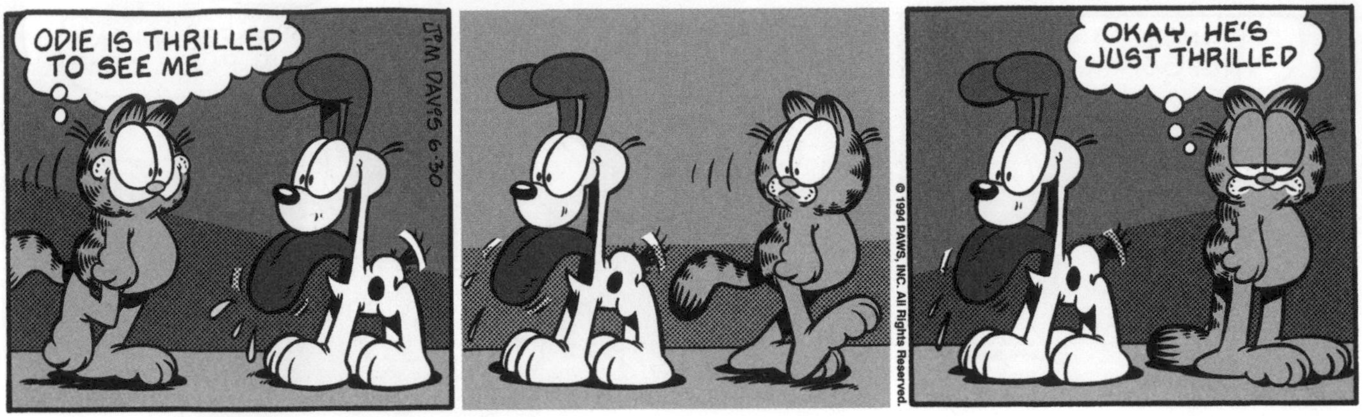
ODIE IS THRILLED TO SEE ME
JIM DAVIS 6-30
© 1994 PAWS, INC. All Rights Reserved.
OKAY, HE'S JUST THRILLED

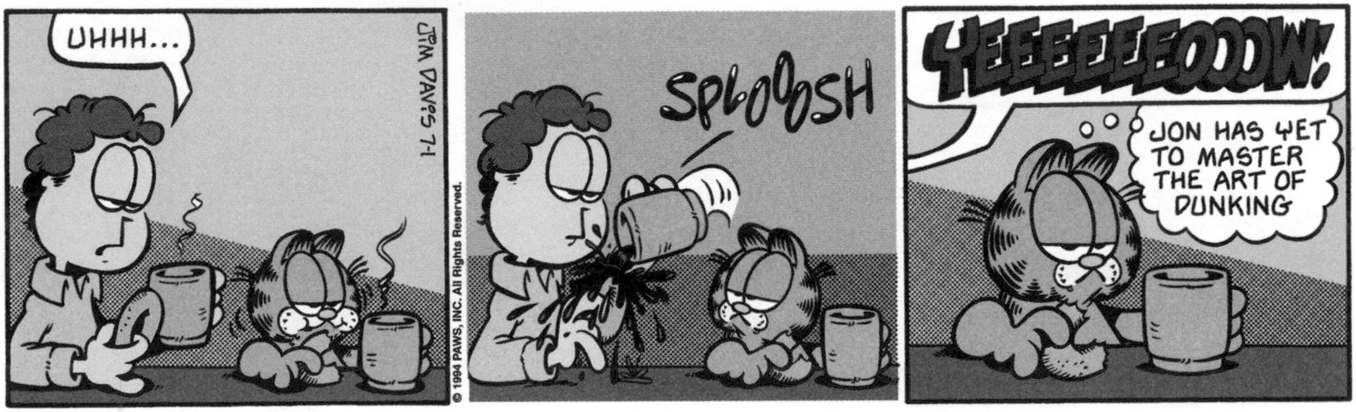
UHHH...
JIM DAVIS 7-1
© 1994 PAWS, INC. All Rights Reserved.
SPLOOOSH
YEEEEEEOOOW!
JON HAS YET TO MASTER THE ART OF DUNKING

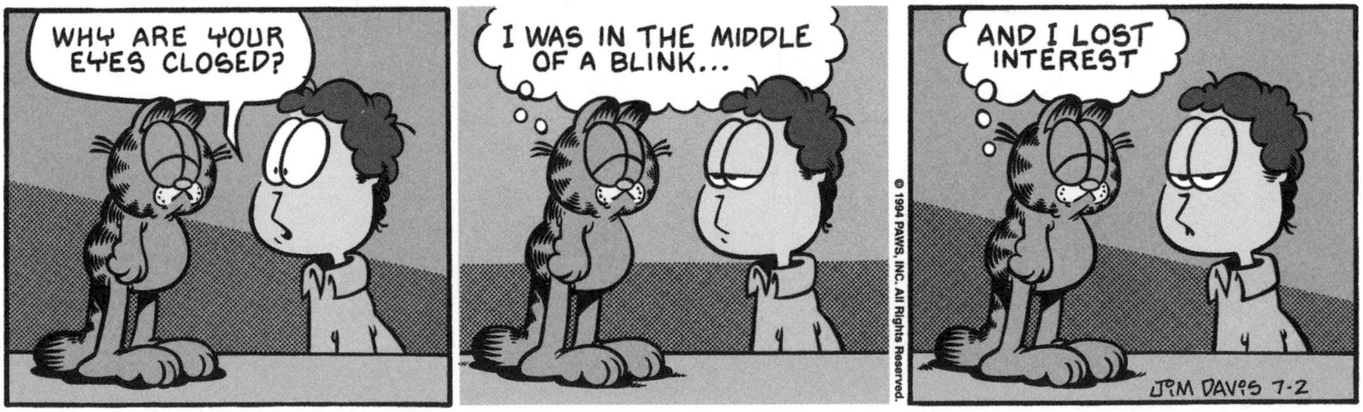
WHY ARE YOUR EYES CLOSED?
I WAS IN THE MIDDLE OF A BLINK...
© 1994 PAWS, INC. All Rights Reserved.
AND I LOST INTEREST
JIM DAVIS 7-2

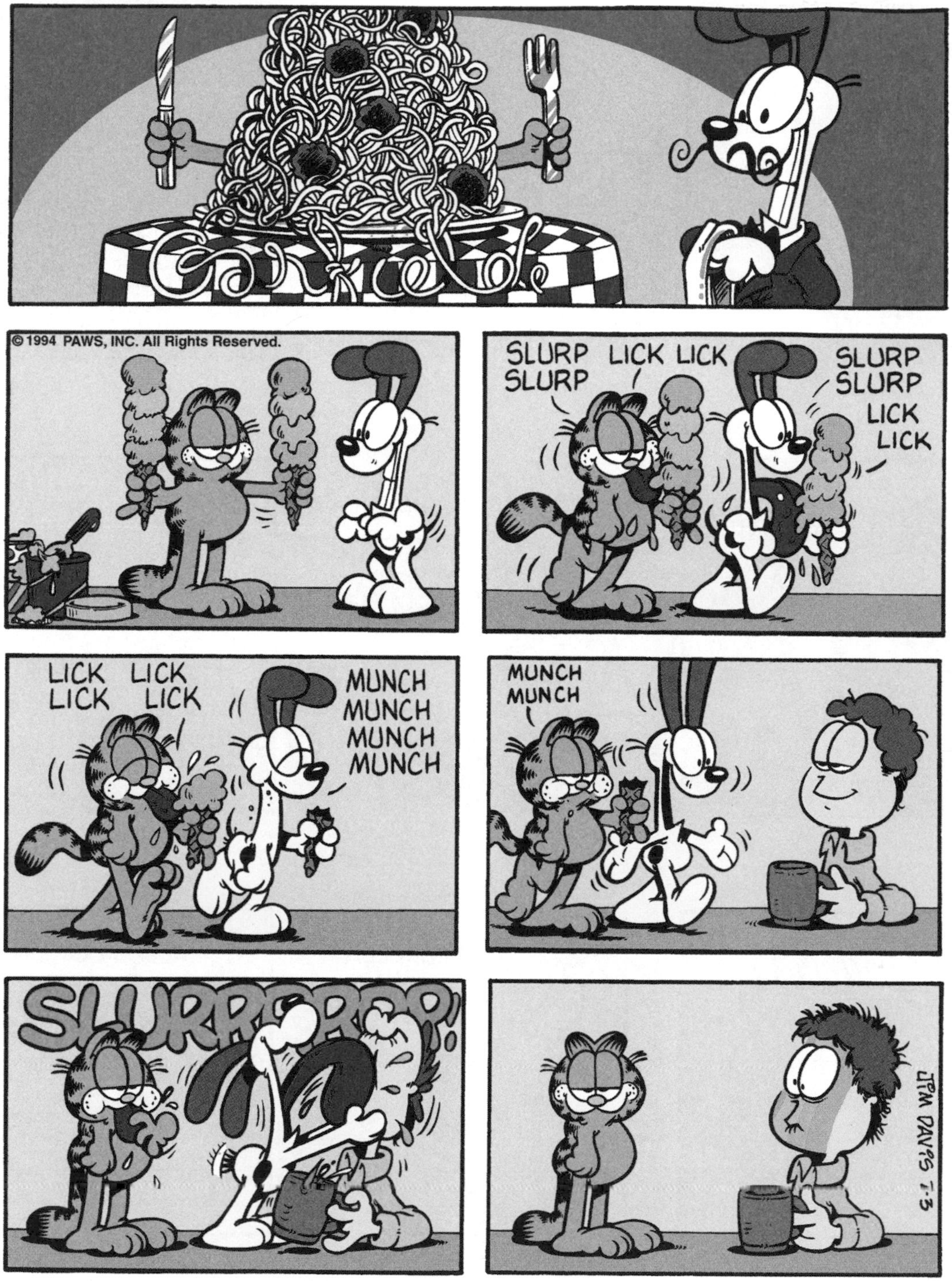
© 1994 PAWS, INC. All Rights Reserved.
SLURP SLURP
LICK LICK
SLURP SLURP
LICK LICK
LICK LICK
LICK LICK
MUNCH MUNCH MUNCH MUNCH
MUNCH MUNCH
SLURRRRRP!
JIM DAVIS 7-3

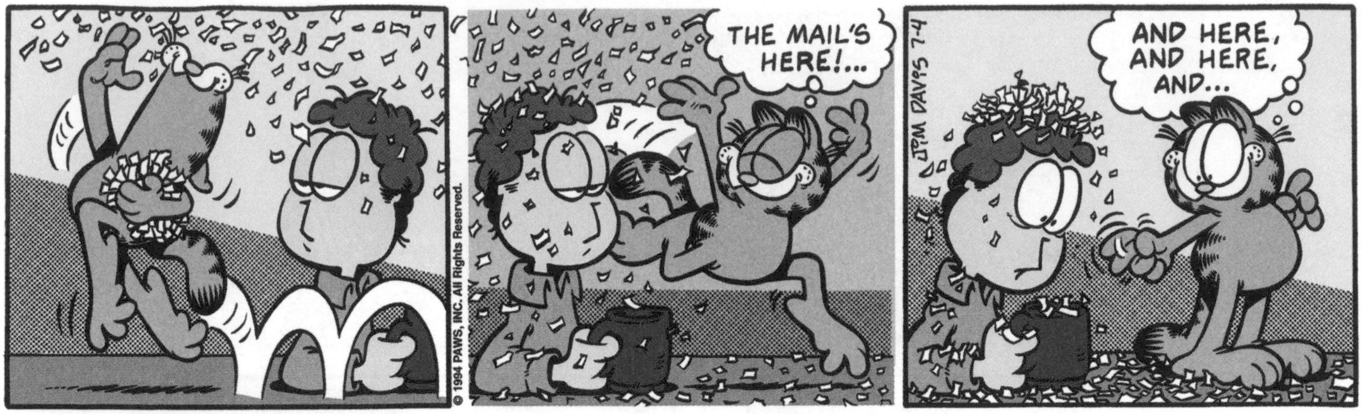
© 1994 PAWS, INC. All Rights Reserved.
THE MAIL'S HERE!...
JIM DAVIS 7-4
AND HERE, AND HERE, AND...

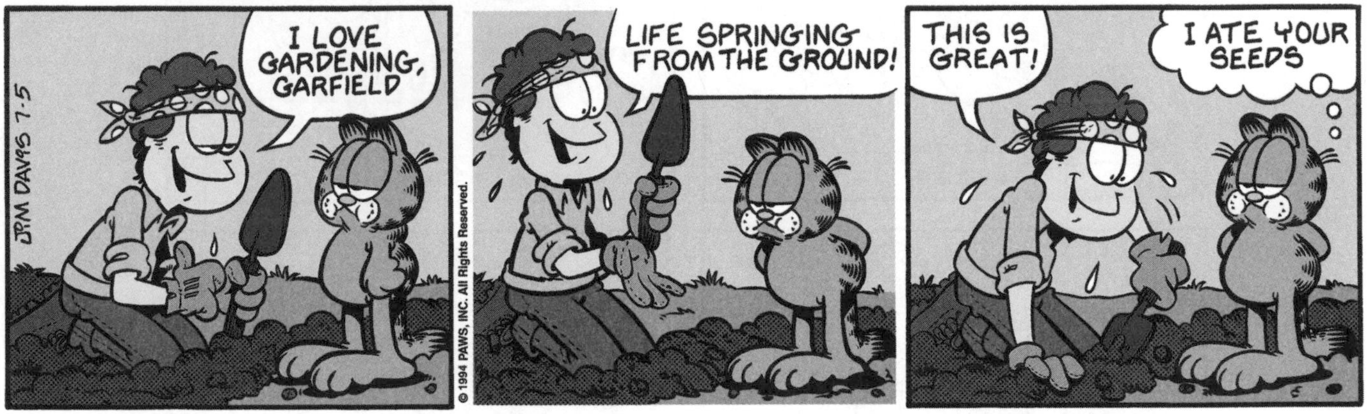
JIM DAVIS 7-5
I LOVE GARDENING, GARFIELD
© 1994 PAWS, INC. All Rights Reserved.
LIFE SPRINGING FROM THE GROUND!
THIS IS GREAT!
I ATE YOUR SEEDS

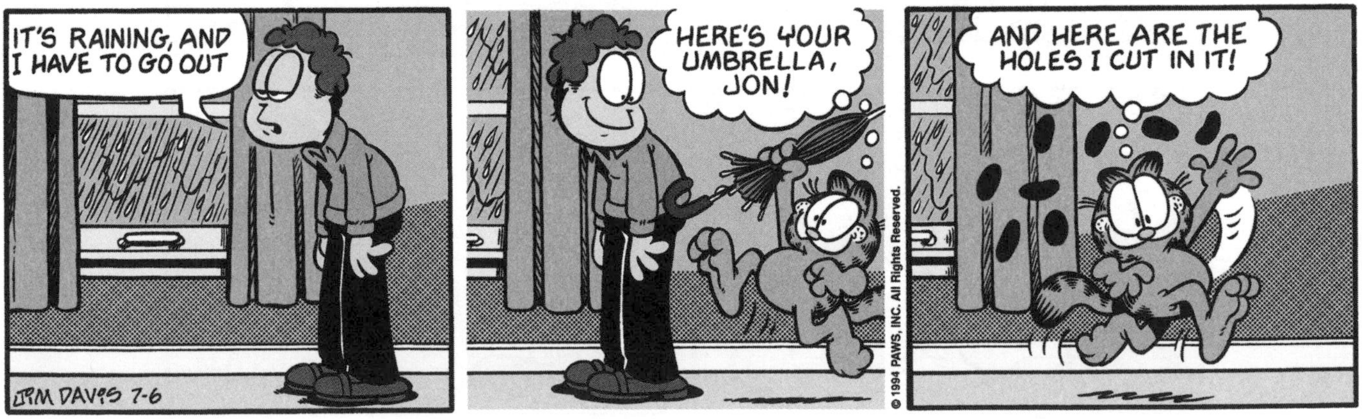
IT'S RAINING, AND I HAVE TO GO OUT
JIM DAVIS 7-6
HERE'S YOUR UMBRELLA, JON!
© 1994 PAWS, INC. All Rights Reserved.
AND HERE ARE THE HOLES I CUT IN IT!

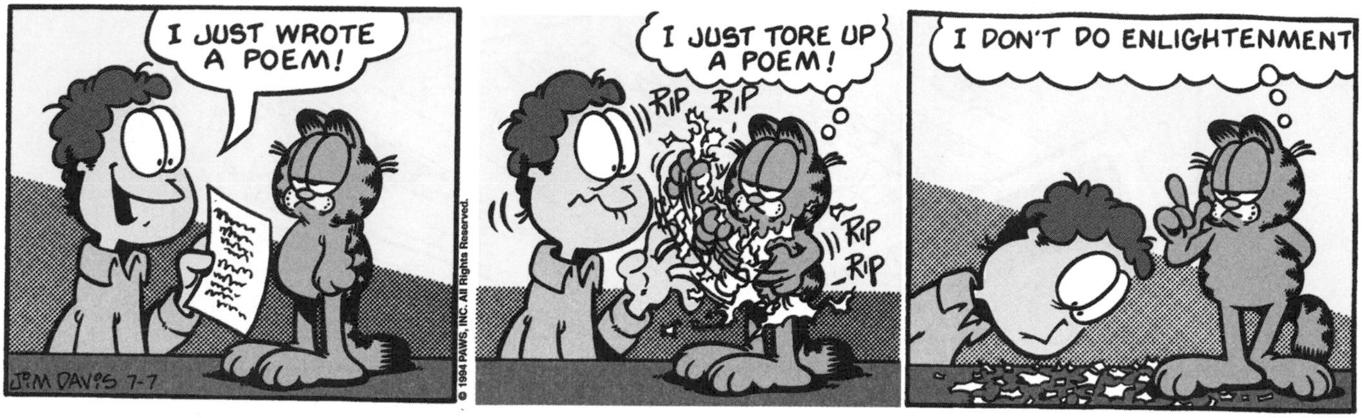
I JUST WROTE A POEM!
JIM DAVIS 7-7
© 1994 PAWS, INC. All Rights Reserved.
I JUST TORE UP A POEM!
RIP RIP
RIP
RIP
I DON'T DO ENLIGHTENMENT

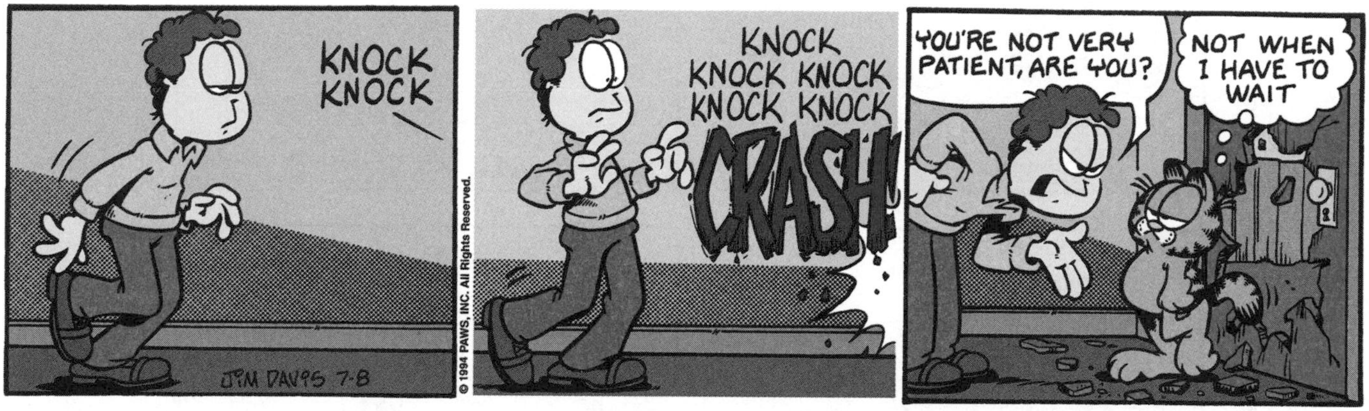
KNOCK KNOCK
JIM DAVIS 7-8
© 1994 PAWS, INC. All Rights Reserved.
KNOCK KNOCK KNOCK KNOCK KNOCK
CRASH!
YOU'RE NOT VERY PATIENT, ARE YOU?
NOT WHEN I HAVE TO WAIT

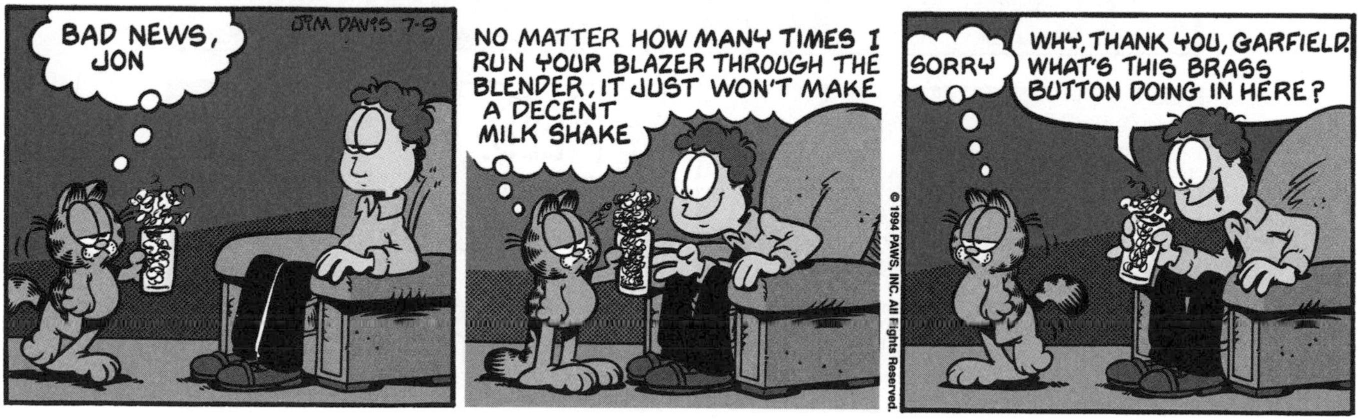
BAD NEWS, JON
JIM DAVIS 7-9
NO MATTER HOW MANY TIMES I RUN YOUR BLAZER THROUGH THE BLENDER, IT JUST WON'T MAKE A DECENT MILK SHAKE
© 1994 PAWS, INC. All Rights Reserved.
SORRY
WHY, THANK YOU, GARFIELD. WHAT'S THIS BRASS BUTTON DOING IN HERE?

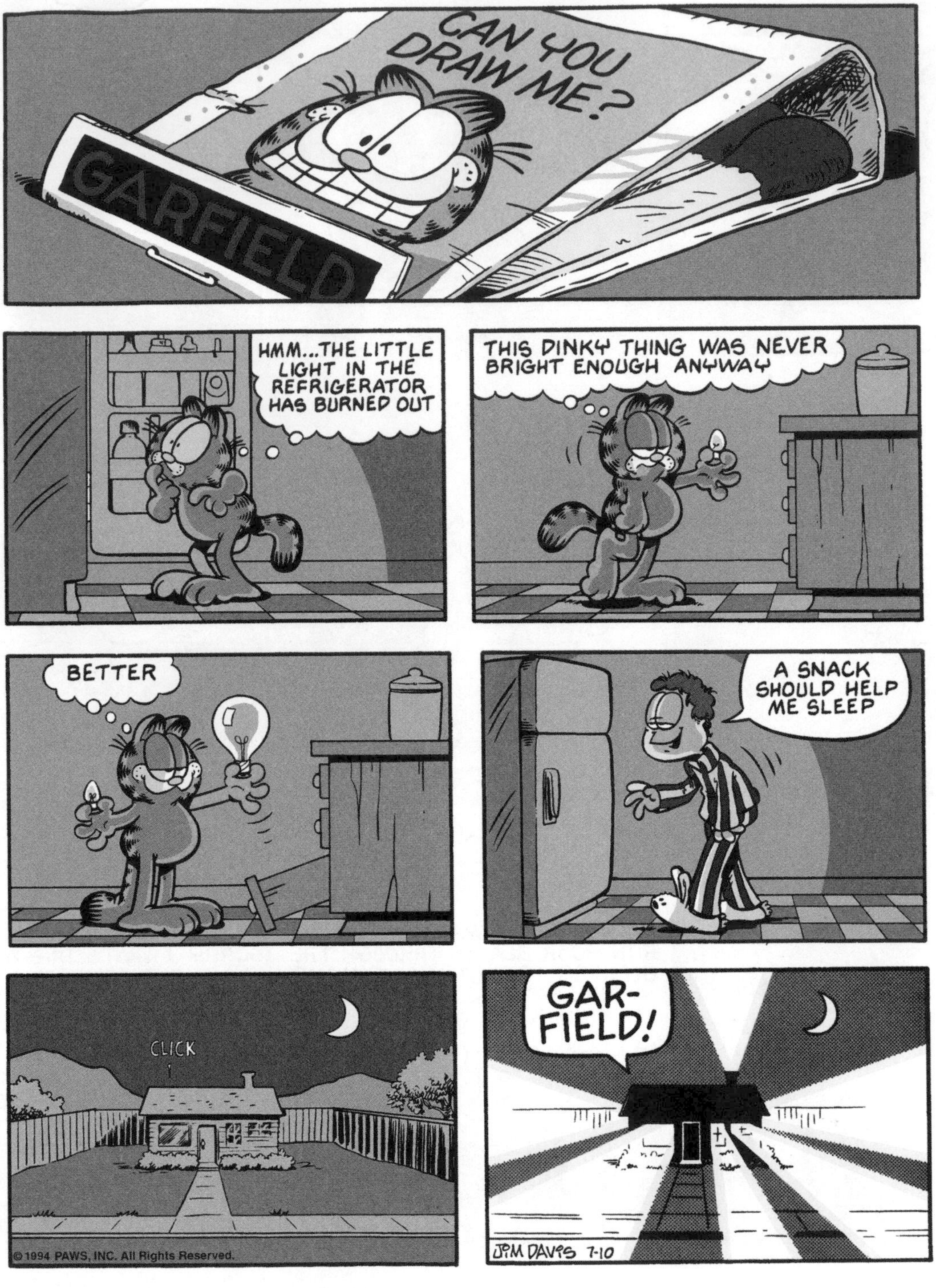
CAN YOU DRAW ME?
GARFIELD
HMM...THE LITTLE LIGHT IN THE REFRIGERATOR HAS BURNED OUT
THIS DINKY THING WAS NEVER BRIGHT ENOUGH ANYWAY
BETTER
A SNACK SHOULD HELP ME SLEEP
CLICK
GAR-FIELD!
JIM DAVIS 7-10

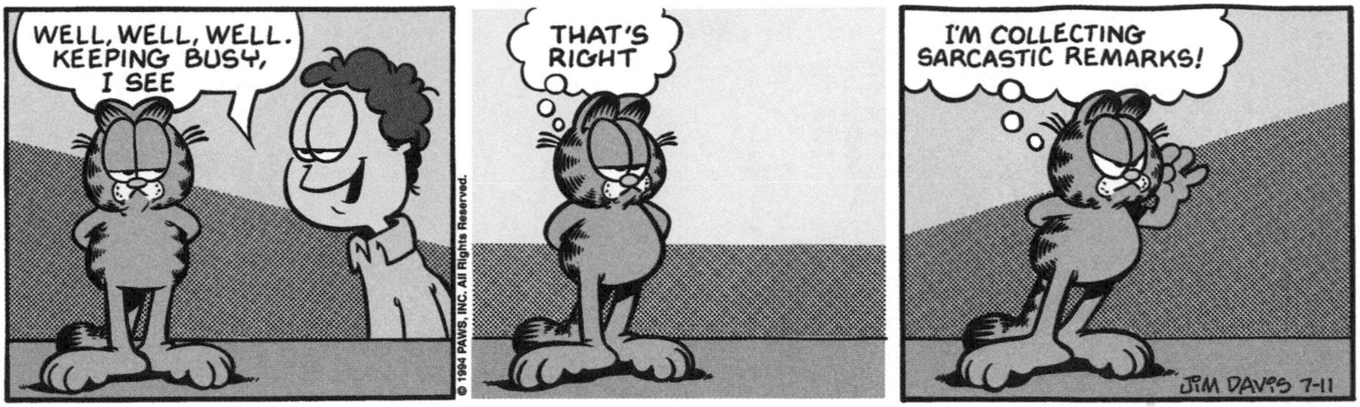
WELL, WELL, WELL. KEEPING BUSY, I SEE
THAT'S RIGHT
I'M COLLECTING SARCASTIC REMARKS!
© 1994 PAWS, INC. All Rights Reserved.
JIM DAVIS 7-11

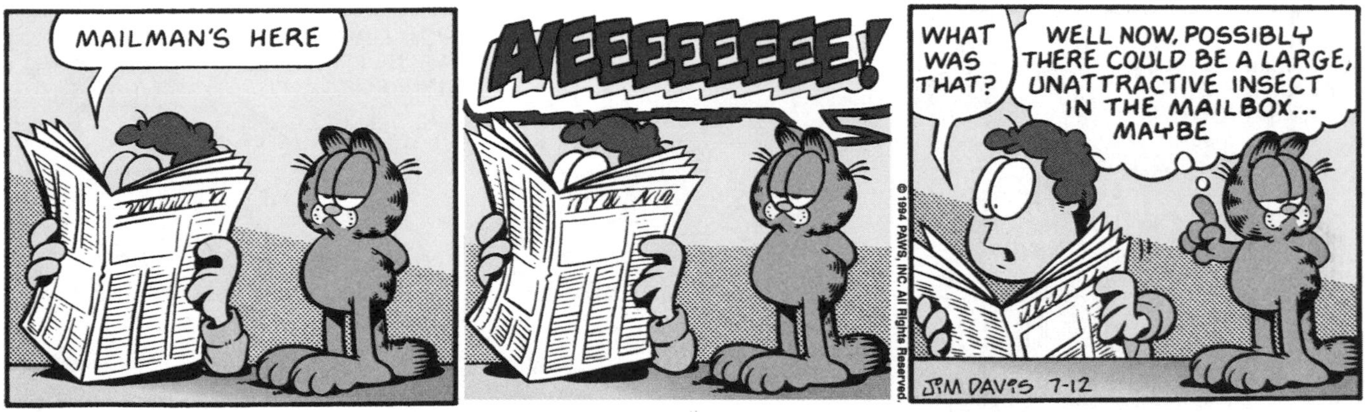
MAILMAN'S HERE
AIEEEEEEEEE!
WHAT WAS THAT?
WELL NOW, POSSIBLY THERE COULD BE A LARGE, UNATTRACTIVE INSECT IN THE MAILBOX... MAYBE
© 1994 PAWS, INC. All Rights Reserved.
JIM DAVIS 7-12

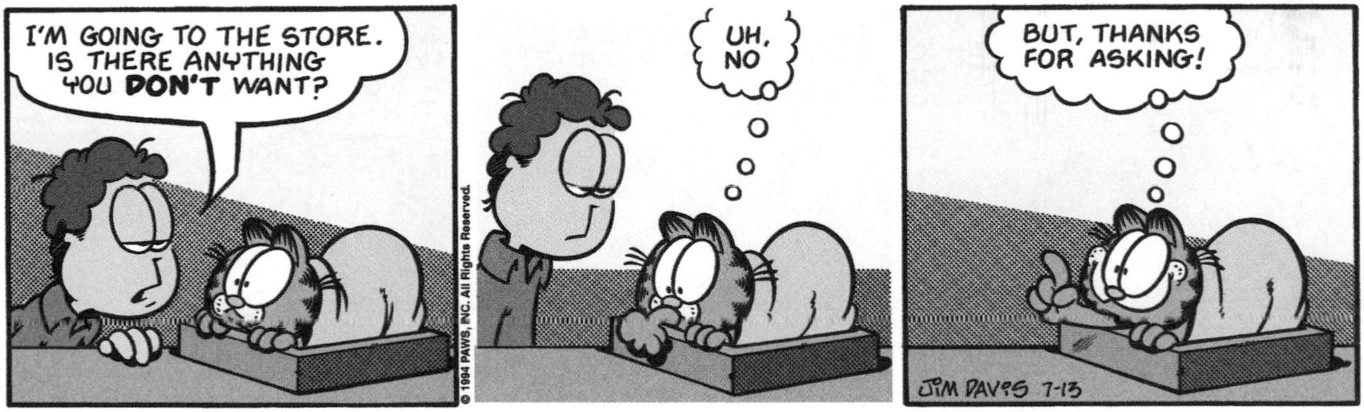
I'M GOING TO THE STORE. IS THERE ANYTHING YOU **DON'T** WANT?
UH, NO
BUT, THANKS FOR ASKING!
© 1994 PAWS, INC. All Rights Reserved.
JIM DAVIS 7-13

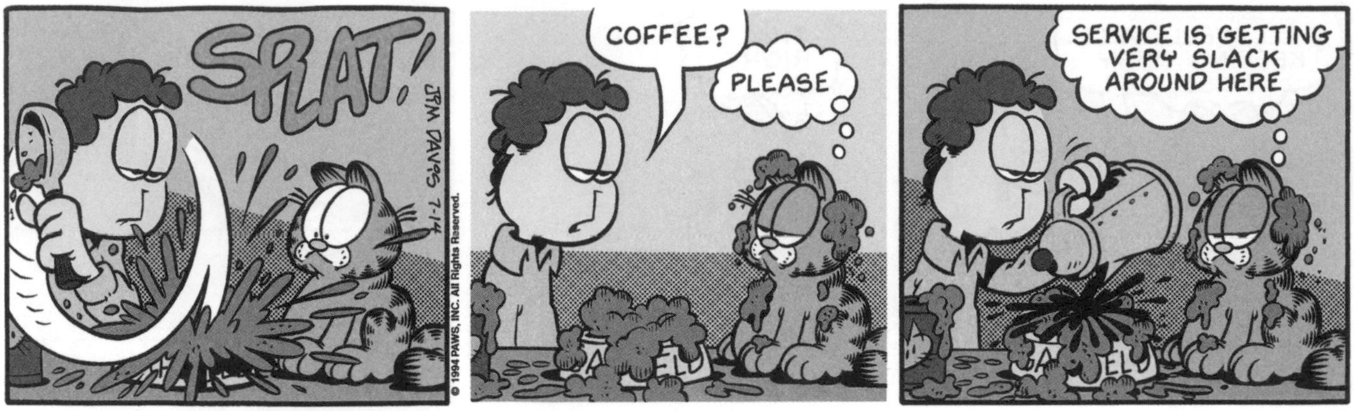
SPLAT!
JIM DAVIS 7-14
© 1994 PAWS, INC. All Rights Reserved.
COFFEE?
PLEASE
SERVICE IS GETTING VERY SLACK AROUND HERE

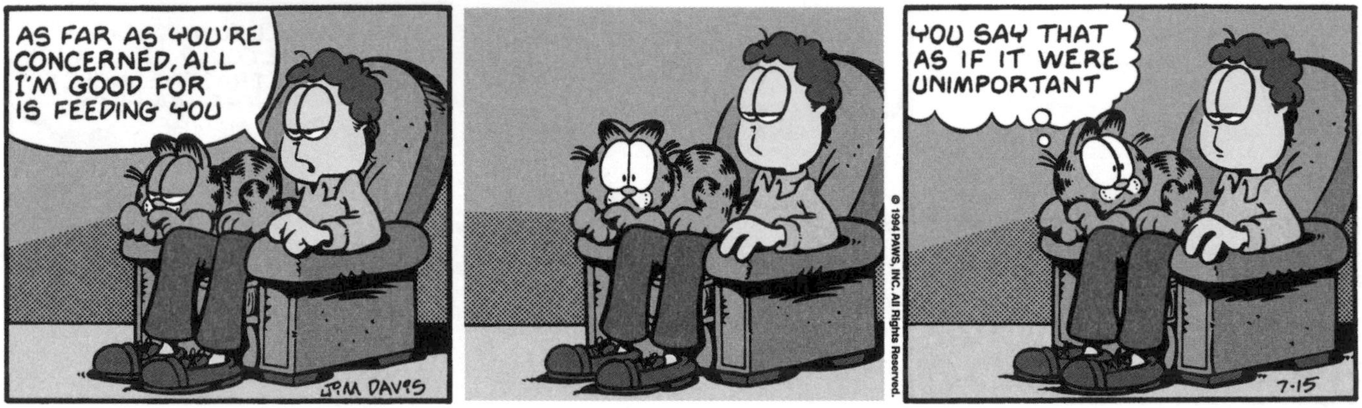
AS FAR AS YOU'RE CONCERNED, ALL I'M GOOD FOR IS FEEDING YOU
JIM DAVIS
© 1994 PAWS, INC. All Rights Reserved.
YOU SAY THAT AS IF IT WERE UNIMPORTANT
7-15

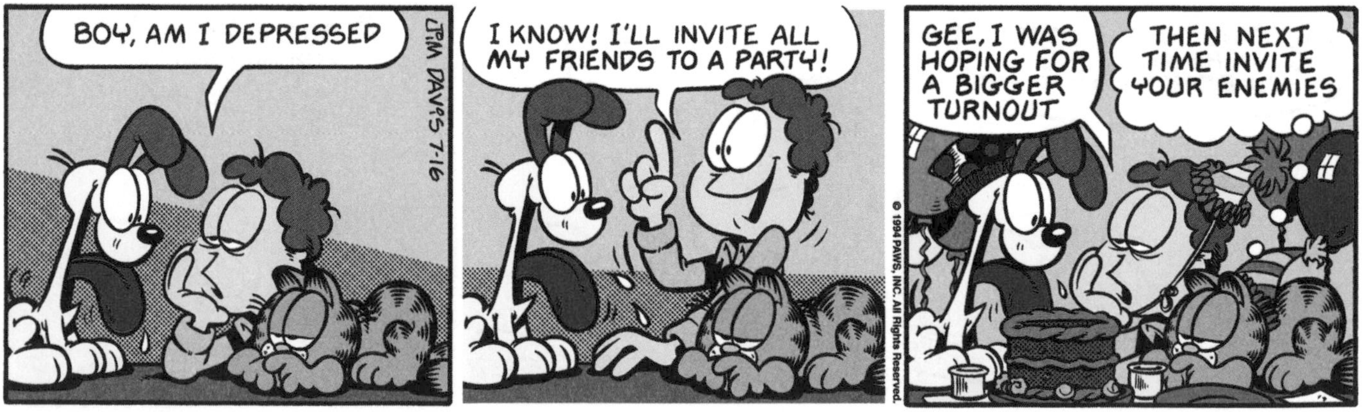
BOY, AM I DEPRESSED
JIM DAVIS 7-16
I KNOW! I'LL INVITE ALL MY FRIENDS TO A PARTY!
© 1994 PAWS, INC. All Rights Reserved.
GEE, I WAS HOPING FOR A BIGGER TURNOUT
THEN NEXT TIME INVITE YOUR ENEMIES

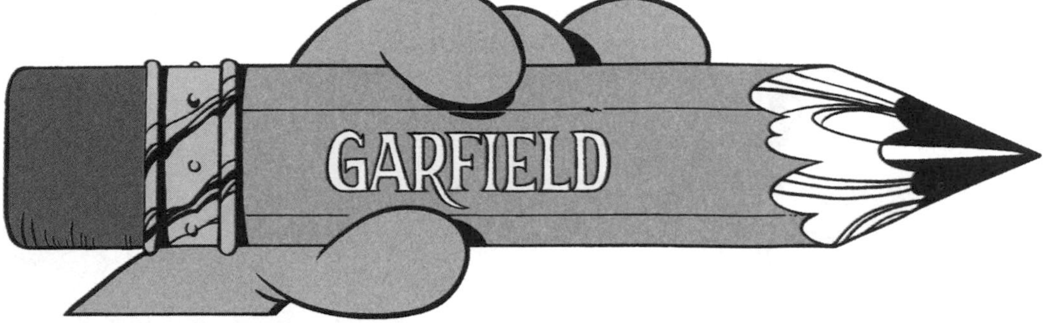
GARFIELD

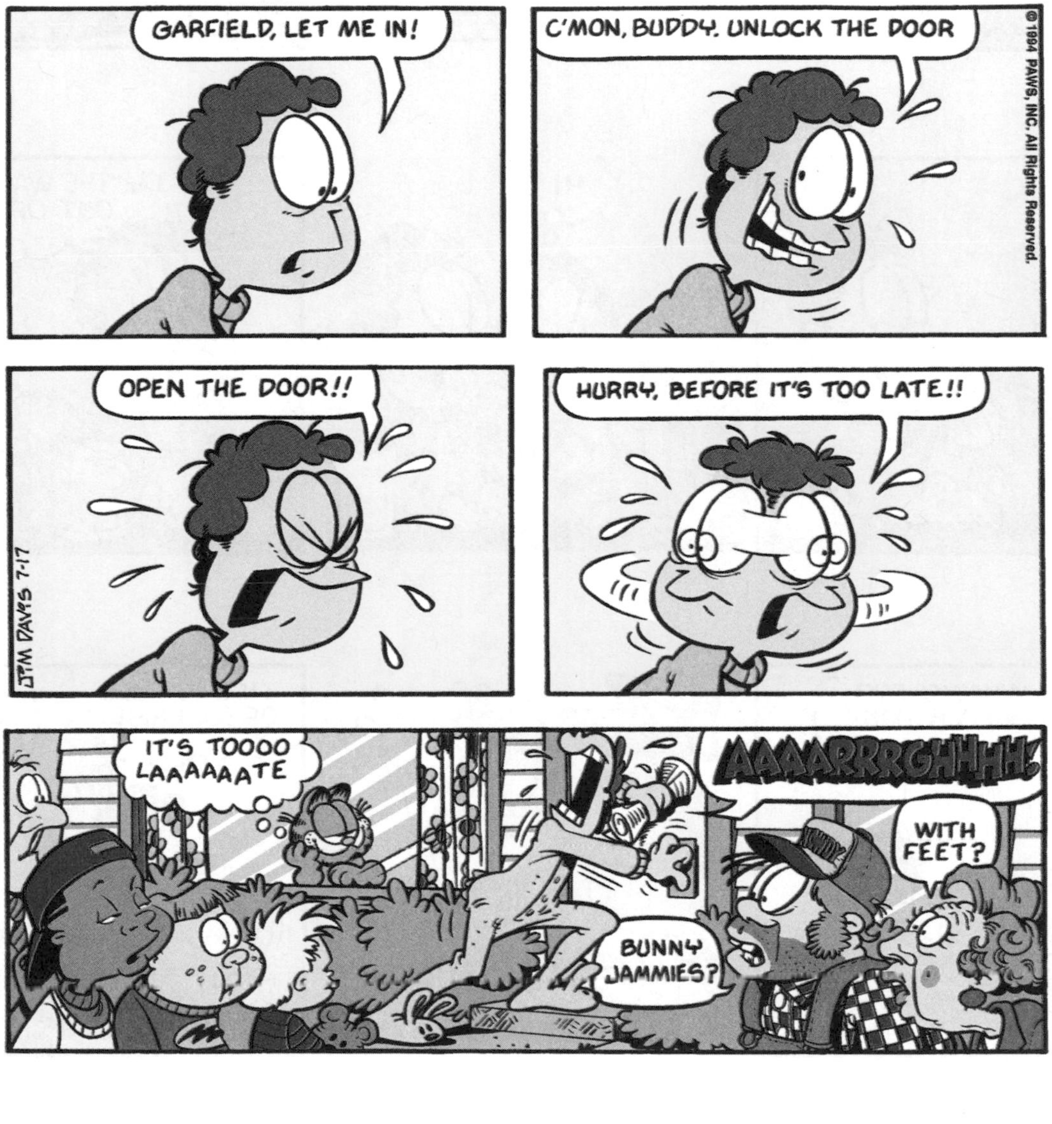
GARFIELD, LET ME IN!
C'MON, BUDDY. UNLOCK THE DOOR
OPEN THE DOOR!!
HURRY, BEFORE IT'S TOO LATE!!
IT'S TOOOO LAAAAAATE
AAAARRRGHHHH!
WITH FEET?
BUNNY JAMMIES?
JIM DAVIS 7-17

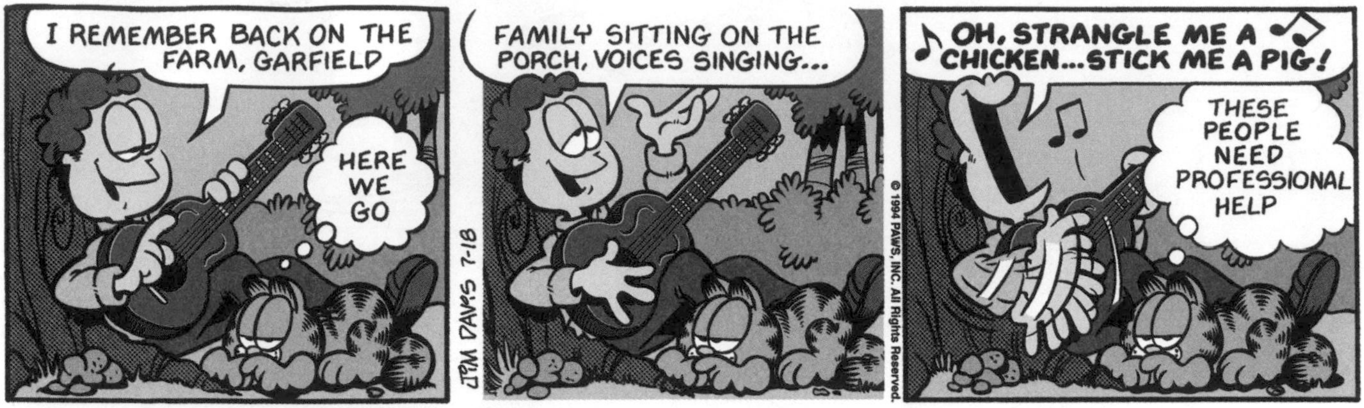
I REMEMBER BACK ON THE FARM, GARFIELD
HERE WE GO
JIM DAVIS 7-18
FAMILY SITTING ON THE PORCH, VOICES SINGING...
© 1994 PAWS, INC. All Rights Reserved.
OH, STRANGLE ME A CHICKEN...STICK ME A PIG!
THESE PEOPLE NEED PROFESSIONAL HELP

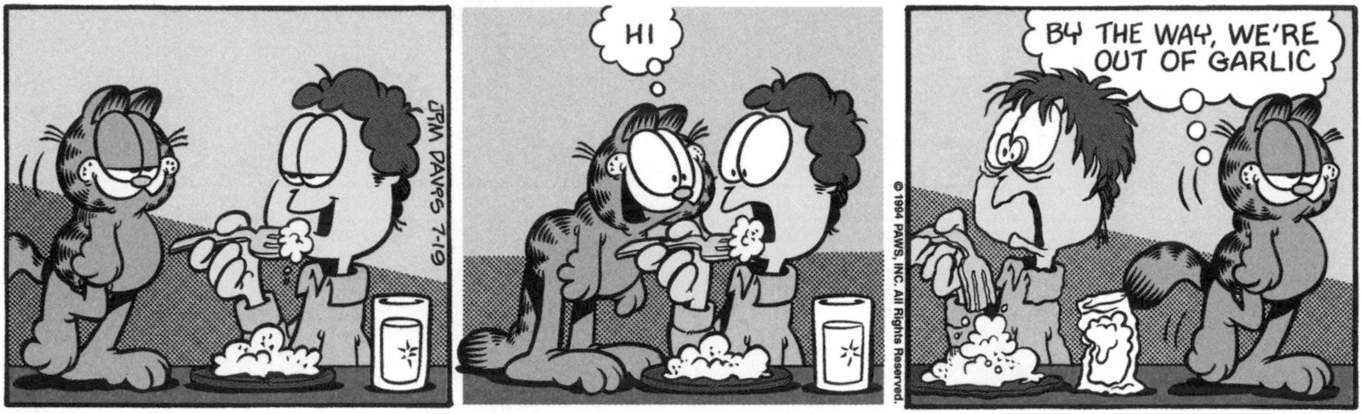
JIM DAVIS 7-19
HI
© 1994 PAWS, INC. All Rights Reserved.
BY THE WAY, WE'RE OUT OF GARLIC

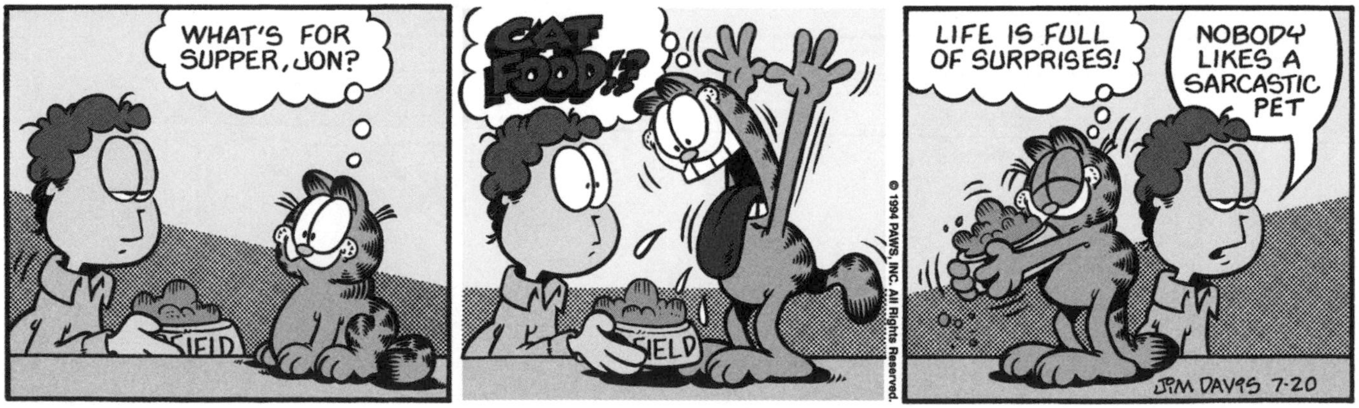
WHAT'S FOR SUPPER, JON?
CAT FOOD!?
© 1994 PAWS, INC. All Rights Reserved.
LIFE IS FULL OF SURPRISES!
NOBODY LIKES A SARCASTIC PET
JIM DAVIS 7-20

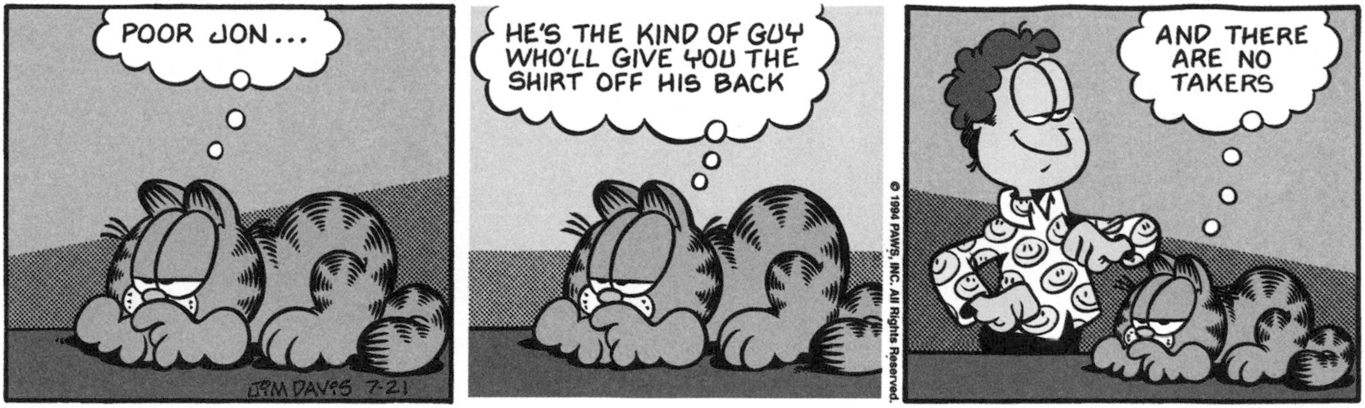
POOR JON...
HE'S THE KIND OF GUY WHO'LL GIVE YOU THE SHIRT OFF HIS BACK
AND THERE ARE NO TAKERS
JIM DAVIS 7-21
© 1994 PAWS, INC. All Rights Reserved.

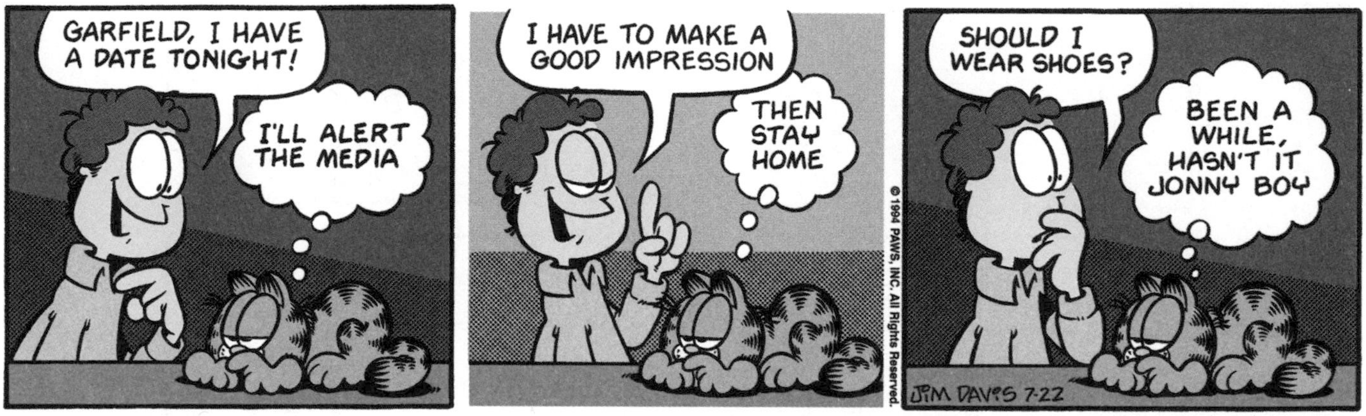
GARFIELD, I HAVE A DATE TONIGHT!
I'LL ALERT THE MEDIA
I HAVE TO MAKE A GOOD IMPRESSION
THEN STAY HOME
SHOULD I WEAR SHOES?
BEEN A WHILE, HASN'T IT JONNY BOY
JIM DAVIS 7-22
© 1994 PAWS, INC. All Rights Reserved.

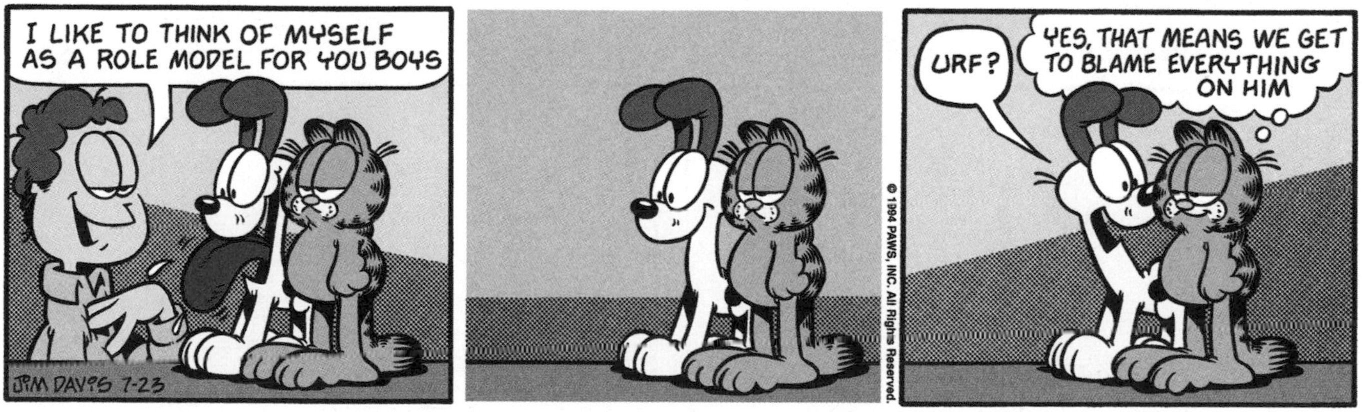
I LIKE TO THINK OF MYSELF AS A ROLE MODEL FOR YOU BOYS
URF?
YES, THAT MEANS WE GET TO BLAME EVERYTHING ON HIM
JIM DAVIS 7-23
© 1994 PAWS, INC. All Rights Reserved.

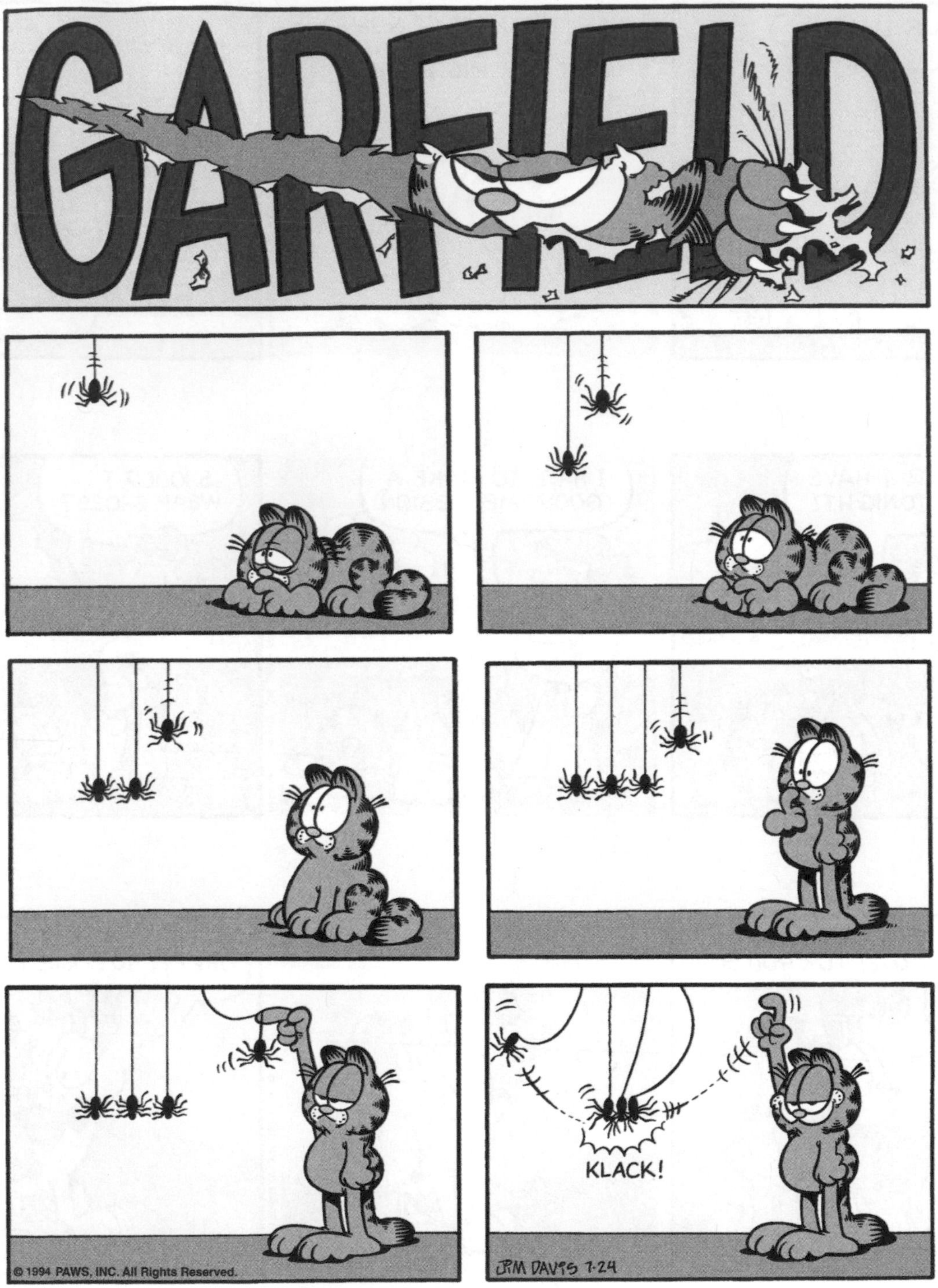
GARFIELD
KLACK!
JPM DAVIS 7-24

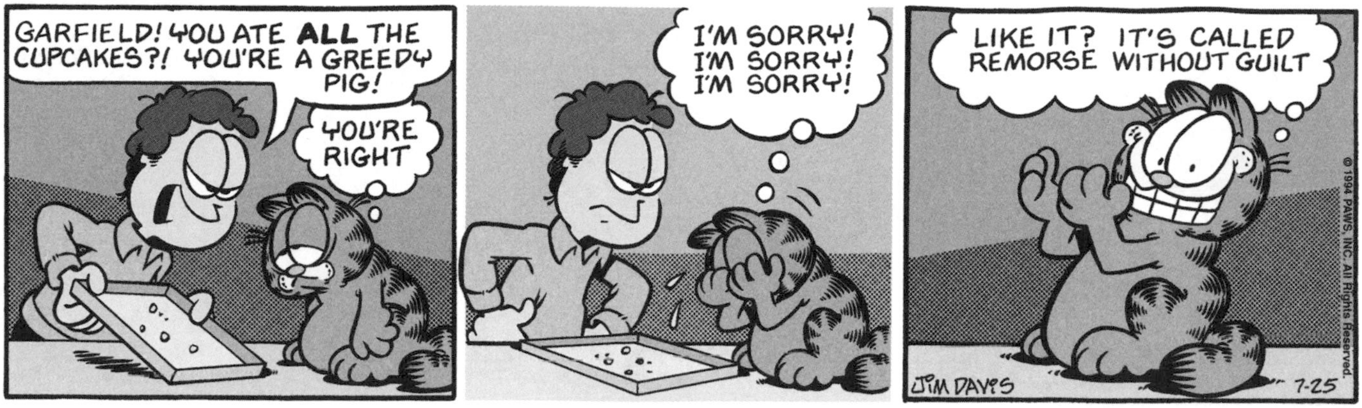
GARFIELD! YOU ATE ALL THE CUPCAKES?! YOU'RE A GREEDY PIG!
YOU'RE RIGHT
I'M SORRY! I'M SORRY! I'M SORRY!
LIKE IT? IT'S CALLED REMORSE WITHOUT GUILT
JIM DAVIS 7-25
© 1994 PAWS, INC. All Rights Reserved.

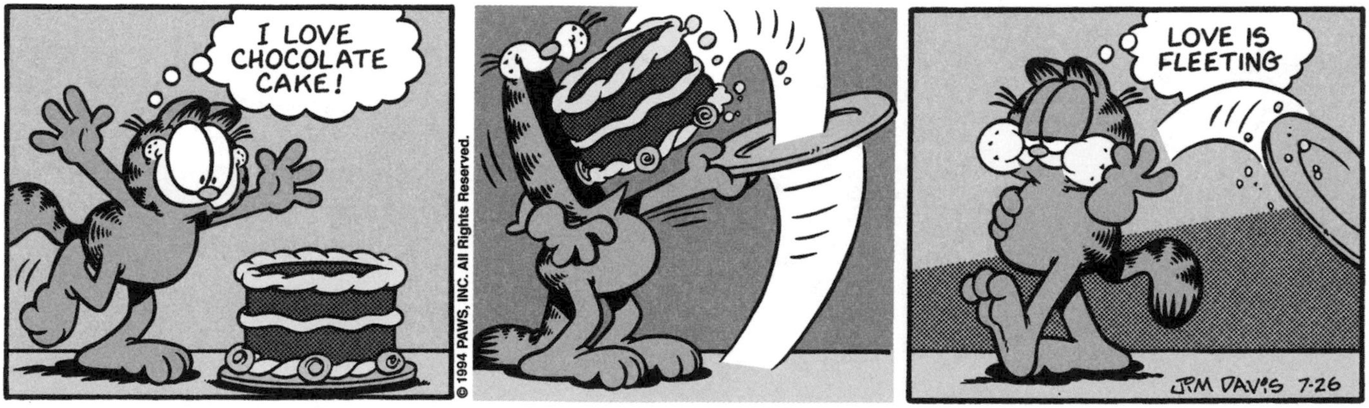
I LOVE CHOCOLATE CAKE!
© 1994 PAWS, INC. All Rights Reserved.
LOVE IS FLEETING
JIM DAVIS 7-26

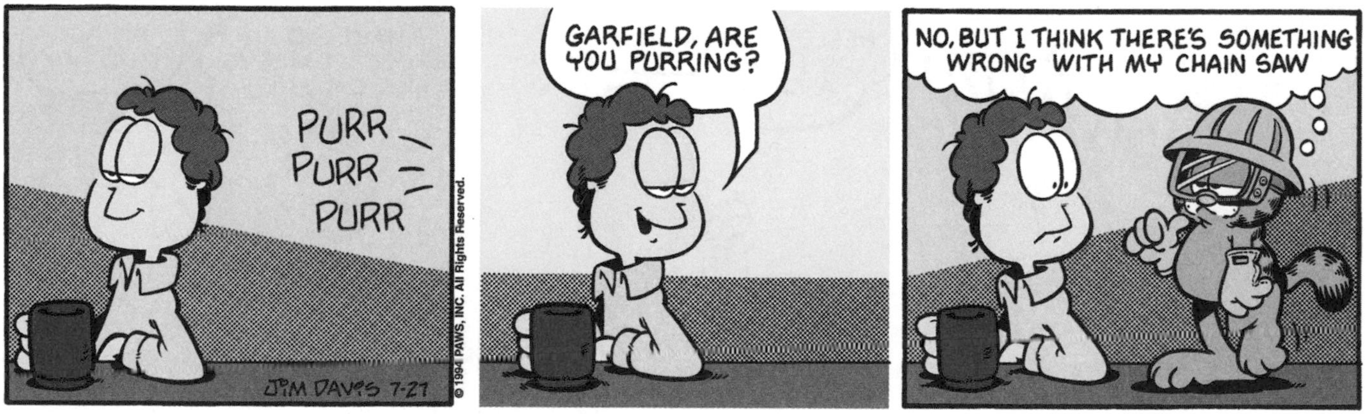
PURR PURR PURR
JIM DAVIS 7-27
© 1994 PAWS, INC. All Rights Reserved.
GARFIELD, ARE YOU PURRING?
NO, BUT I THINK THERE'S SOMETHING WRONG WITH MY CHAIN SAW

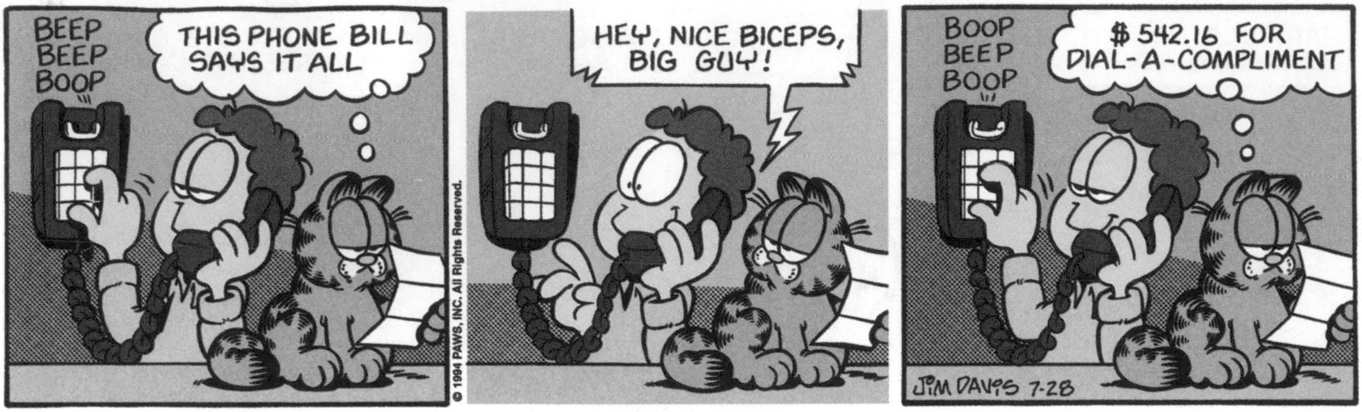
BEEP BEEP BOOP
THIS PHONE BILL SAYS IT ALL
© 1994 PAWS, INC. All Rights Reserved.
HEY, NICE BICEPS, BIG GUY!
BOOP BEEP BOOP
$ 542.16 FOR DIAL-A-COMPLIMENT
JIM DAVIS 7-28

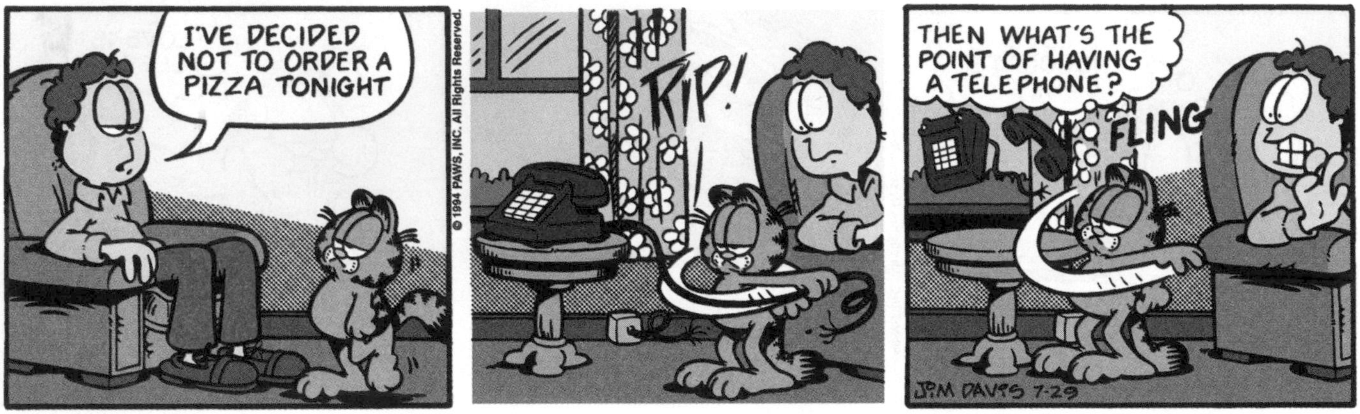
I'VE DECIDED NOT TO ORDER A PIZZA TONIGHT
© 1994 PAWS, INC. All Rights Reserved.
RIP!
THEN WHAT'S THE POINT OF HAVING A TELEPHONE?
FLING
JIM DAVIS 7-29

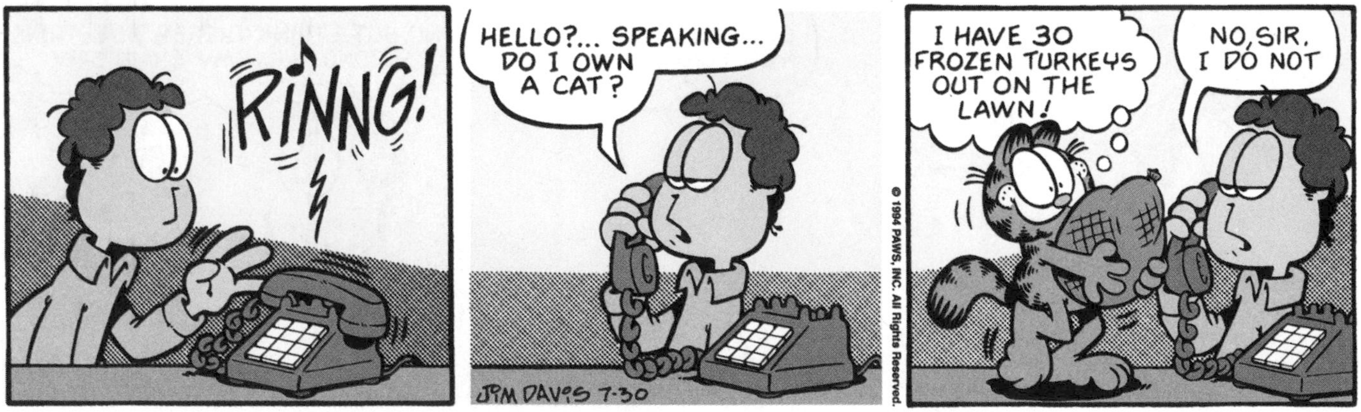
RINNG!
HELLO?... SPEAKING... DO I OWN A CAT?
JIM DAVIS 7-30
© 1994 PAWS, INC. All Rights Reserved.
I HAVE 30 FROZEN TURKEYS OUT ON THE LAWN!
NO, SIR, I DO NOT

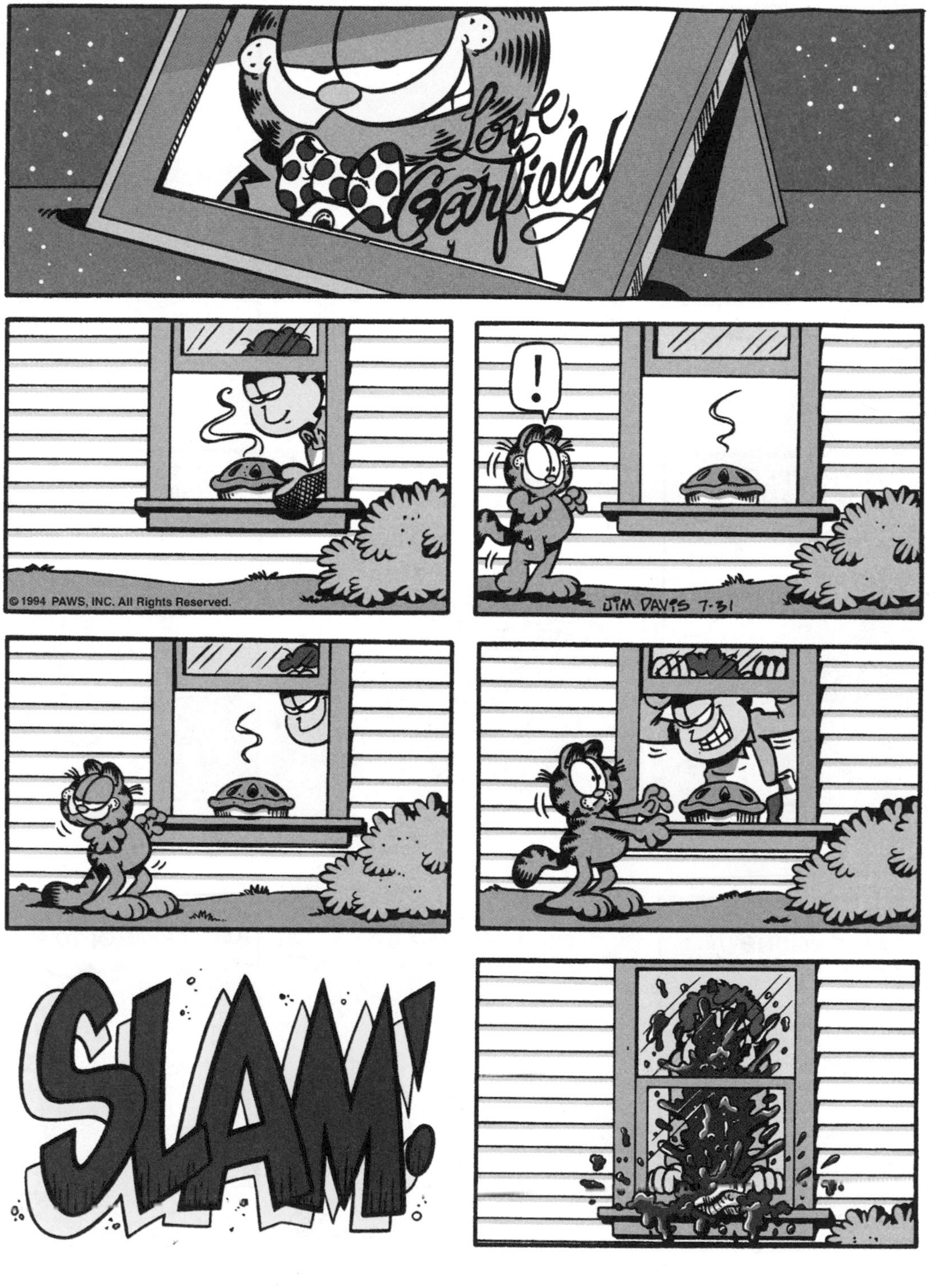
Love,
Garfield
© 1994 PAWS, INC. All Rights Reserved.
!
JIM DAVIS 7-31
SLAM!

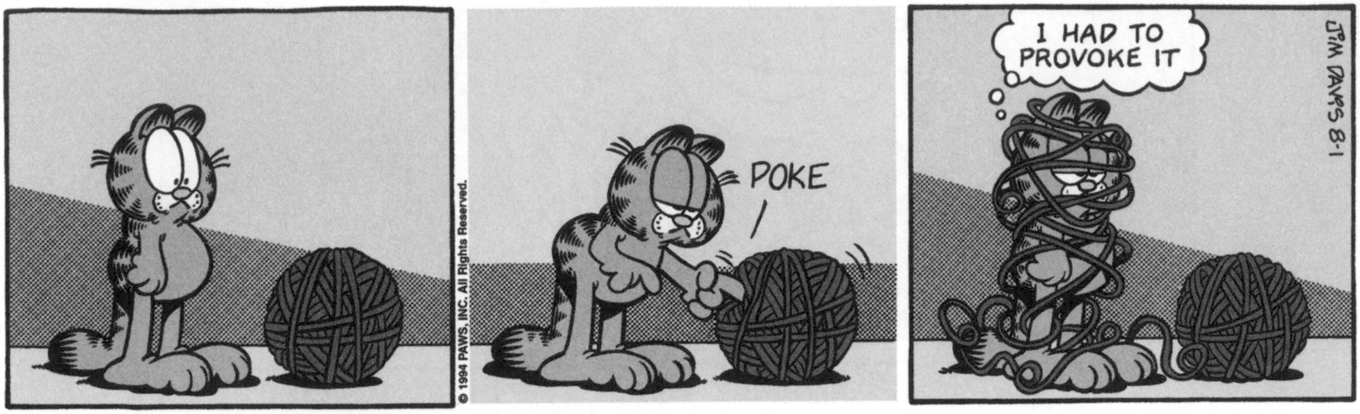
© 1994 PAWS, INC. All Rights Reserved.
POKE
I HAD TO PROVOKE IT
JIM DAVIS 8-1

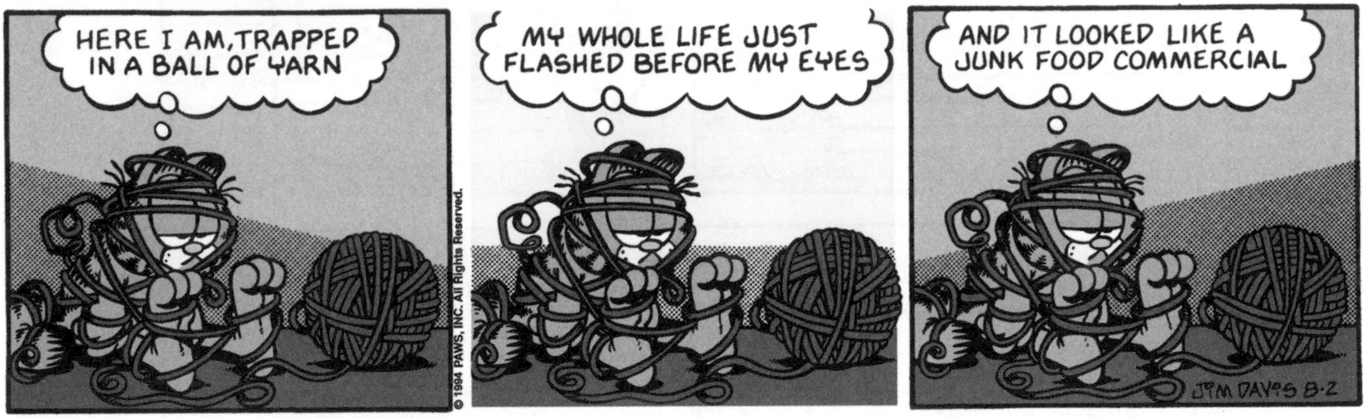
HERE I AM, TRAPPED IN A BALL OF YARN
© 1994 PAWS, INC. All Rights Reserved.
MY WHOLE LIFE JUST FLASHED BEFORE MY EYES
AND IT LOOKED LIKE A JUNK FOOD COMMERCIAL
JIM DAVIS 8-2

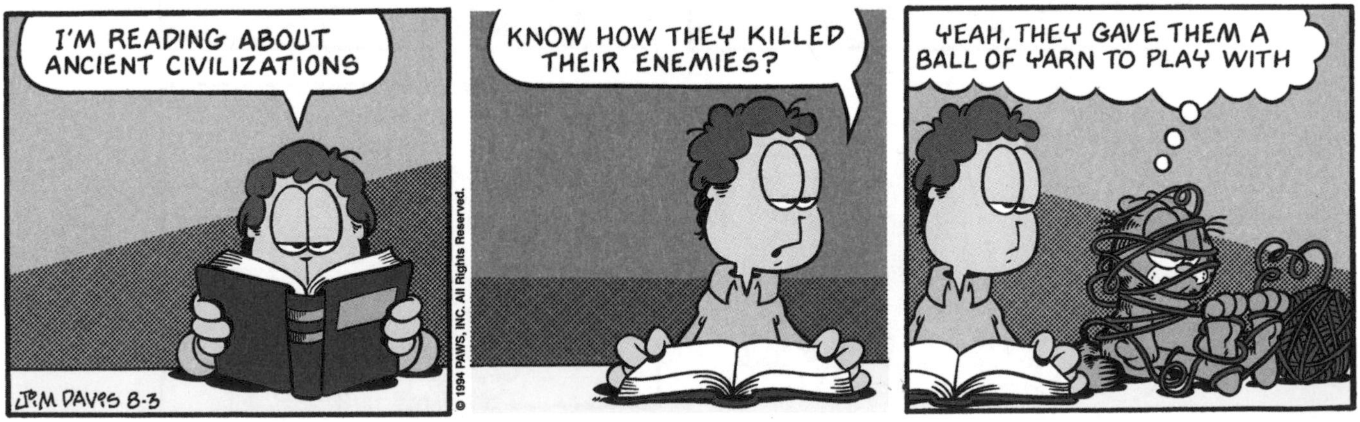
I'M READING ABOUT ANCIENT CIVILIZATIONS
JIM DAVIS 8-3
© 1994 PAWS, INC. All Rights Reserved.
KNOW HOW THEY KILLED THEIR ENEMIES?
YEAH, THEY GAVE THEM A BALL OF YARN TO PLAY WITH

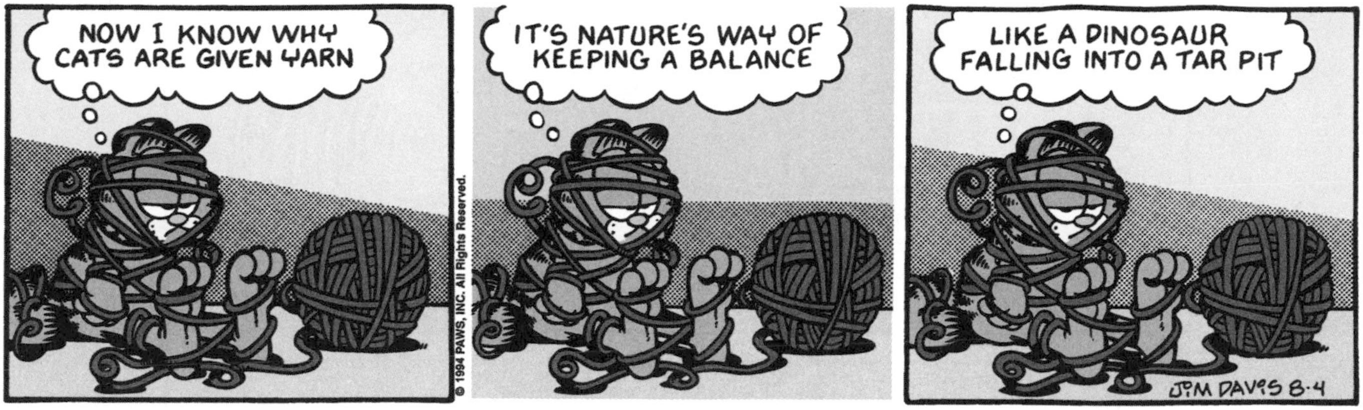
NOW I KNOW WHY CATS ARE GIVEN YARN
IT'S NATURE'S WAY OF KEEPING A BALANCE
LIKE A DINOSAUR FALLING INTO A TAR PIT
© 1994 PAWS, INC. All Rights Reserved.
JIM DAVIS 8·4

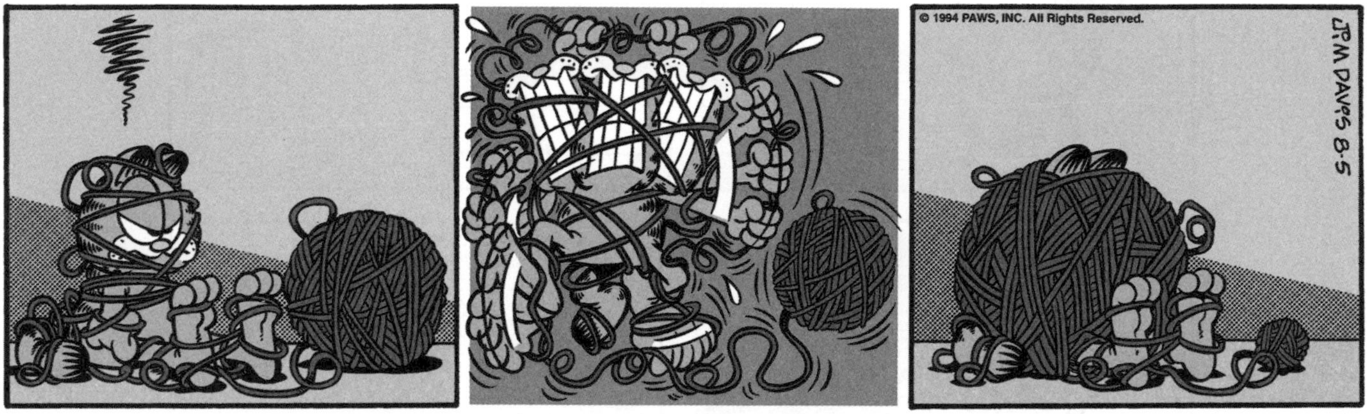
© 1994 PAWS, INC. All Rights Reserved.
JIM DAVIS 8·5

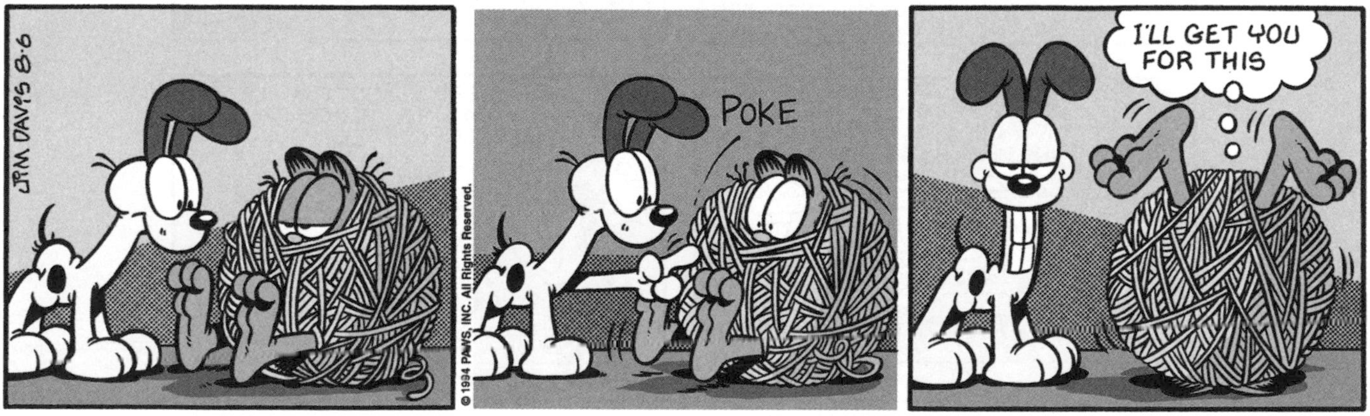
JIM DAVIS 8·6
© 1994 PAWS, INC. All Rights Reserved.
POKE
I'LL GET YOU FOR THIS

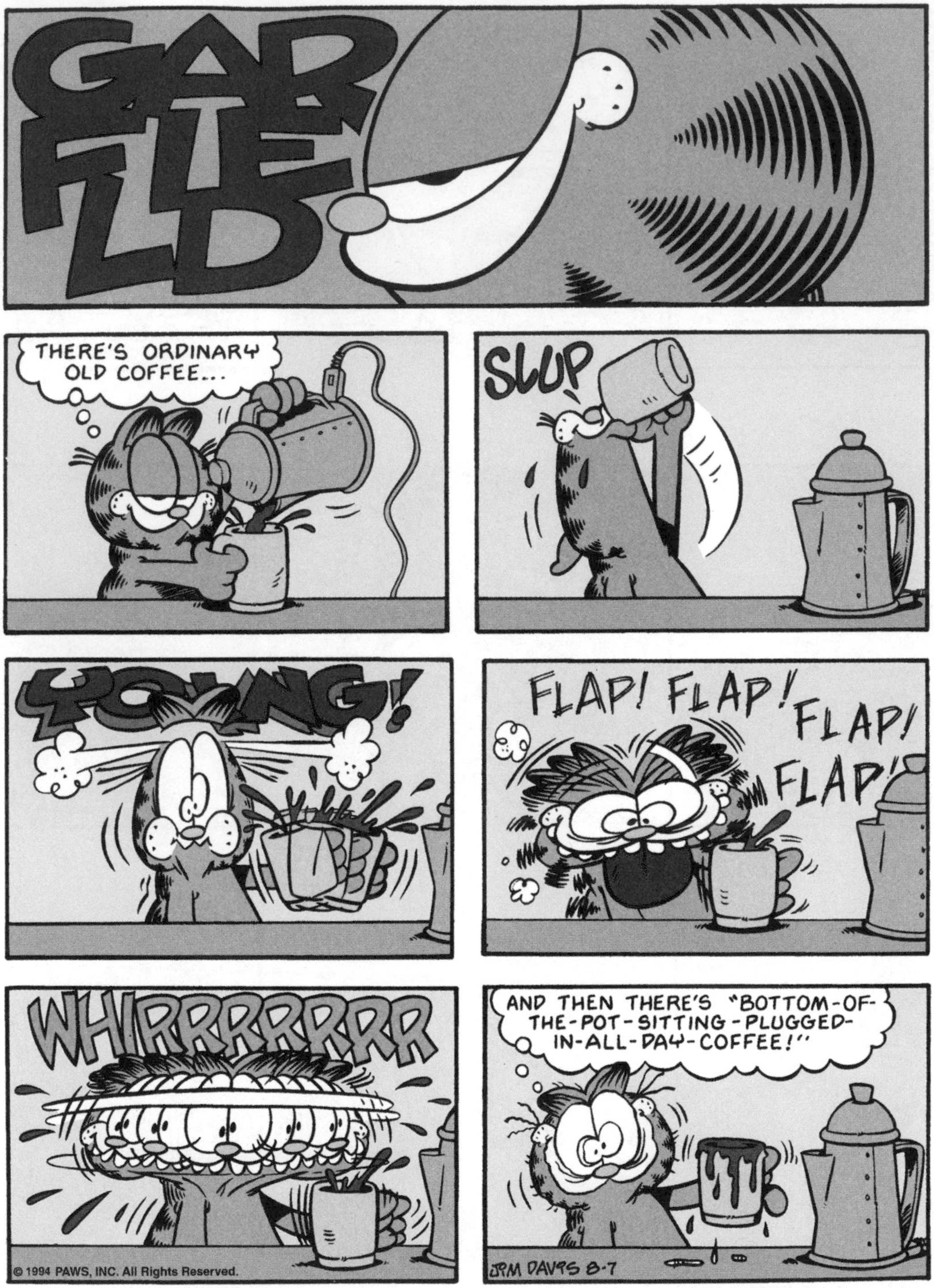
GARFIELD
THERE'S ORDINARY OLD COFFEE...
SLUP
YOING!
FLAP! FLAP! FLAP! FLAP!
WHIRRRRRRR
AND THEN THERE'S "BOTTOM-OF-THE-POT-SITTING-PLUGGED-IN-ALL-DAY-COFFEE!"
JPM DAVPS 8-7

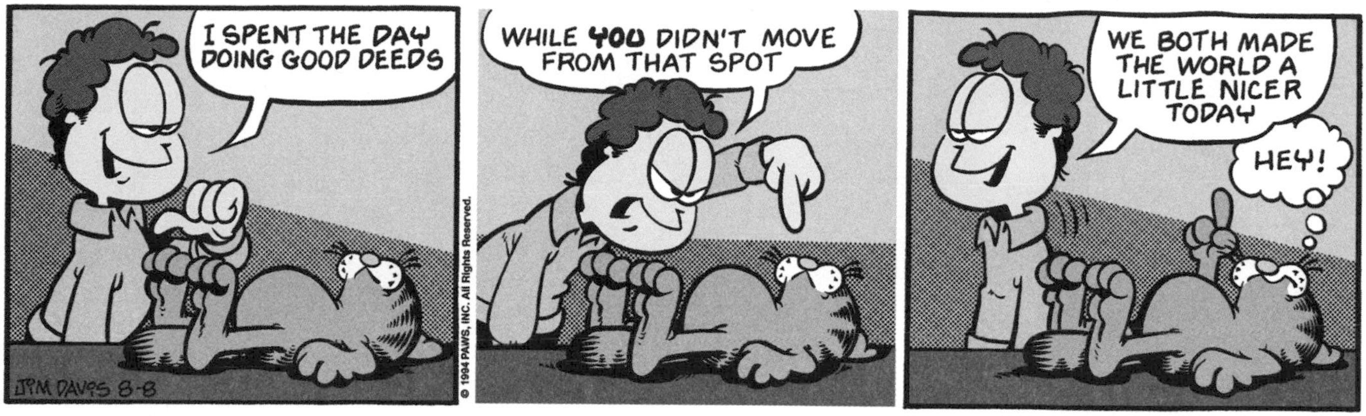
I SPENT THE DAY DOING GOOD DEEDS
WHILE YOU DIDN'T MOVE FROM THAT SPOT
WE BOTH MADE THE WORLD A LITTLE NICER TODAY
HEY!
JIM DAVIS 8-8
© 1994 PAWS, INC. All Rights Reserved.

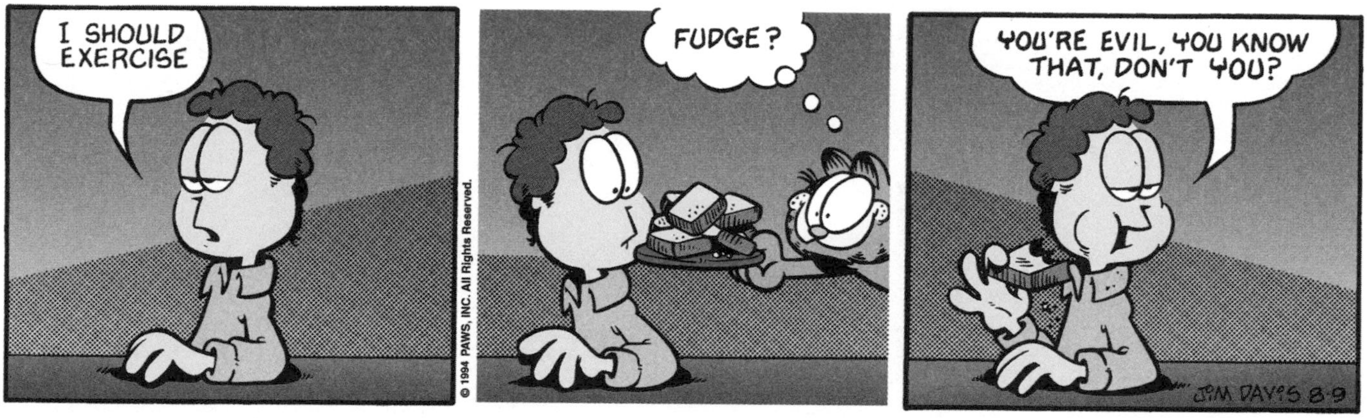
I SHOULD EXERCISE
FUDGE?
YOU'RE EVIL, YOU KNOW THAT, DON'T YOU?
JIM DAVIS 8-9
© 1994 PAWS, INC. All Rights Reserved.

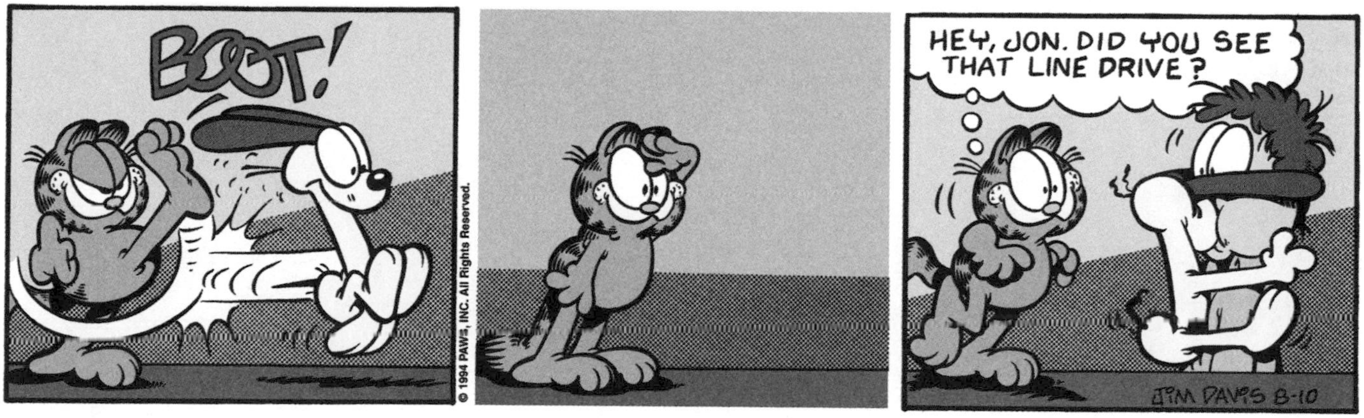
BOOT!
HEY, JON. DID YOU SEE THAT LINE DRIVE?
JIM DAVIS 8-10
© 1994 PAWS, INC. All Rights Reserved.

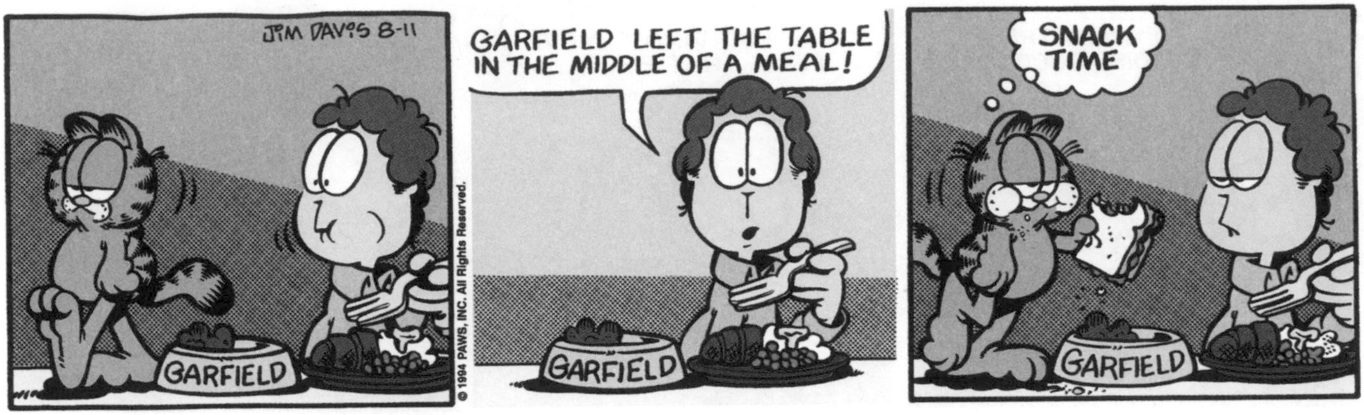
JIM DAVIS 8-11
© 1994 PAWS, INC. All Rights Reserved.
GARFIELD
GARFIELD LEFT THE TABLE IN THE MIDDLE OF A MEAL!
GARFIELD
SNACK TIME
GARFIELD

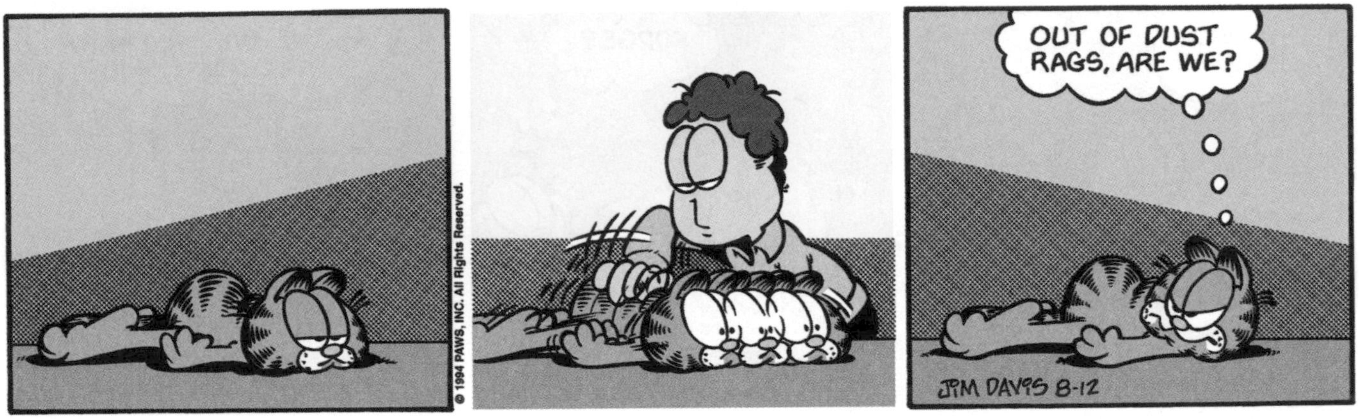
© 1994 PAWS, INC. All Rights Reserved.
OUT OF DUST RAGS, ARE WE?
JIM DAVIS 8-12

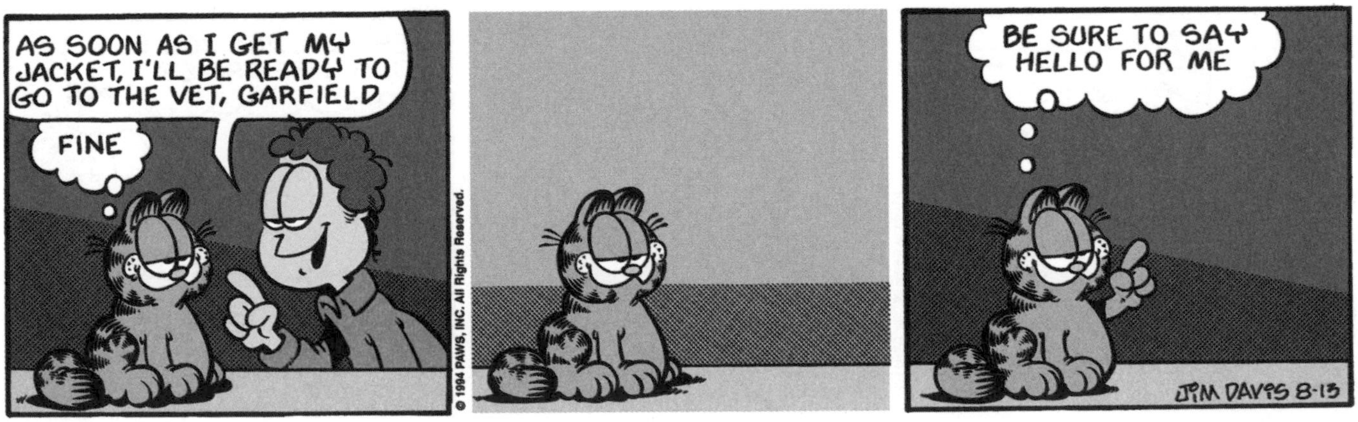
AS SOON AS I GET MY JACKET, I'LL BE READY TO GO TO THE VET, GARFIELD
FINE
© 1994 PAWS, INC. All Rights Reserved.
BE SURE TO SAY HELLO FOR ME
JIM DAVIS 8-13

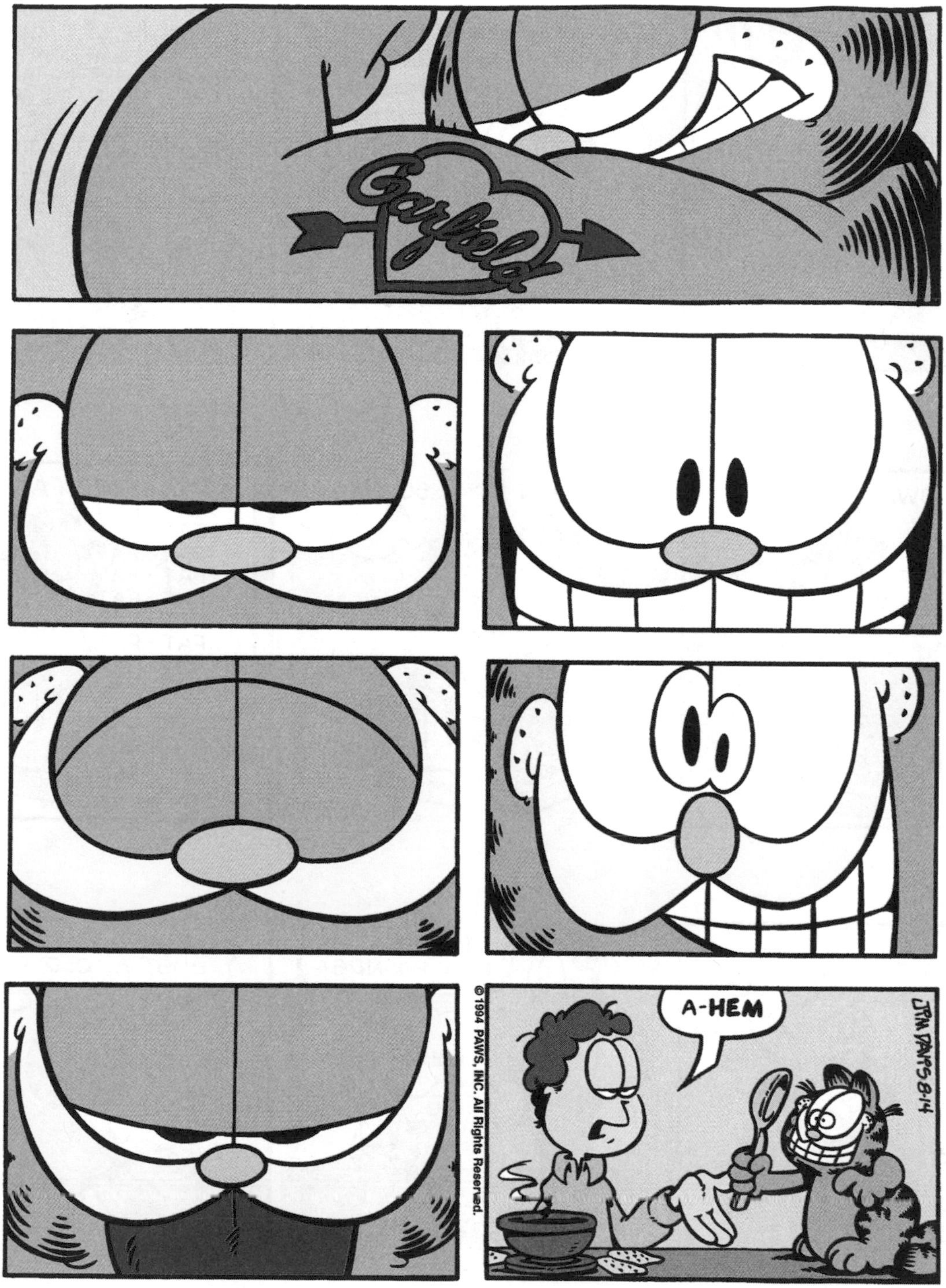
Garfield
A-HEM

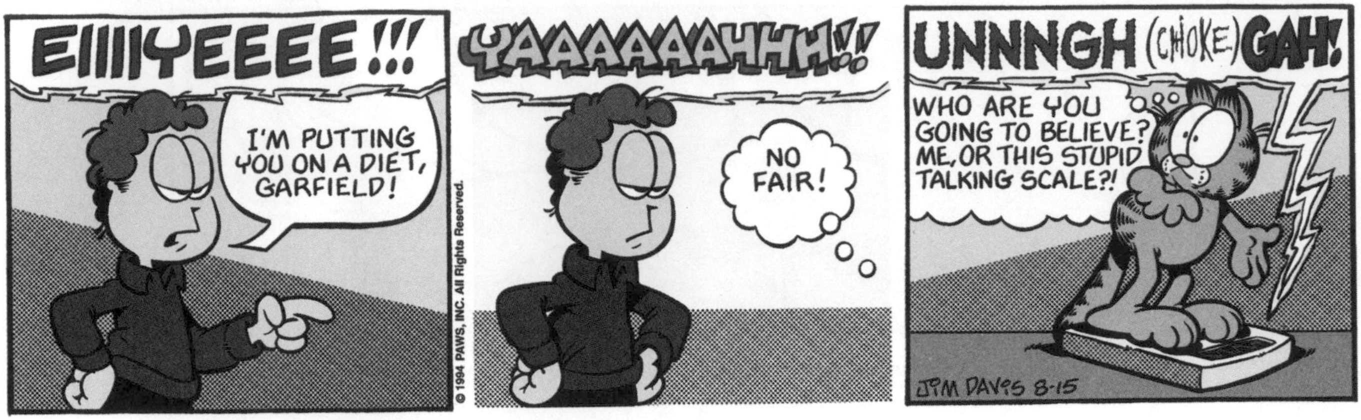
EIIIIYEEEE!!!
I'M PUTTING YOU ON A DIET, GARFIELD!
YAAAAAAHHH!!!
NO FAIR!
UNNNGH (CHOKE) GAH!
WHO ARE YOU GOING TO BELIEVE? ME, OR THIS STUPID TALKING SCALE?!
© 1994 PAWS, INC. All Rights Reserved.
JIM DAVIS 8-15

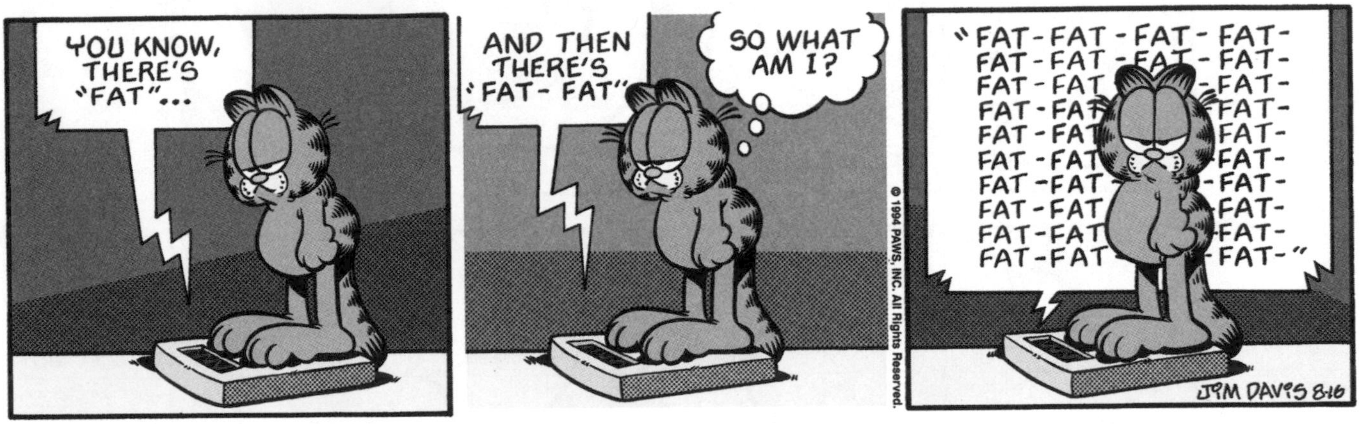
YOU KNOW, THERE'S "FAT"...
AND THEN THERE'S "FAT-FAT"
SO WHAT AM I?
"FAT-FAT-FAT-FAT-
FAT-FAT-FAT-FAT-
FAT-FAT-FAT-
FAT-FAT-FAT-
FAT-FAT-FAT-
FAT-FAT-FAT-
FAT-FAT-FAT-
FAT-FAT-FAT-
FAT-FAT-FAT-
FAT-FAT-FAT-"
© 1994 PAWS, INC. All Rights Reserved.
JIM DAVIS 8-16

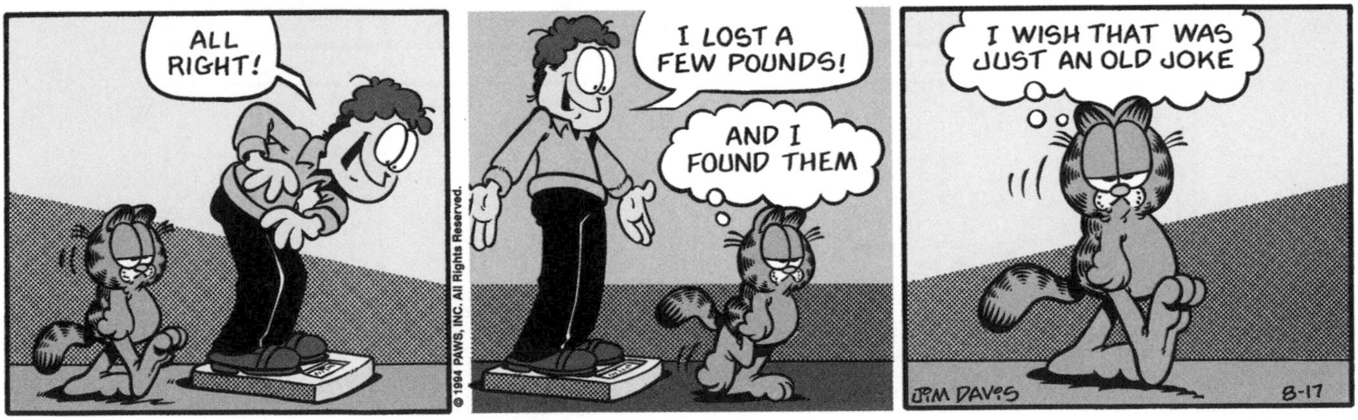
ALL RIGHT!
I LOST A FEW POUNDS!
AND I FOUND THEM
I WISH THAT WAS JUST AN OLD JOKE
© 1994 PAWS, INC. All Rights Reserved.
JIM DAVIS 8-17

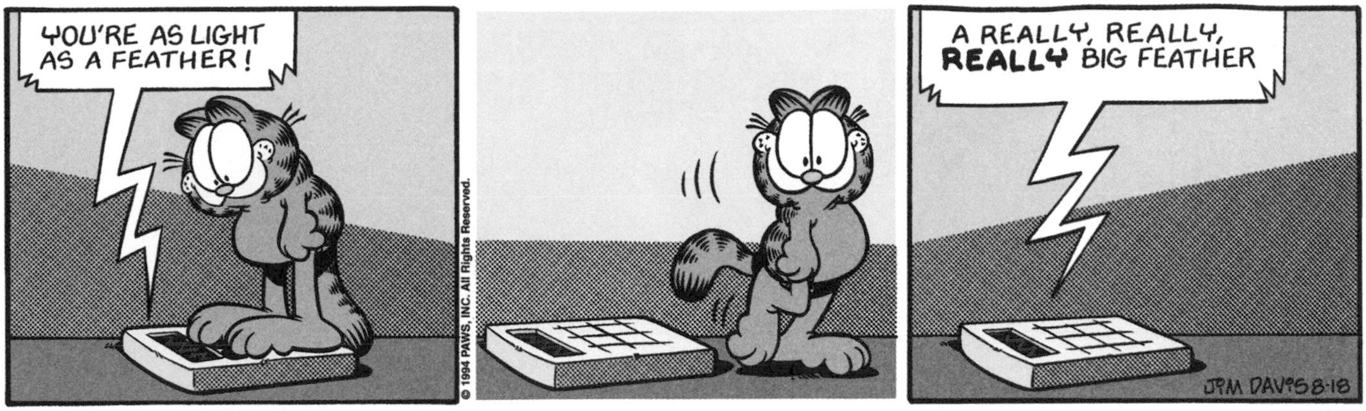
YOU'RE AS LIGHT AS A FEATHER!
© 1994 PAWS, INC. All Rights Reserved.
A REALLY, REALLY, **REALLY** BIG FEATHER
JIM DAVIS 8-18

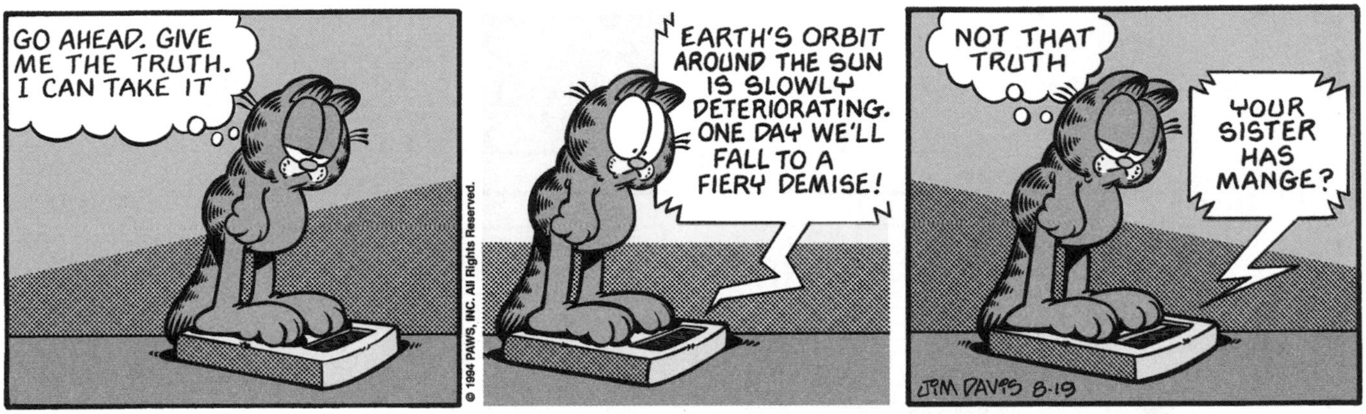
GO AHEAD. GIVE ME THE TRUTH. I CAN TAKE IT
© 1994 PAWS, INC. All Rights Reserved.
EARTH'S ORBIT AROUND THE SUN IS SLOWLY DETERIORATING. ONE DAY WE'LL FALL TO A FIERY DEMISE!
NOT THAT TRUTH
YOUR SISTER HAS MANGE?
JIM DAVIS 8-19

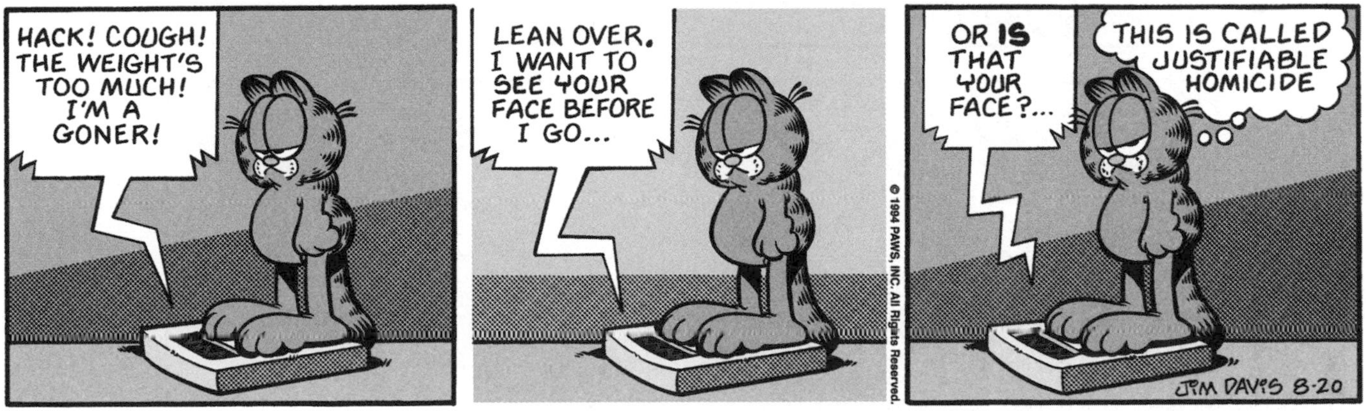
HACK! COUGH! THE WEIGHT'S TOO MUCH! I'M A GONER!
LEAN OVER. I WANT TO SEE YOUR FACE BEFORE I GO...
© 1994 PAWS, INC. All Rights Reserved.
OR **IS** THAT YOUR FACE?...
THIS IS CALLED JUSTIFIABLE HOMICIDE
JIM DAVIS 8-20

GARFIELD
I WONDER IF JON FIXED THE TOASTER?
CLICK
KA-CHOINNG!
© 1994 PAWS, INC. All Rights Reserved.
PWANG!
PWING!
YAAAHHHH!
CRASH!
YIPE!
PWING!
PWANG!
CRAAASHH!
YUP
JIM DAVIS 8-21

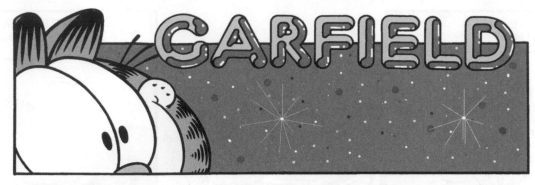

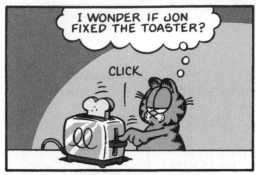

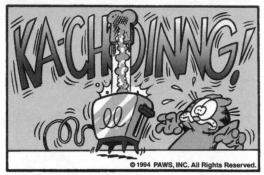

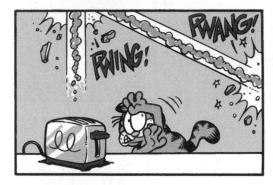

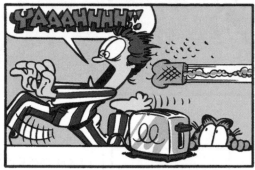

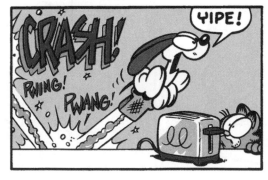

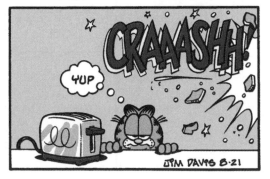

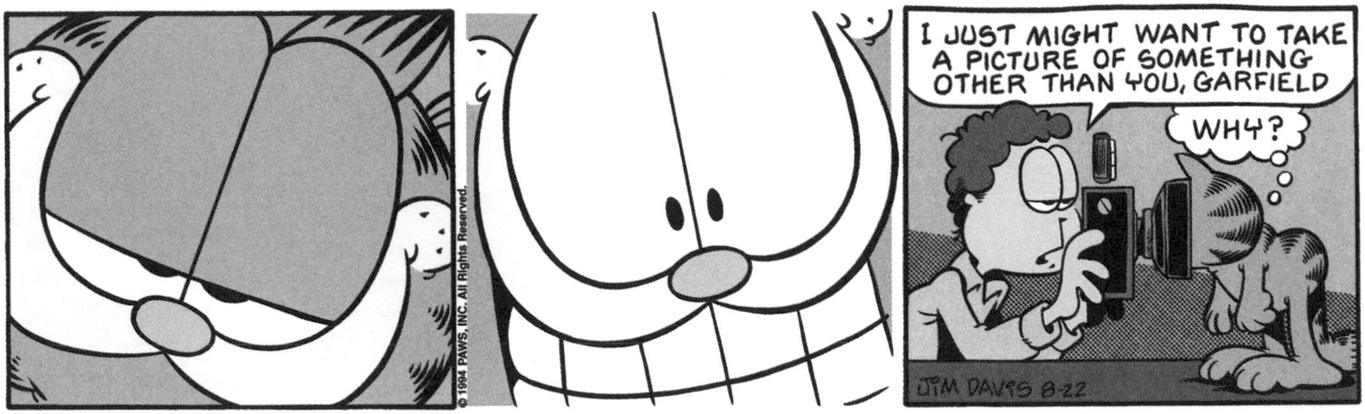
© 1994 PAWS, INC. All Rights Reserved.
I JUST MIGHT WANT TO TAKE A PICTURE OF SOMETHING OTHER THAN YOU, GARFIELD
WHY?
JIM DAVIS 8-22

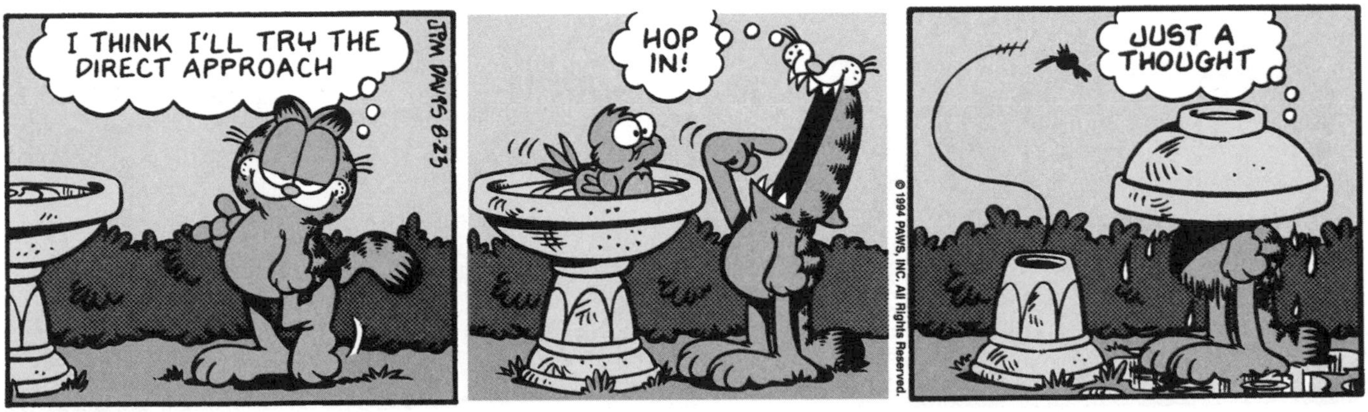
I THINK I'LL TRY THE DIRECT APPROACH
JIM DAVIS 8-23
HOP IN!
© 1994 PAWS, INC. All Rights Reserved.
JUST A THOUGHT

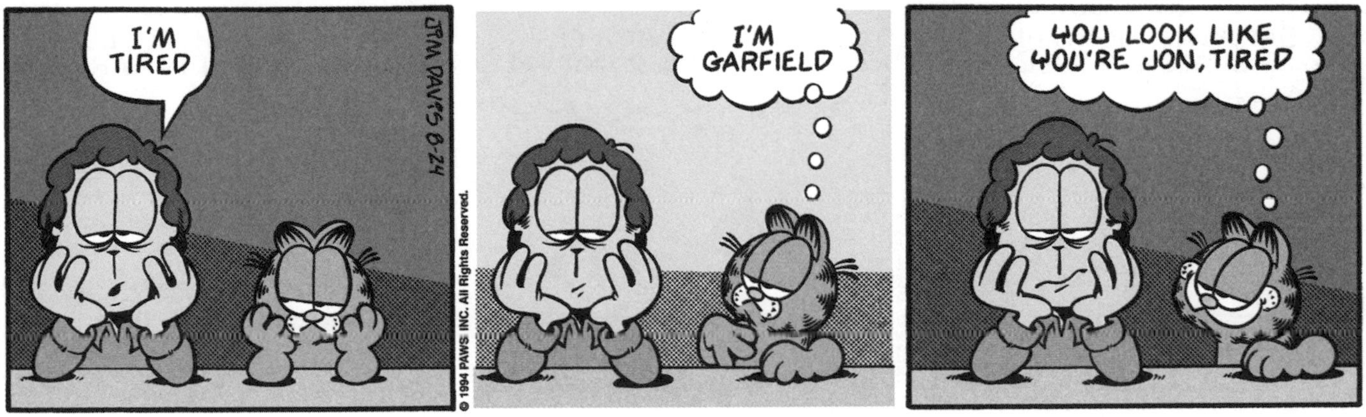
I'M TIRED
JIM DAVIS 8-24
© 1994 PAWS, INC. All Rights Reserved.
I'M GARFIELD
YOU LOOK LIKE YOU'RE JON, TIRED

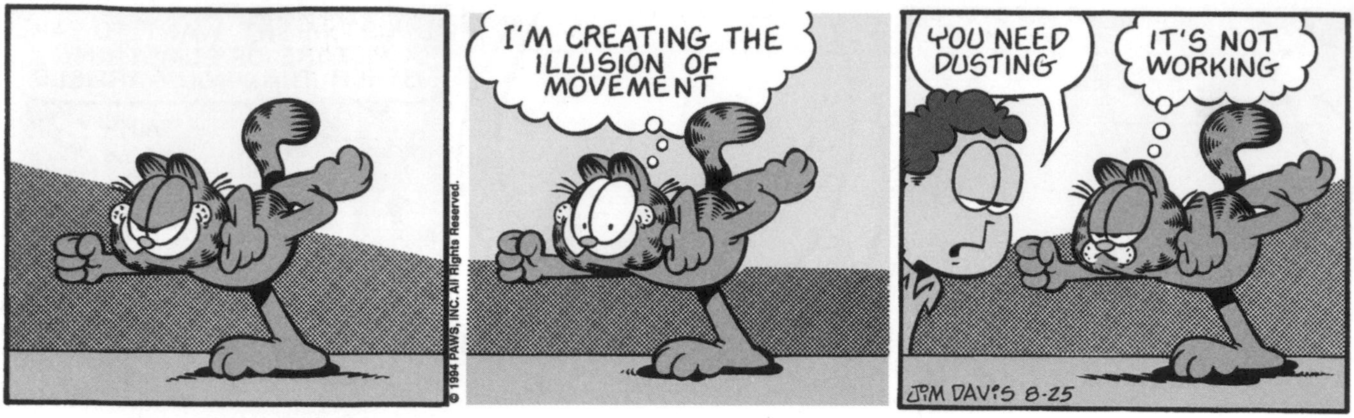
I'M CREATING THE ILLUSION OF MOVEMENT
YOU NEED DUSTING
IT'S NOT WORKING
JIM DAVIS 8-25
© 1994 PAWS, INC. All Rights Reserved.

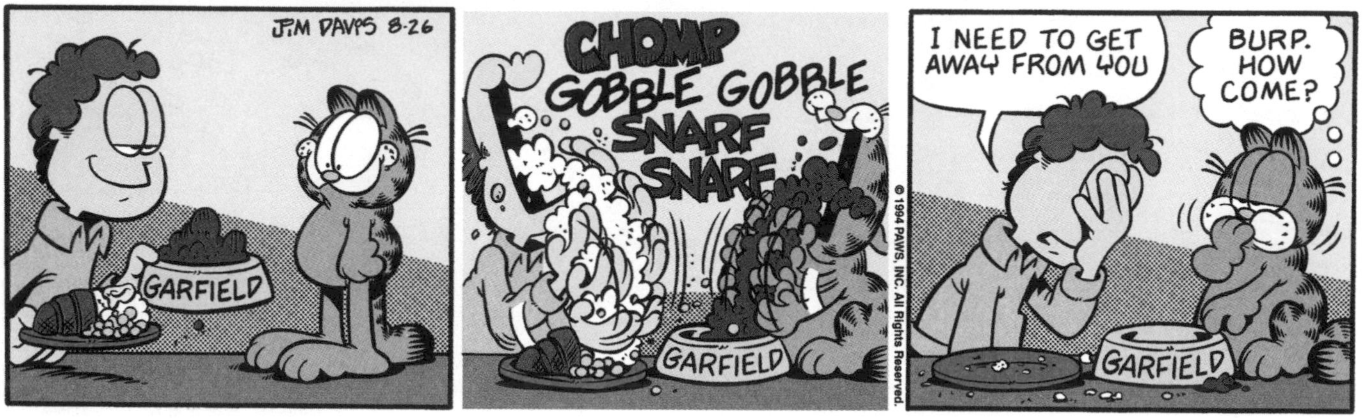
JIM DAVIS 8-26
GARFIELD
CHOMP
GOBBLE GOBBLE
SNARF
SNARF
GARFIELD
I NEED TO GET AWAY FROM YOU
BURP. HOW COME?
GARFIELD
© 1994 PAWS, INC. All Rights Reserved.

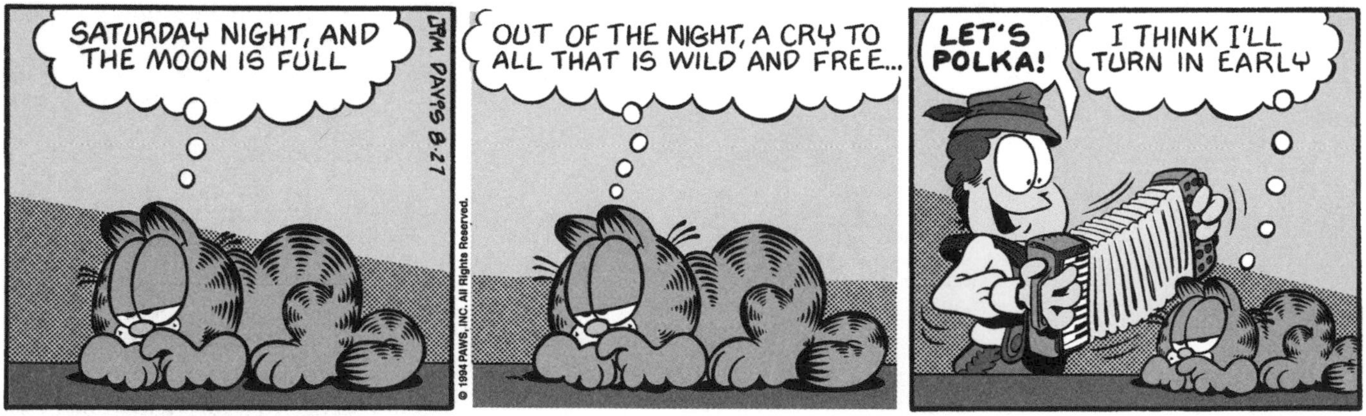
SATURDAY NIGHT, AND THE MOON IS FULL
JIM DAVIS 8-27
OUT OF THE NIGHT, A CRY TO ALL THAT IS WILD AND FREE...
LET'S POLKA!
I THINK I'LL TURN IN EARLY
© 1994 PAWS, INC. All Rights Reserved.

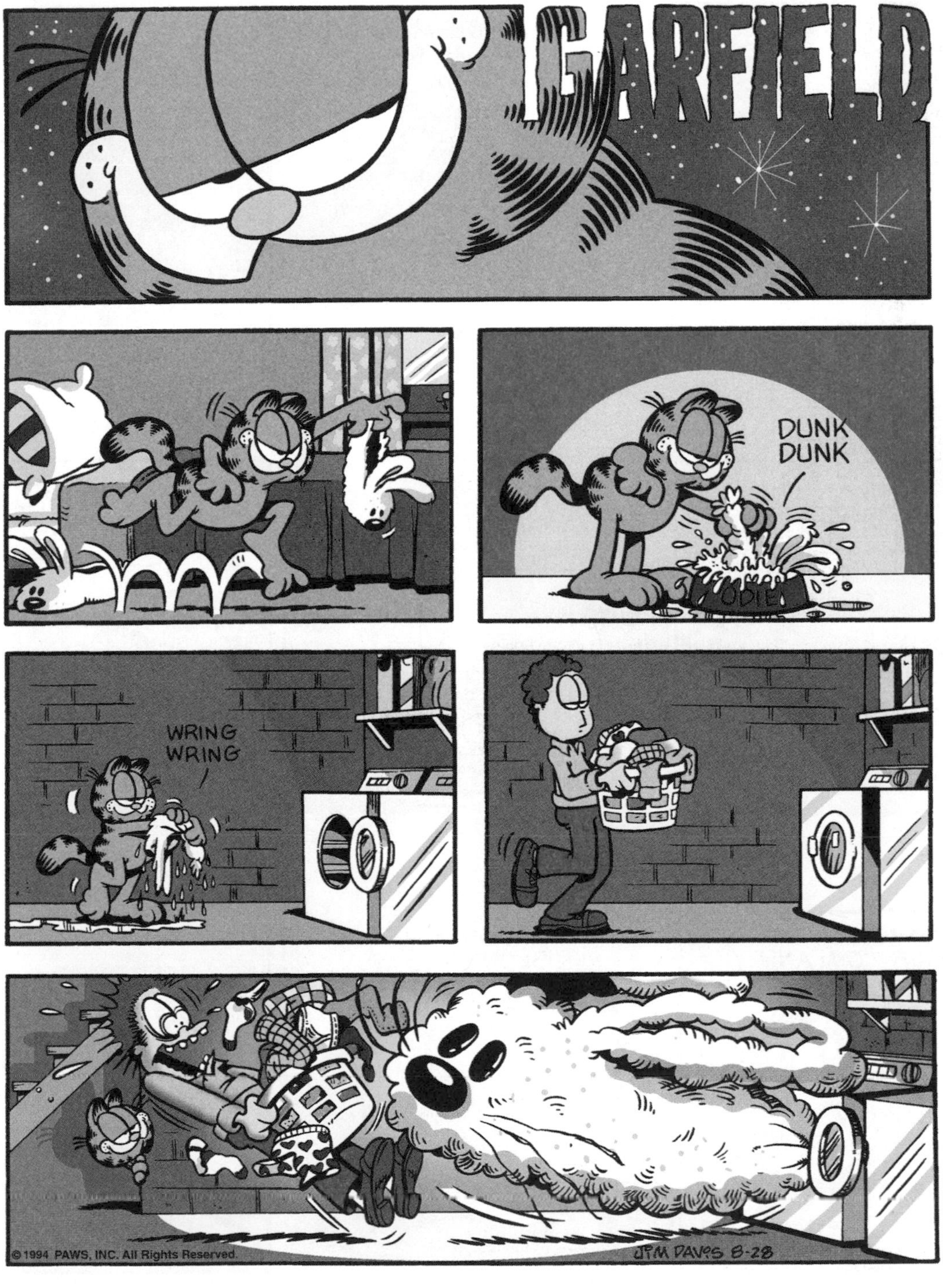
GARFIELD
DUNK DUNK
ODIE
WRING WRING
© 1994 PAWS, INC. All Rights Reserved.
JIM DAVIS 8-28

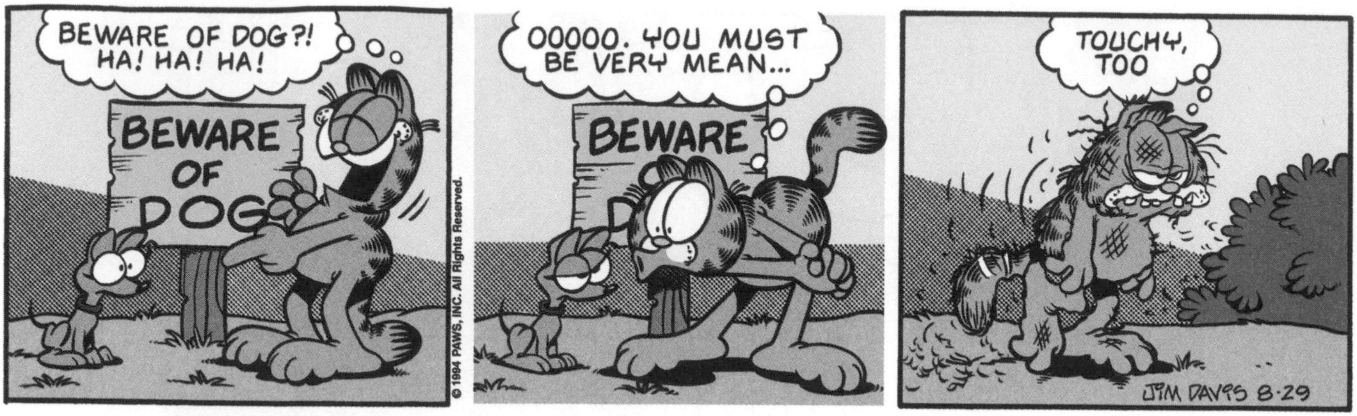
BEWARE OF DOG?! HA! HA! HA!
BEWARE OF DOG
© 1994 PAWS, INC. All Rights Reserved.
OOOOO. YOU MUST BE VERY MEAN...
BEWARE
TOUCHY, TOO
JIM DAVIS 8-29

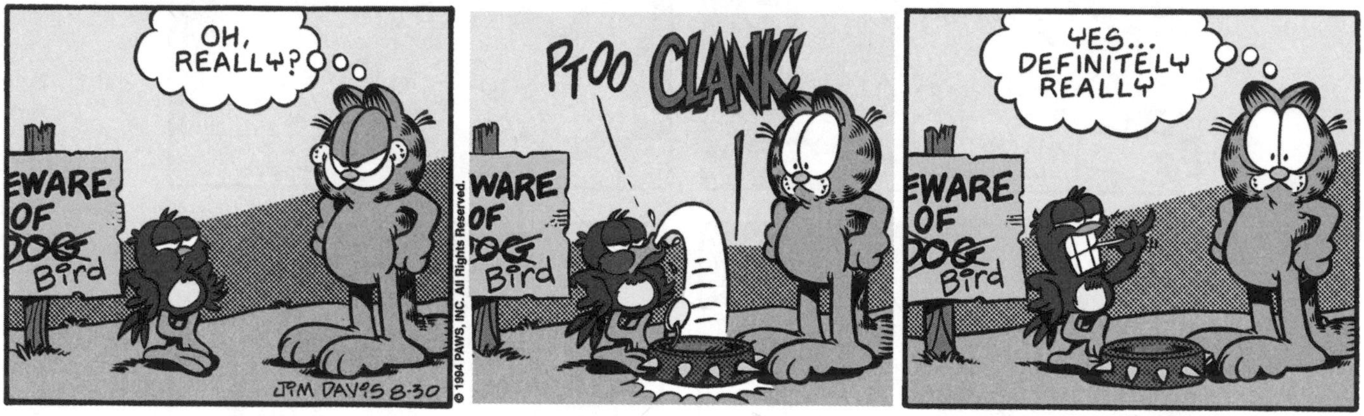
OH, REALLY?
EWARE OF DOG Bird
JIM DAVIS 8-30
© 1994 PAWS, INC. All Rights Reserved.
PTOO
CLANK!
WARE OF DOG Bird
YES... DEFINITELY REALLY
EWARE OF DOG Bird

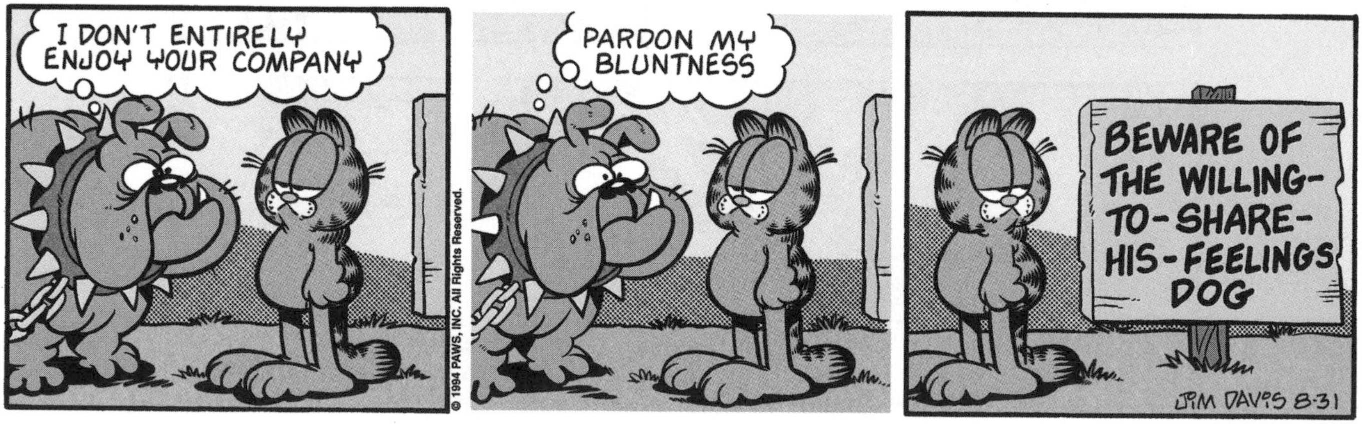
I DON'T ENTIRELY ENJOY YOUR COMPANY
© 1994 PAWS, INC. All Rights Reserved.
PARDON MY BLUNTNESS
BEWARE OF THE WILLING-TO-SHARE-HIS-FEELINGS DOG
JIM DAVIS 8-31

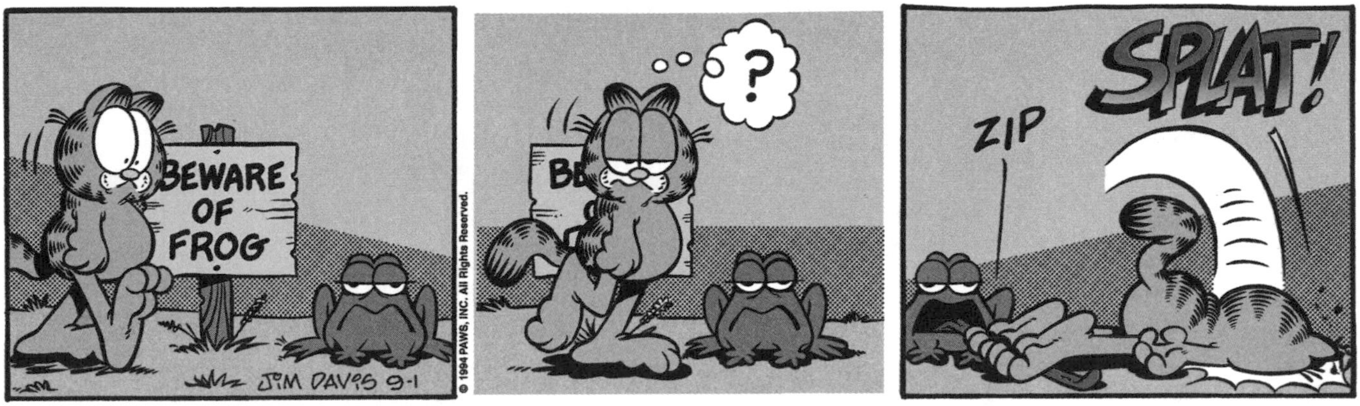
BEWARE OF FROG
JIM DAVIS 9-1
© 1994 PAWS, INC. All Rights Reserved.
?
ZIP
SPLAT!

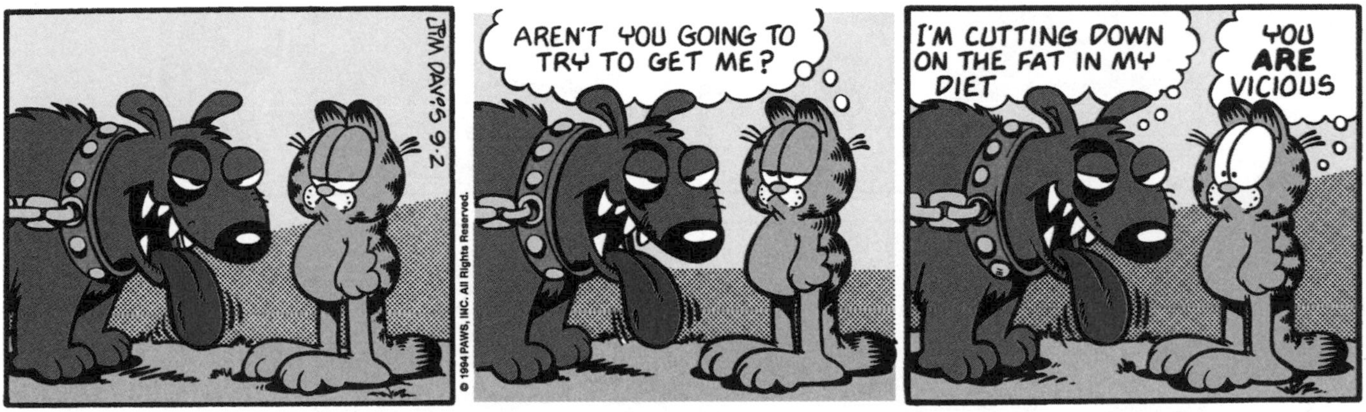
JIM DAVIS 9-2
© 1994 PAWS, INC. All Rights Reserved.
AREN'T YOU GOING TO TRY TO GET ME?
I'M CUTTING DOWN ON THE FAT IN MY DIET
YOU **ARE** VICIOUS

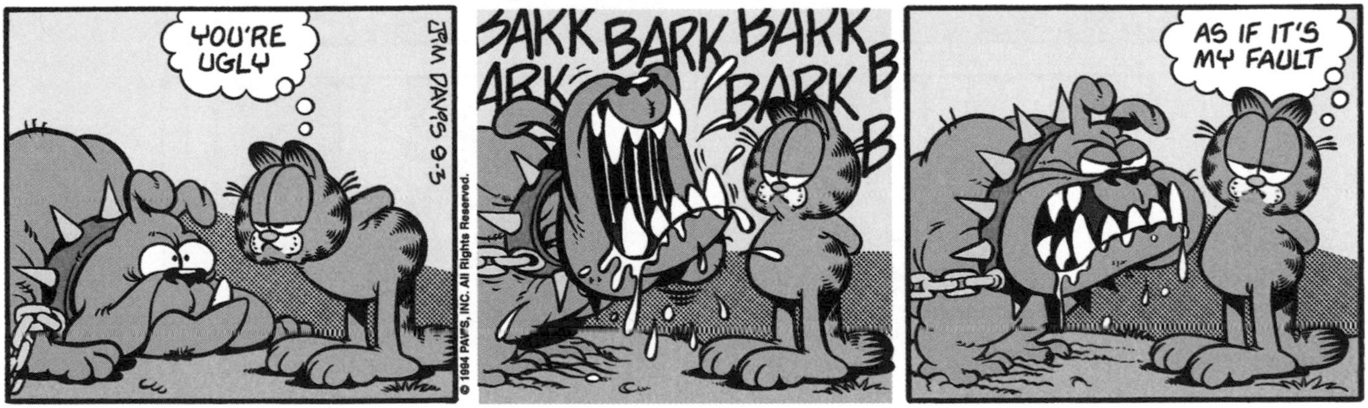
YOU'RE UGLY
JIM DAVIS 9-3
© 1994 PAWS, INC. All Rights Reserved.
BARK BARK BARK
BARK B B
AS IF IT'S MY FAULT

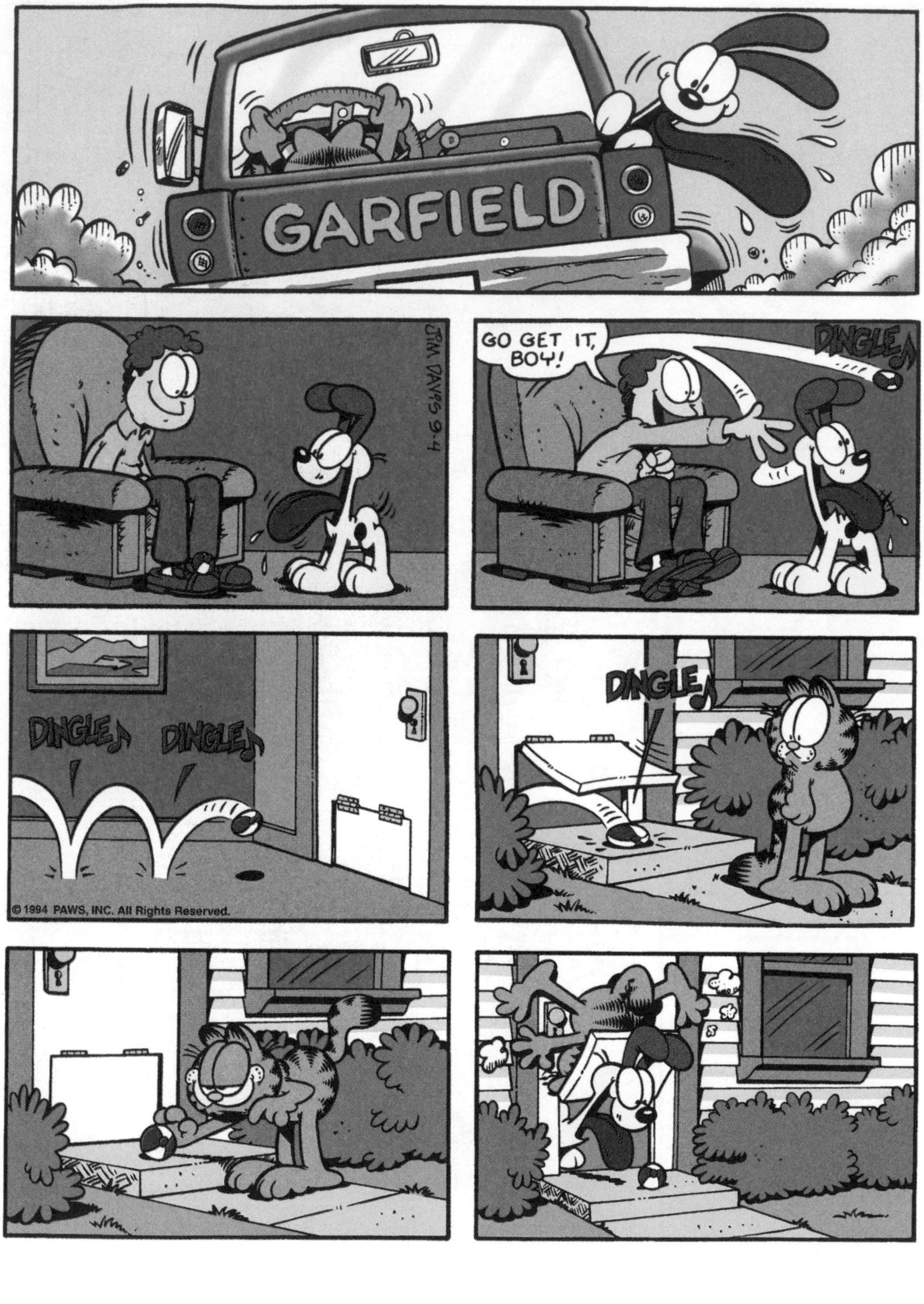
GARFIELD
JIM DAVIS 9-4
GO GET IT, BOY!
DINGLE
DINGLE DINGLE
DINGLE
© 1994 PAWS, INC. All Rights Reserved.

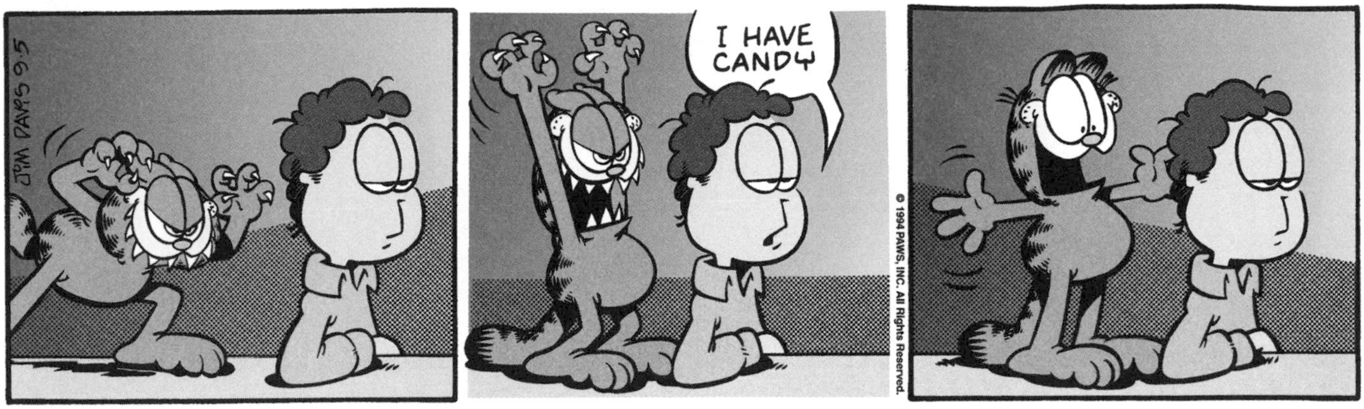
JIM DAVIS 9-5
I HAVE CANDY
© 1994 PAWS, INC. All Rights Reserved.

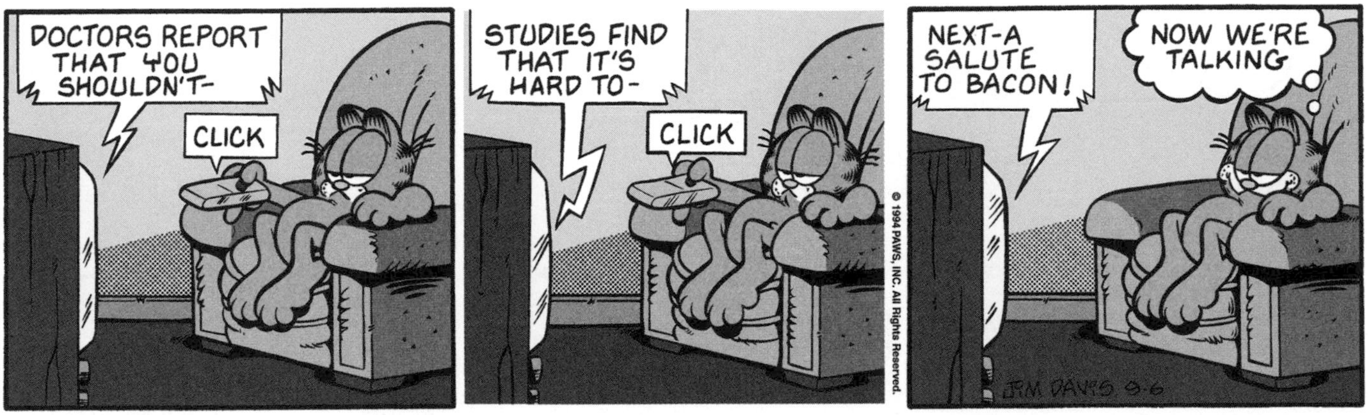
DOCTORS REPORT THAT YOU SHOULDN'T-
CLICK
STUDIES FIND THAT IT'S HARD TO-
CLICK
NEXT-A SALUTE TO BACON!
NOW WE'RE TALKING
JIM DAVIS 9-6
© 1994 PAWS, INC. All Rights Reserved.

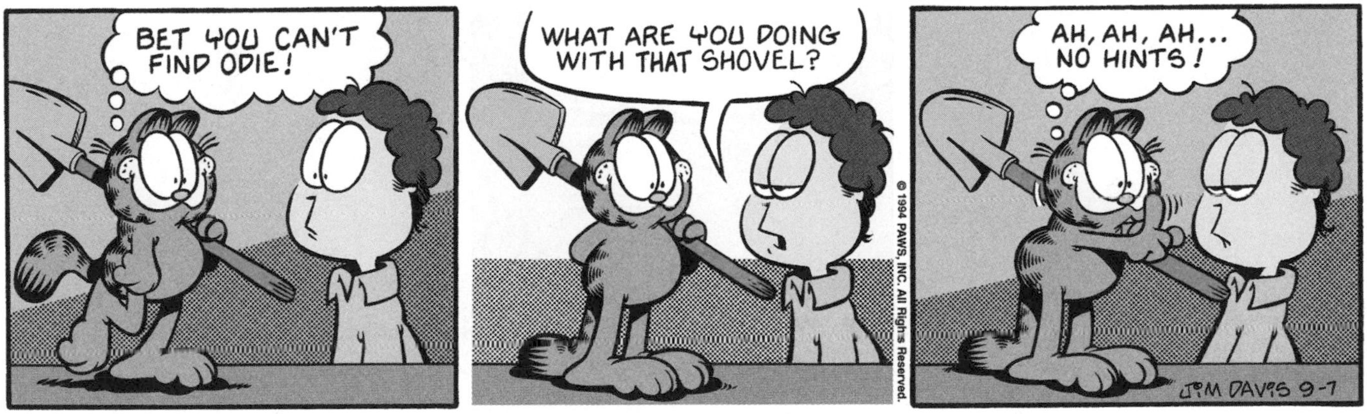
BET YOU CAN'T FIND ODIE!
WHAT ARE YOU DOING WITH THAT SHOVEL?
AH, AH, AH... NO HINTS!
JIM DAVIS 9-7
© 1994 PAWS, INC. All Rights Reserved.

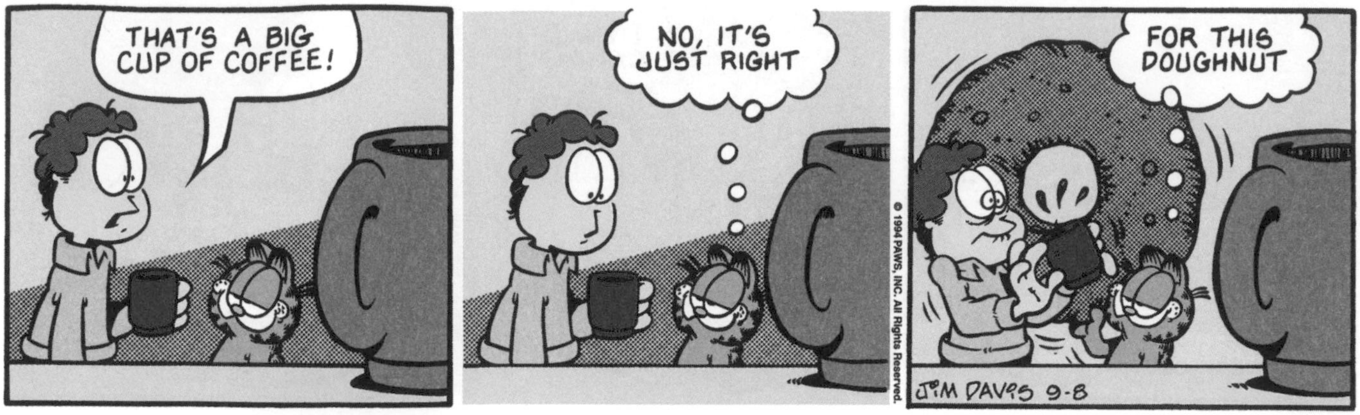
THAT'S A BIG CUP OF COFFEE!
NO, IT'S JUST RIGHT
FOR THIS DOUGHNUT
© 1994 PAWS, INC. All Rights Reserved.
JIM DAVIS 9-8

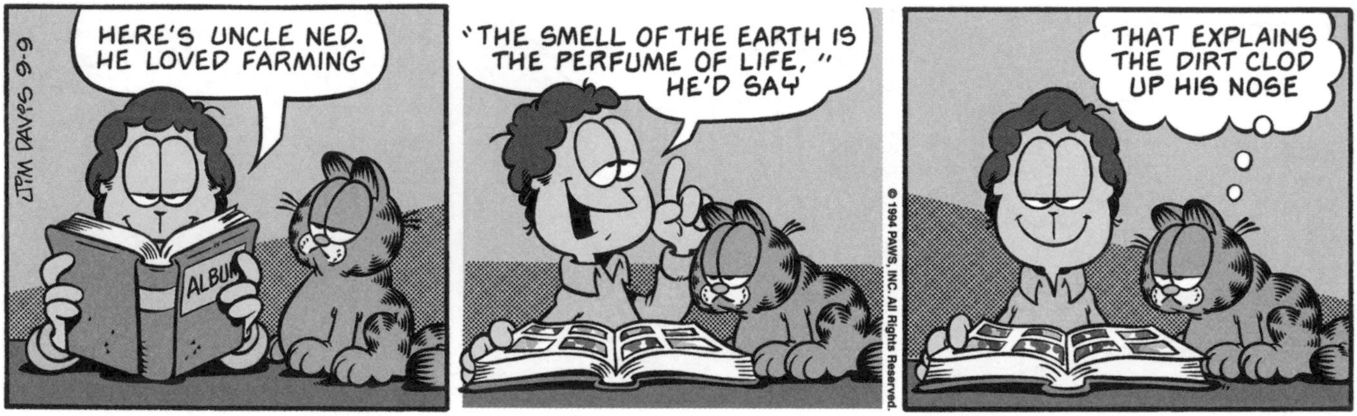
JIM DAVIS 9-9
HERE'S UNCLE NED. HE LOVED FARMING
ALBUM
"THE SMELL OF THE EARTH IS THE PERFUME OF LIFE," HE'D SAY
© 1994 PAWS, INC. All Rights Reserved.
THAT EXPLAINS THE DIRT CLOD UP HIS NOSE

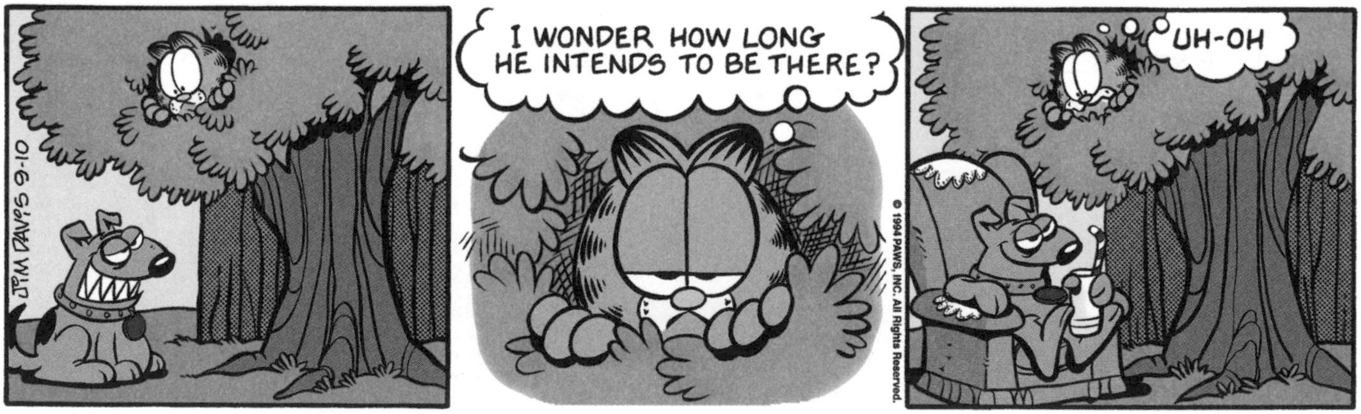
JIM DAVIS 9-10
I WONDER HOW LONG HE INTENDS TO BE THERE?
© 1994 PAWS, INC. All Rights Reserved.
UH-OH

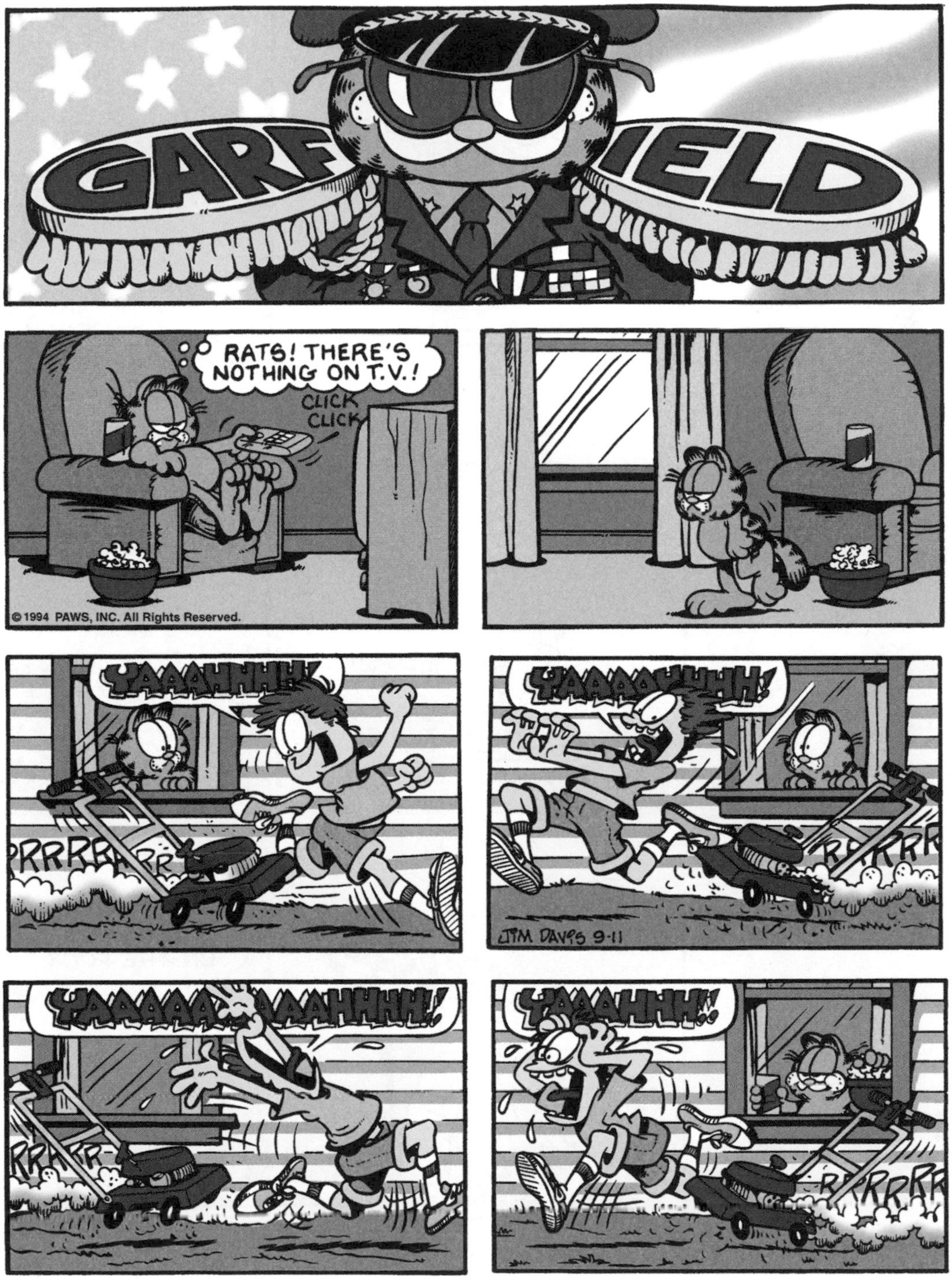
GARFIELD
RATS! THERE'S NOTHING ON T.V.!
CLICK CLICK
YAAAHHHH!
RRRRRRRR
YAAAAHHHH!
RRRRR
JIM DAVIS 9-11
YAAAAAAAAHHHHH!
RRRR
YAAAHHH!
RRRRRR

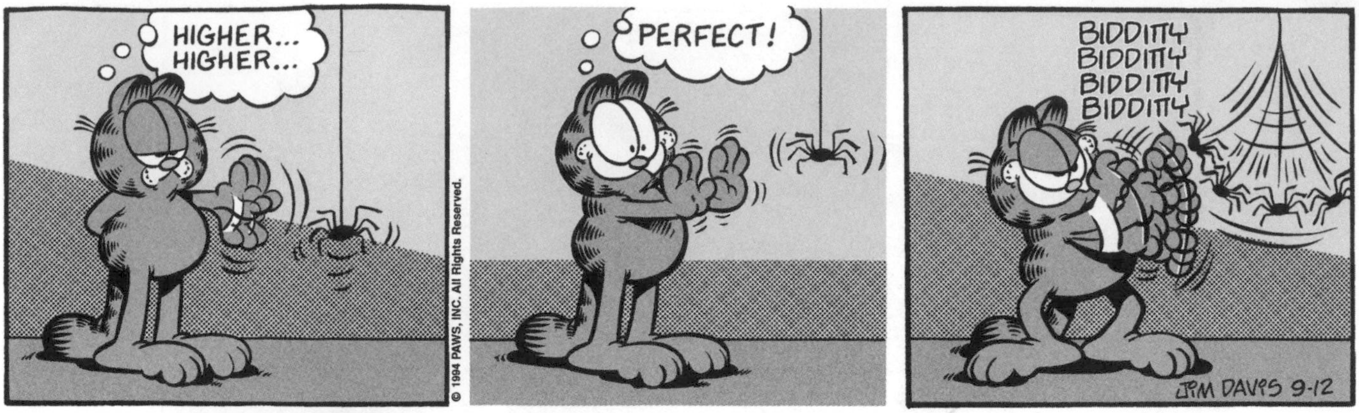
HIGHER... HIGHER...
© 1994 PAWS, INC. All Rights Reserved.
PERFECT!
BIDDITTY BIDDITTY BIDDITTY BIDDITTY
JIM DAVIS 9-12

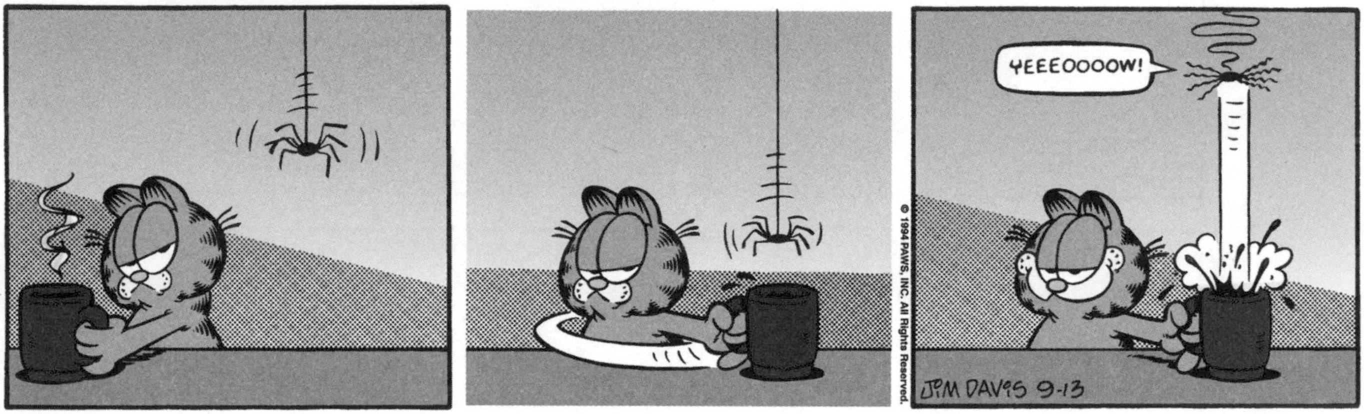
© 1994 PAWS, INC. All Rights Reserved.
YEEEOOOOW!
JIM DAVIS 9-13

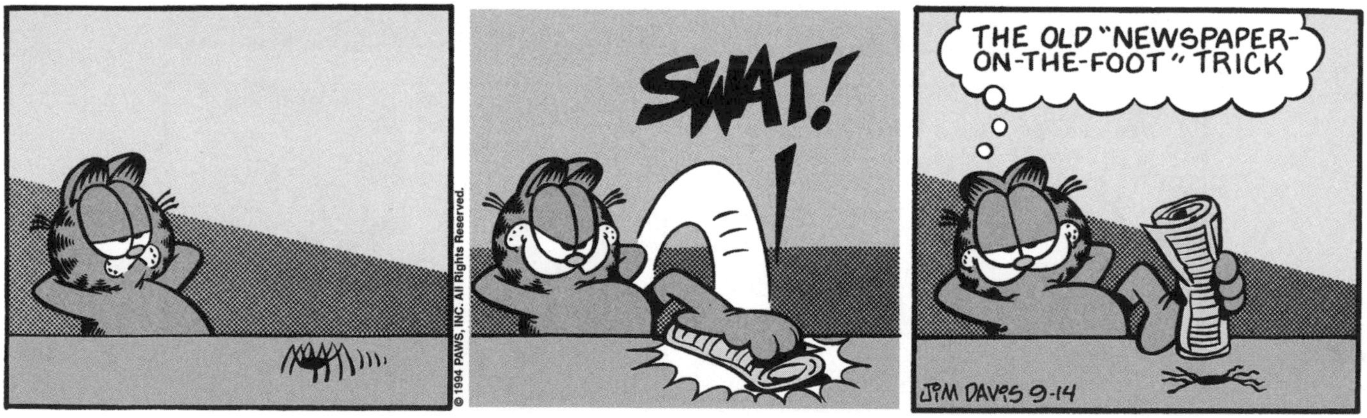
© 1994 PAWS, INC. All Rights Reserved.
SWAT!
THE OLD "NEWSPAPER-ON-THE-FOOT" TRICK
JIM DAVIS 9-14

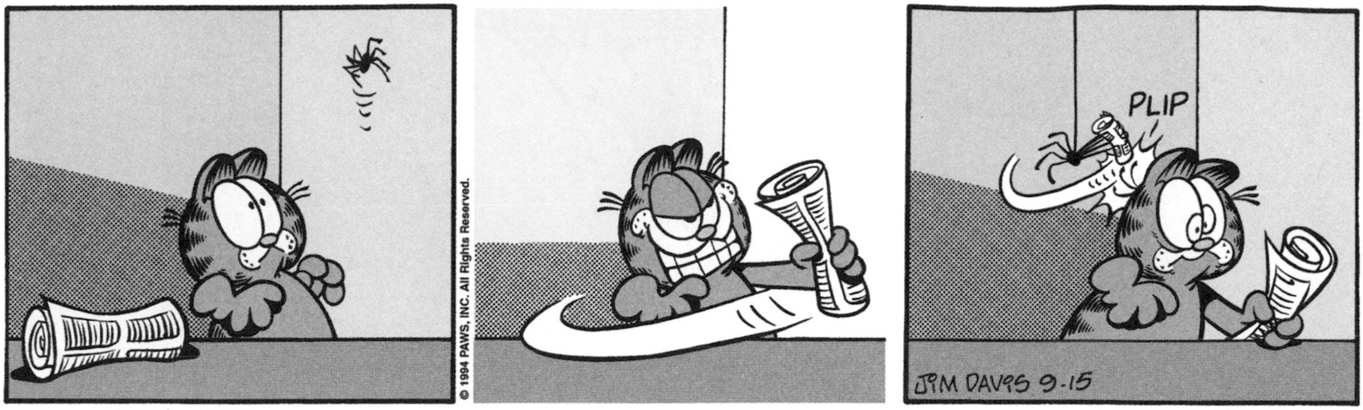
PLIP
JIM DAVIS 9-15

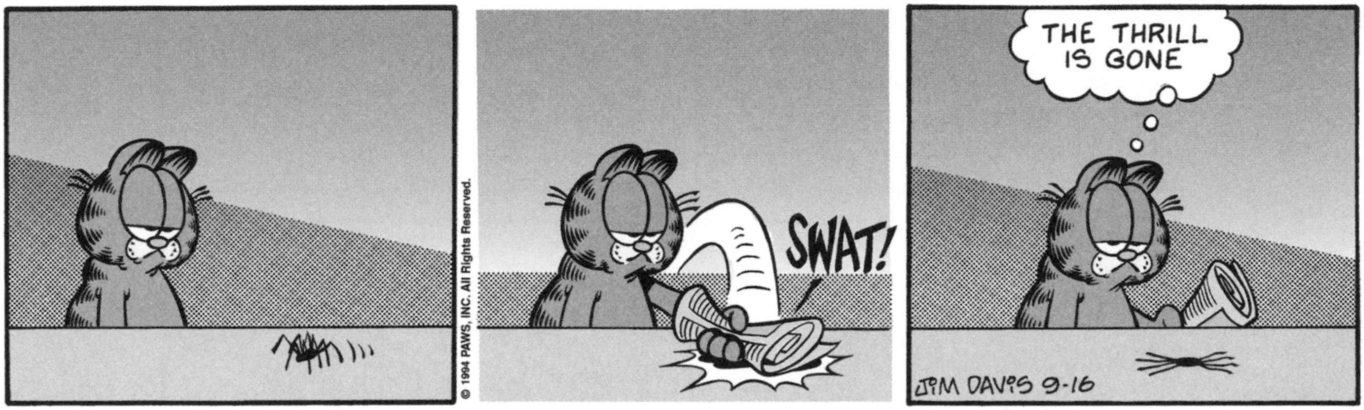
SWAT!
THE THRILL IS GONE
JIM DAVIS 9-16

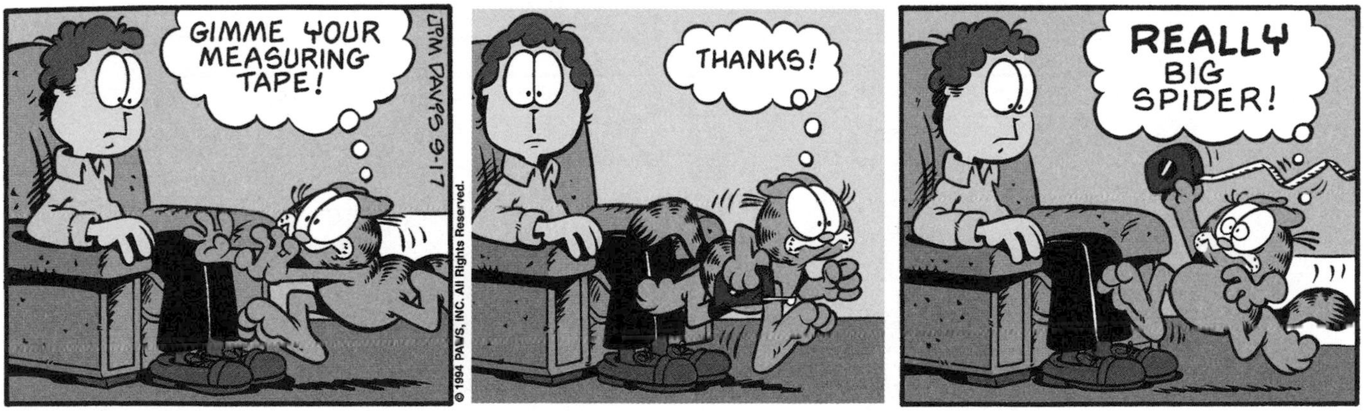
GIMME YOUR MEASURING TAPE!
JIM DAVIS 9-17
THANKS!
REALLY BIG SPIDER!

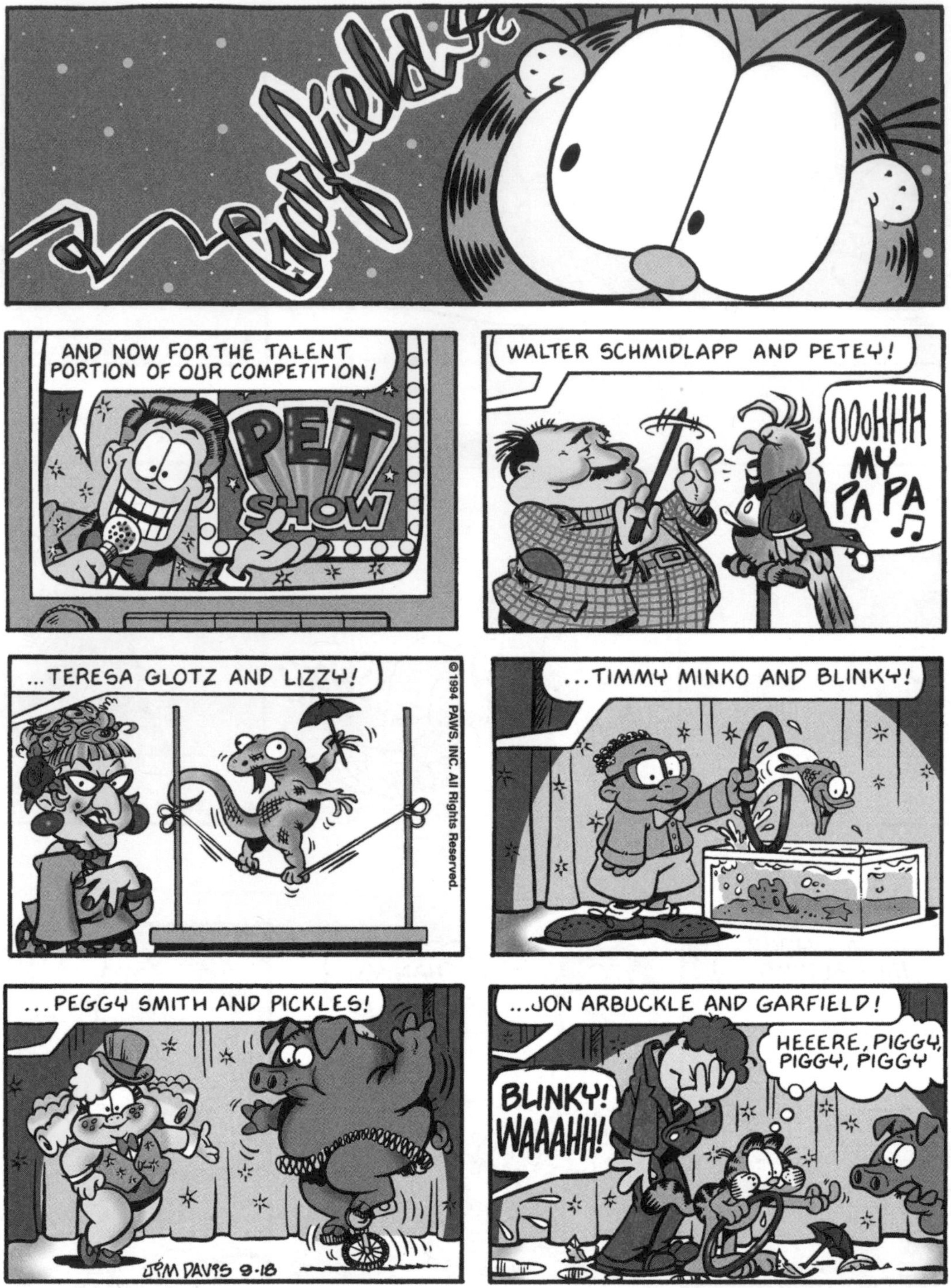
GARFIELD
AND NOW FOR THE TALENT PORTION OF OUR COMPETITION!
PET SHOW
WALTER SCHMIDLAPP AND PETEY!
OOoHHH MY PA PA ♫
...TERESA GLOTZ AND LIZZY!
© 1994 PAWS, INC. All Rights Reserved.
...TIMMY MINKO AND BLINKY!
...PEGGY SMITH AND PICKLES!
JIM DAVIS 9-18
...JON ARBUCKLE AND GARFIELD!
HEEERE, PIGGY, PIGGY, PIGGY
BLINKY! WAAAHH!

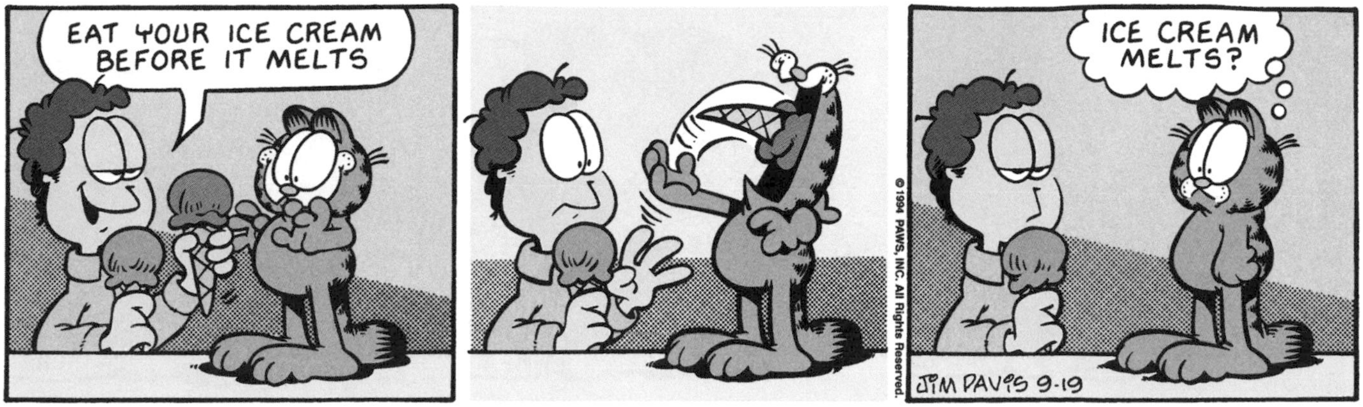
EAT YOUR ICE CREAM BEFORE IT MELTS
ICE CREAM MELTS?
JIM DAVIS 9-19

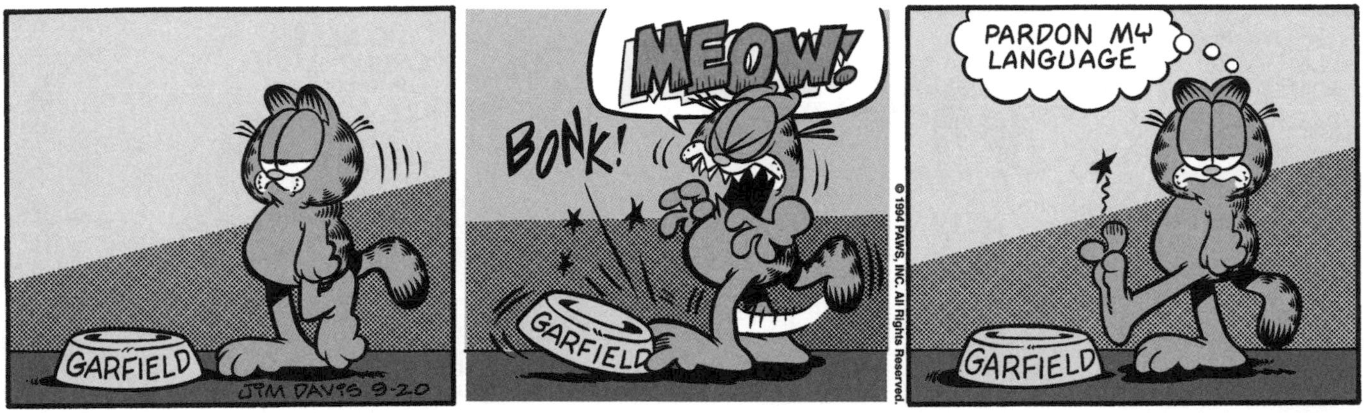
GARFIELD
JIM DAVIS 9-20
BONK!
MEOW!
GARFIELD
PARDON MY LANGUAGE
GARFIELD

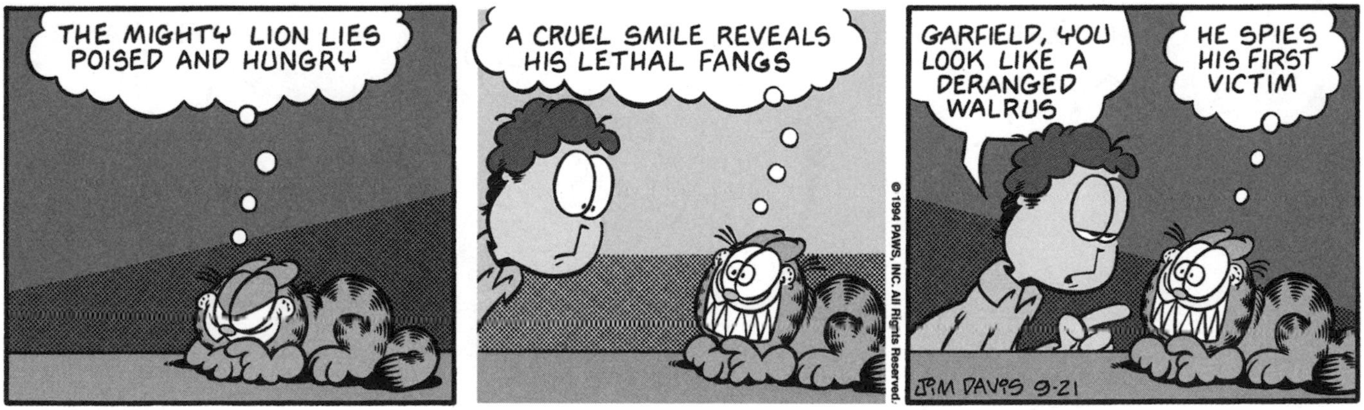
THE MIGHTY LION LIES POISED AND HUNGRY
A CRUEL SMILE REVEALS HIS LETHAL FANGS
GARFIELD, YOU LOOK LIKE A DERANGED WALRUS
HE SPIES HIS FIRST VICTIM
JIM DAVIS 9-21

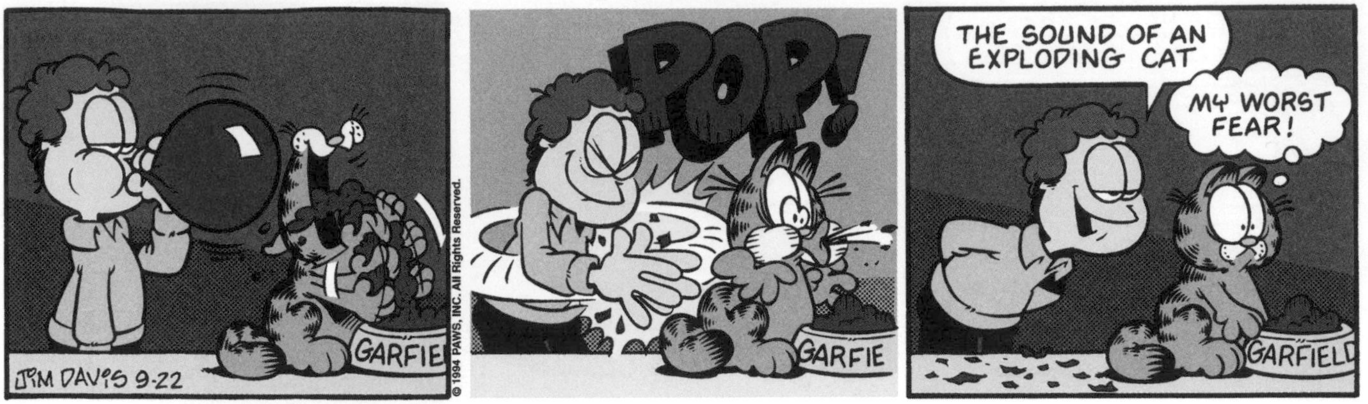
GARFIE
JIM DAVIS 9-22
POP!
© 1994 PAWS, INC. All Rights Reserved.
GARFIE
THE SOUND OF AN EXPLODING CAT
MY WORST FEAR!
GARFIELD

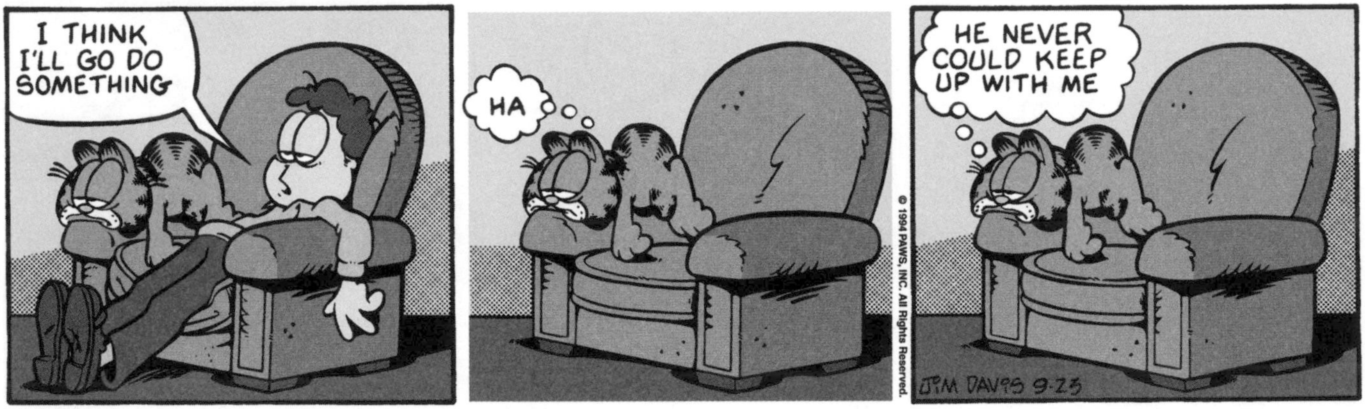
I THINK I'LL GO DO SOMETHING
HA
© 1994 PAWS, INC. All Rights Reserved.
HE NEVER COULD KEEP UP WITH ME
JIM DAVIS 9-23

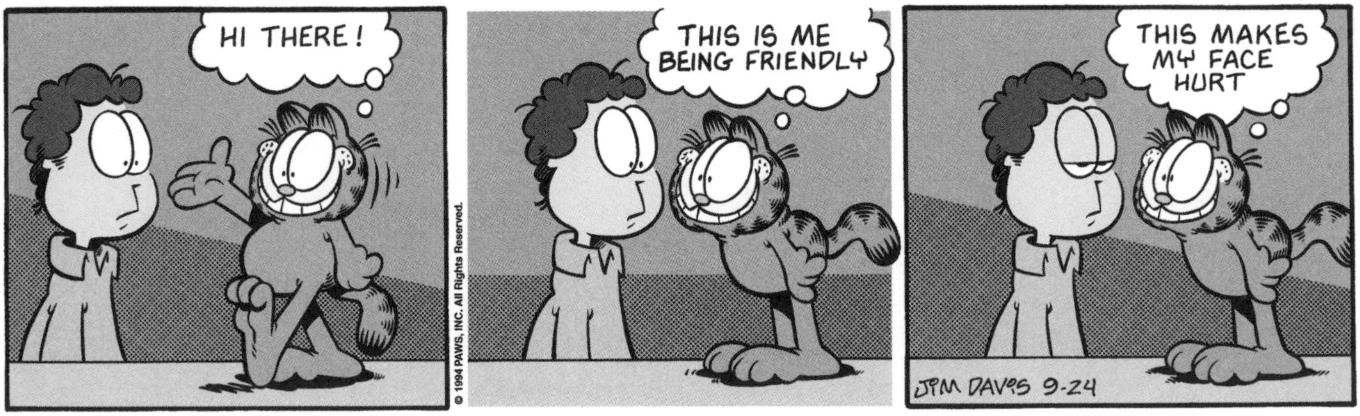
HI THERE!
© 1994 PAWS, INC. All Rights Reserved.
THIS IS ME BEING FRIENDLY
THIS MAKES MY FACE HURT
JIM DAVIS 9-24

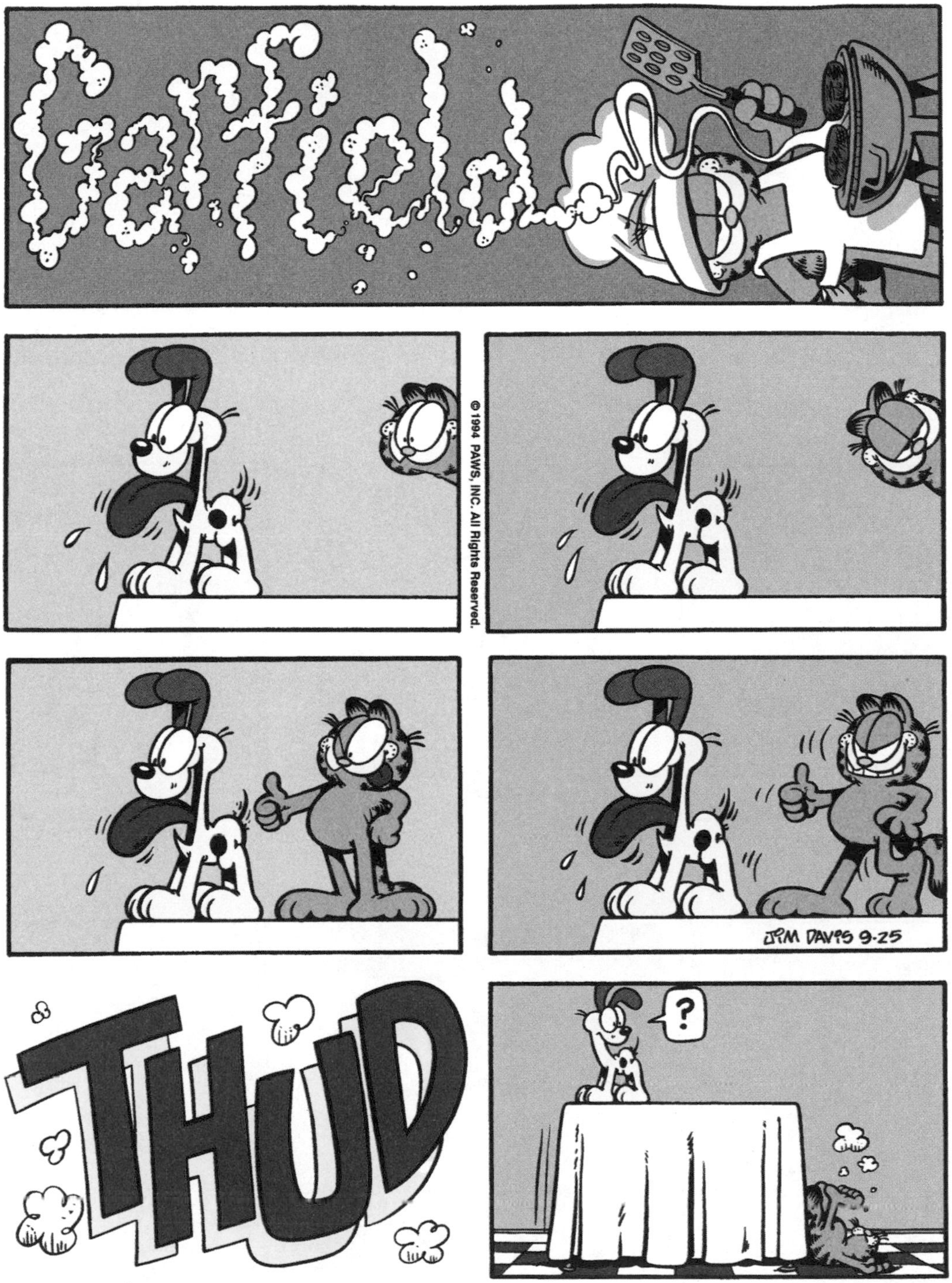
Garfield
© 1994 PAWS, INC. All Rights Reserved.
JIM DAVIS 9-25
THUD
?

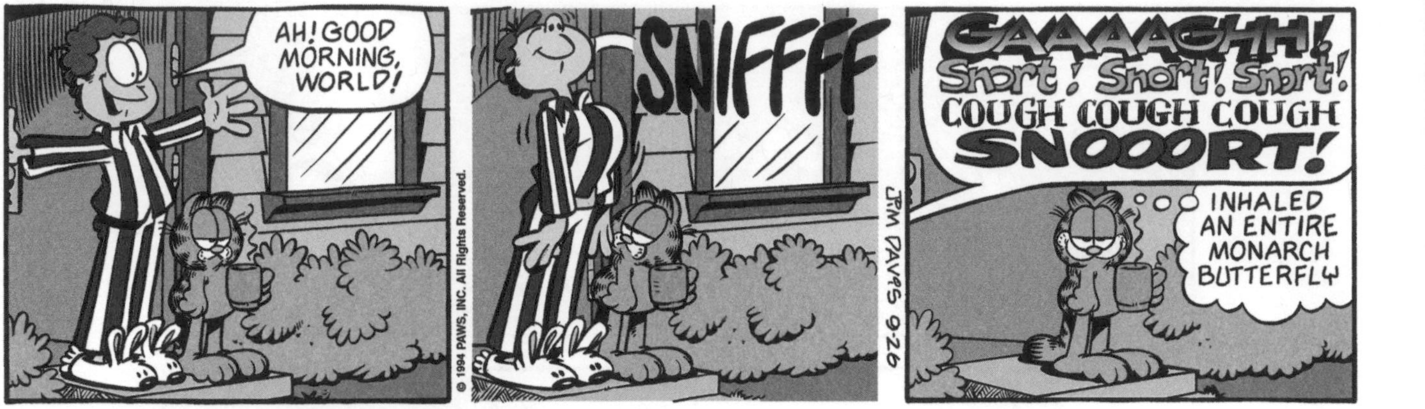
AH! GOOD MORNING, WORLD!
SNIFFFF
GAAAAGHH! Snort! Snort! Snort! COUGH COUGH COUGH SNOOORT!
INHALED AN ENTIRE MONARCH BUTTERFLY
© 1994 PAWS, INC. All Rights Reserved.
JIM DAVIS 9-26

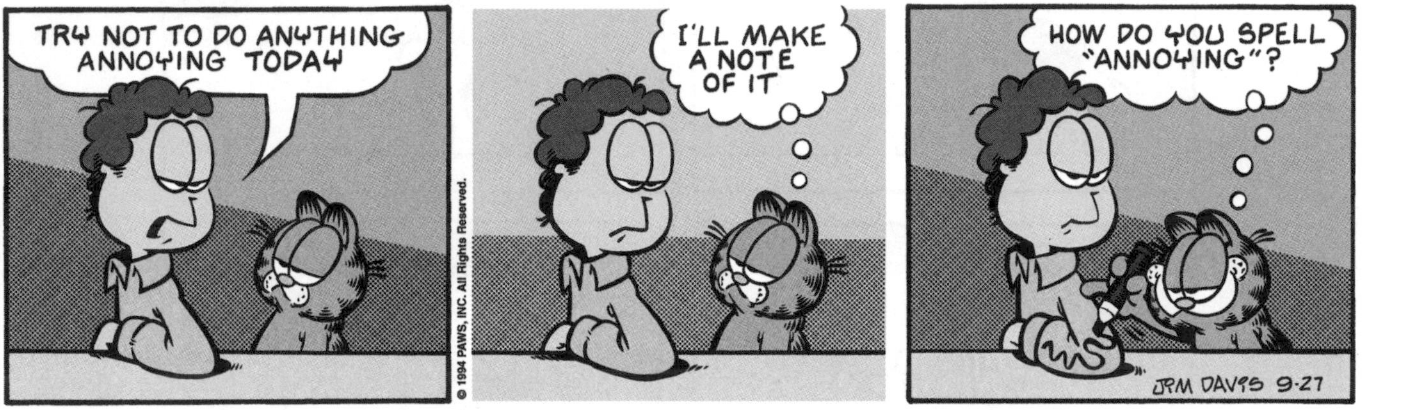
TRY NOT TO DO ANYTHING ANNOYING TODAY
I'LL MAKE A NOTE OF IT
HOW DO YOU SPELL "ANNOYING"?
© 1994 PAWS, INC. All Rights Reserved.
JIM DAVIS 9-27

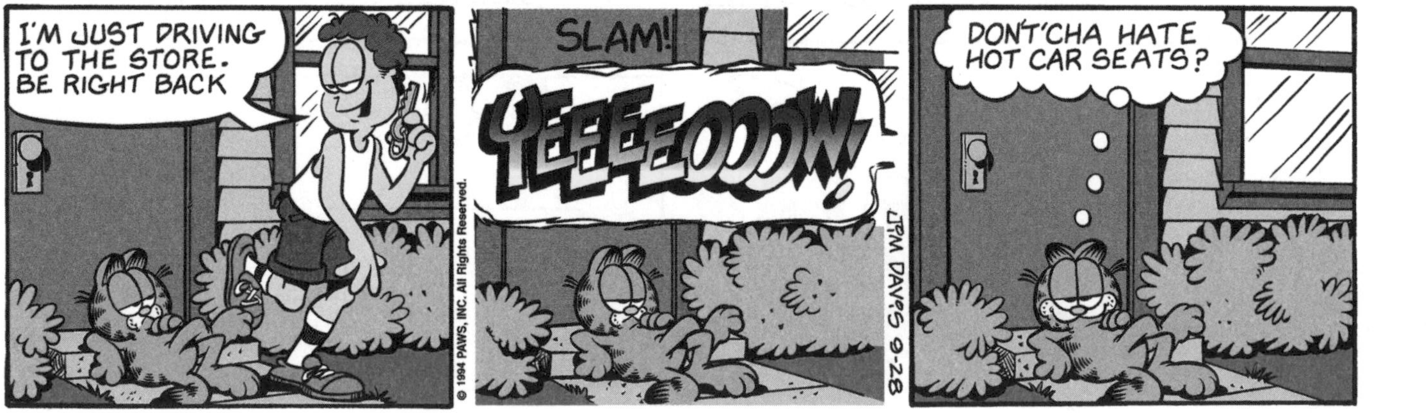
I'M JUST DRIVING TO THE STORE. BE RIGHT BACK
SLAM!
YEEEEOOOW!
DON'T'CHA HATE HOT CAR SEATS?
© 1994 PAWS, INC. All Rights Reserved.
JIM DAVIS 9-28

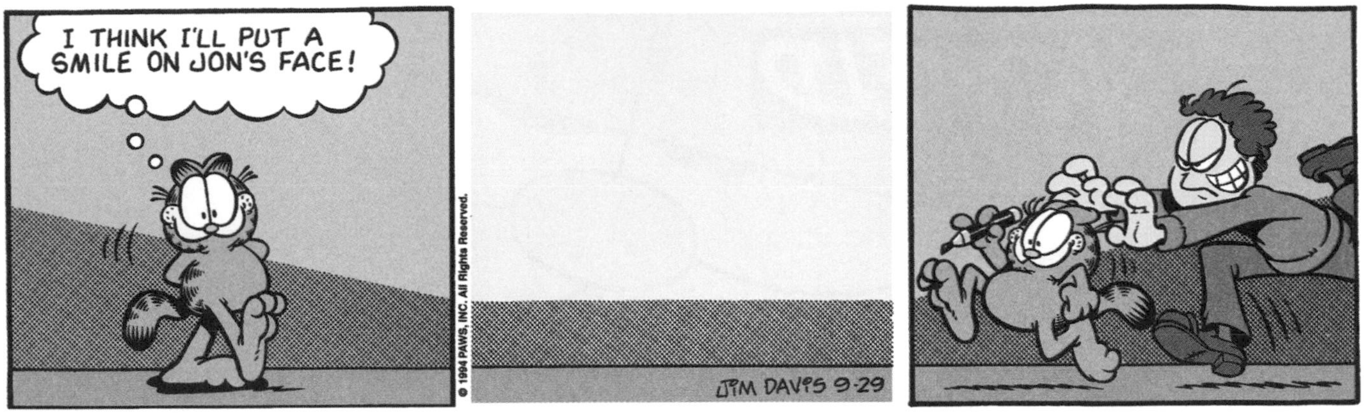
I THINK I'LL PUT A SMILE ON JON'S FACE!
© 1994 PAWS, INC. All Rights Reserved.
JIM DAVIS 9-29

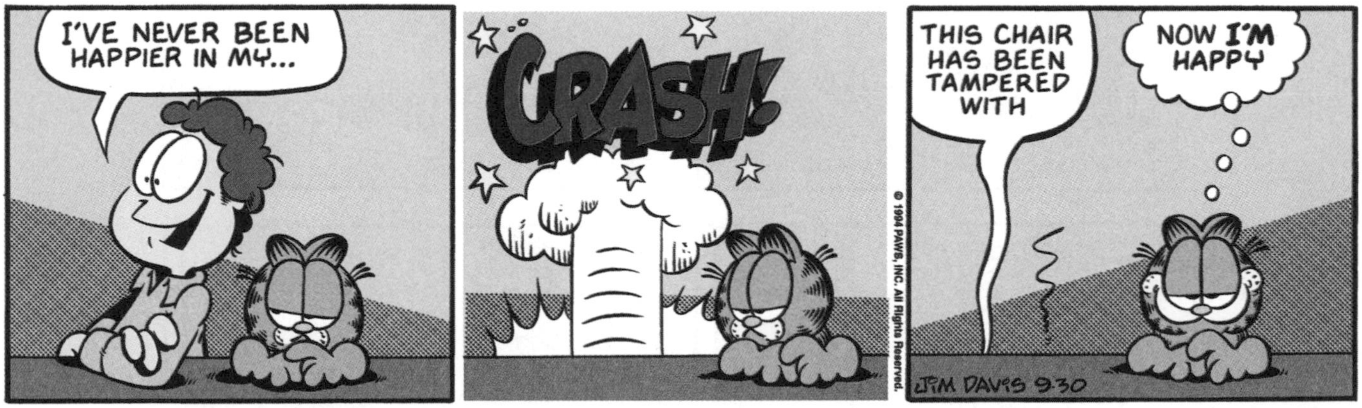
I'VE NEVER BEEN HAPPIER IN MY...
CRASH!
© 1994 PAWS, INC. All Rights Reserved.
THIS CHAIR HAS BEEN TAMPERED WITH
NOW **I'M** HAPPY
JIM DAVIS 9-30

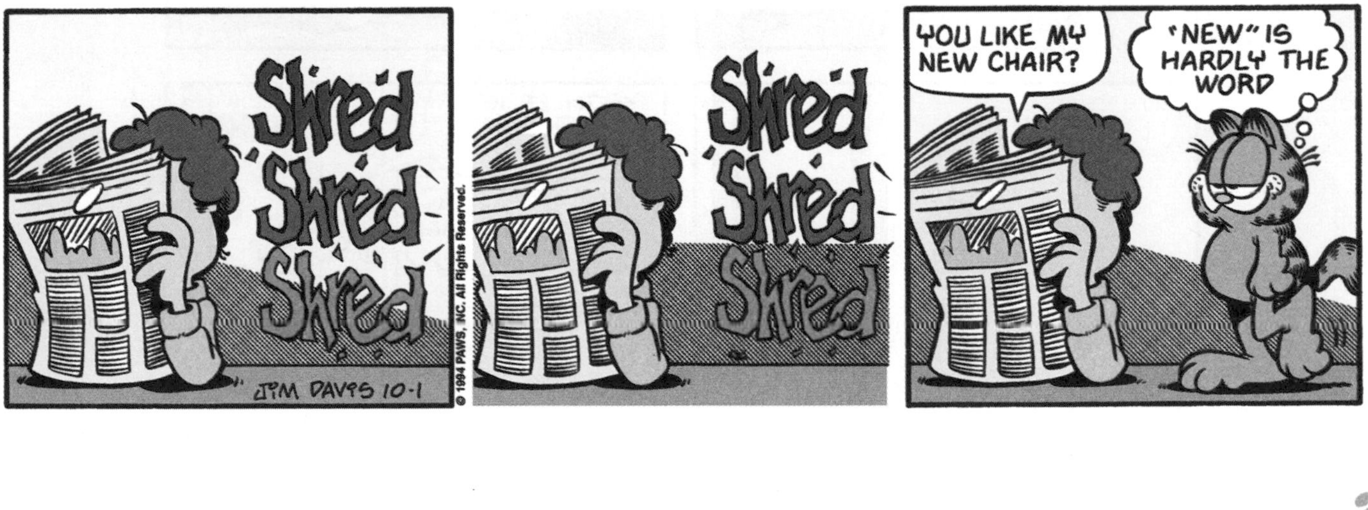
Shred
Shred
Shred
JIM DAVIS 10-1
© 1994 PAWS, INC. All Rights Reserved.
Shred
Shred
Shred
YOU LIKE MY NEW CHAIR?
"NEW" IS HARDLY THE WORD

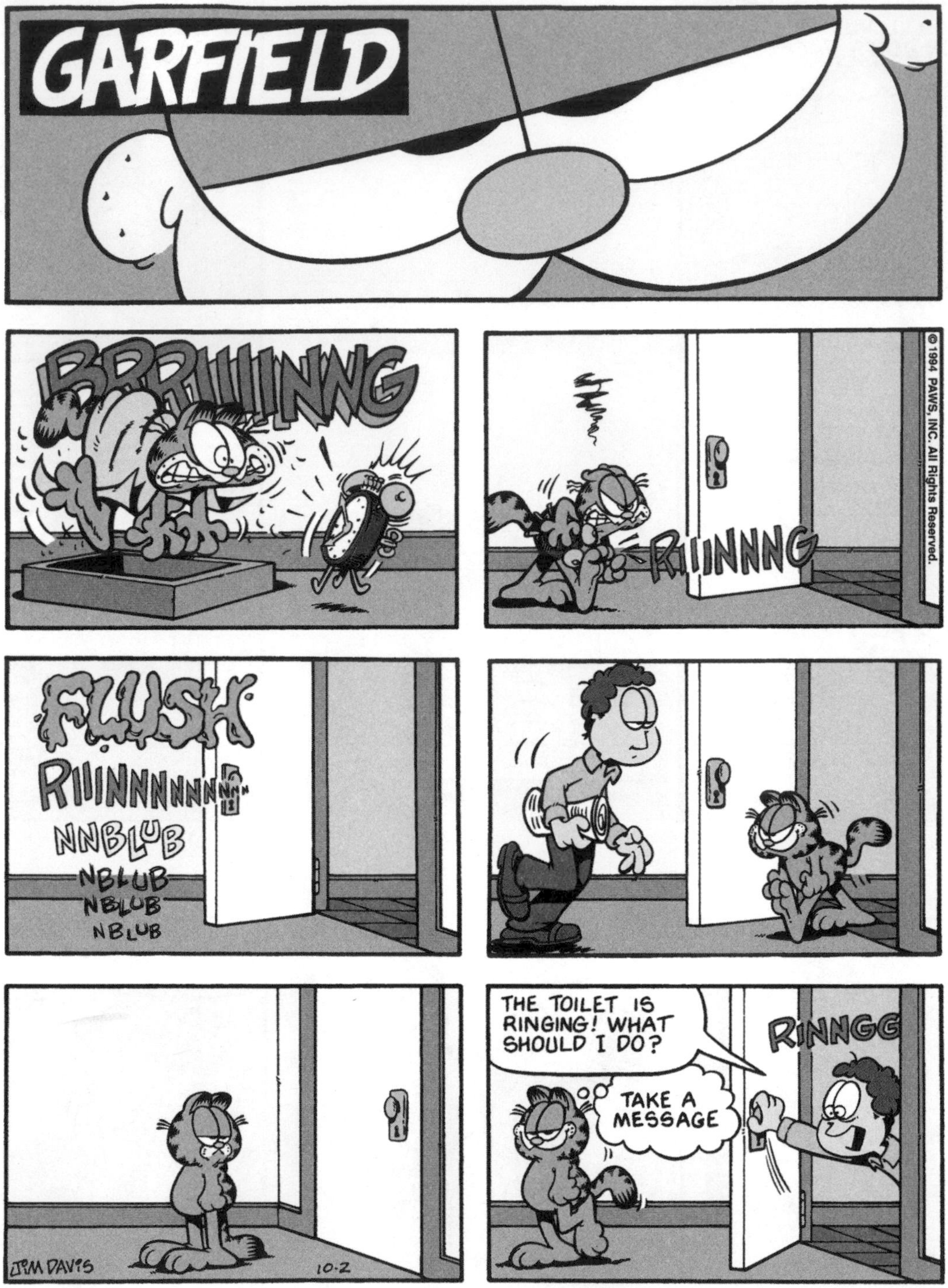
GARFIELD
BRRIIIIINNG
RIIINNNG
© 1994 PAWS, INC. All Rights Reserved.
FLUSH
RIIINNNNNNN
NNBLUB
NBLUB
NBLUB
NBLUB
JIM DAVIS
10-2
THE TOILET IS RINGING! WHAT SHOULD I DO?
RINNGG
TAKE A MESSAGE

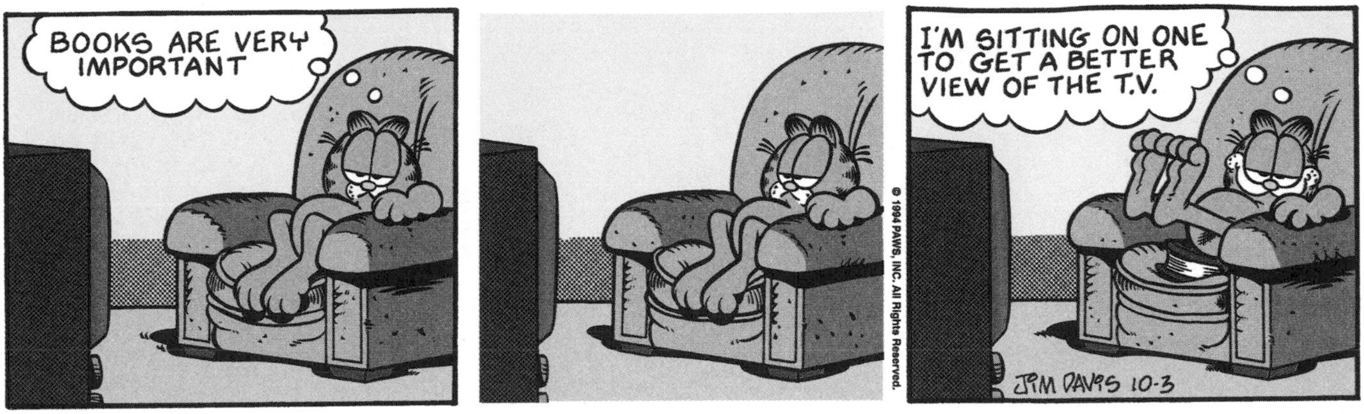
BOOKS ARE VERY IMPORTANT
I'M SITTING ON ONE TO GET A BETTER VIEW OF THE T.V.
© 1994 PAWS, INC. All Rights Reserved.
JIM DAVIS 10-3

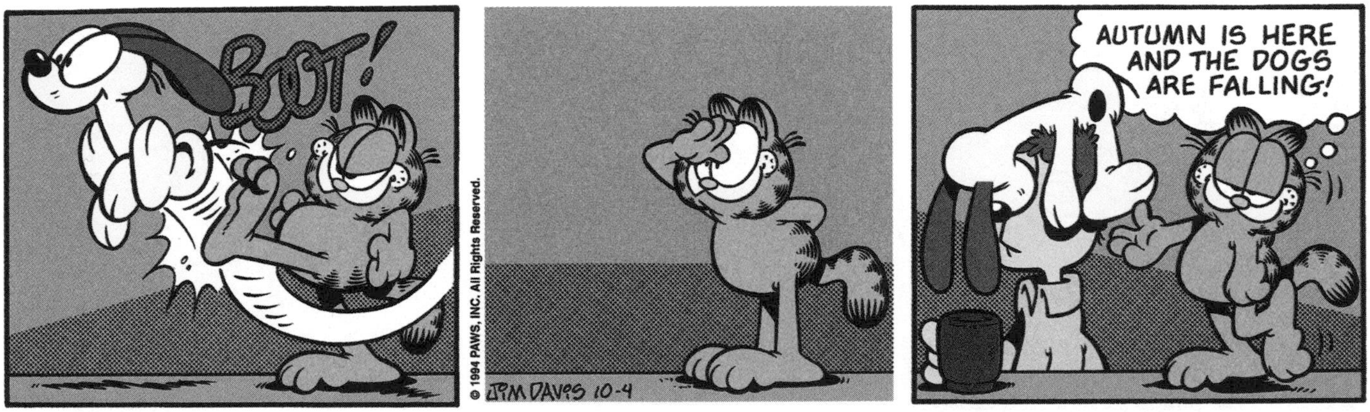
BOOT!
© 1994 PAWS, INC. All Rights Reserved.
JIM DAVIS 10-4
AUTUMN IS HERE AND THE DOGS ARE FALLING!

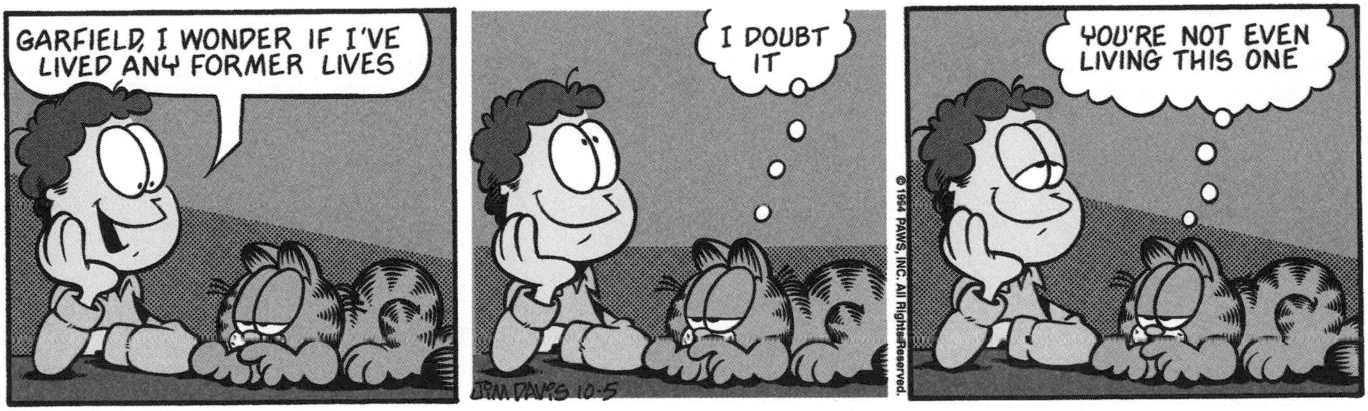
GARFIELD, I WONDER IF I'VE LIVED ANY FORMER LIVES
I DOUBT IT
JIM DAVIS 10-5
© 1994 PAWS, INC. All Rights Reserved.
YOU'RE NOT EVEN LIVING THIS ONE

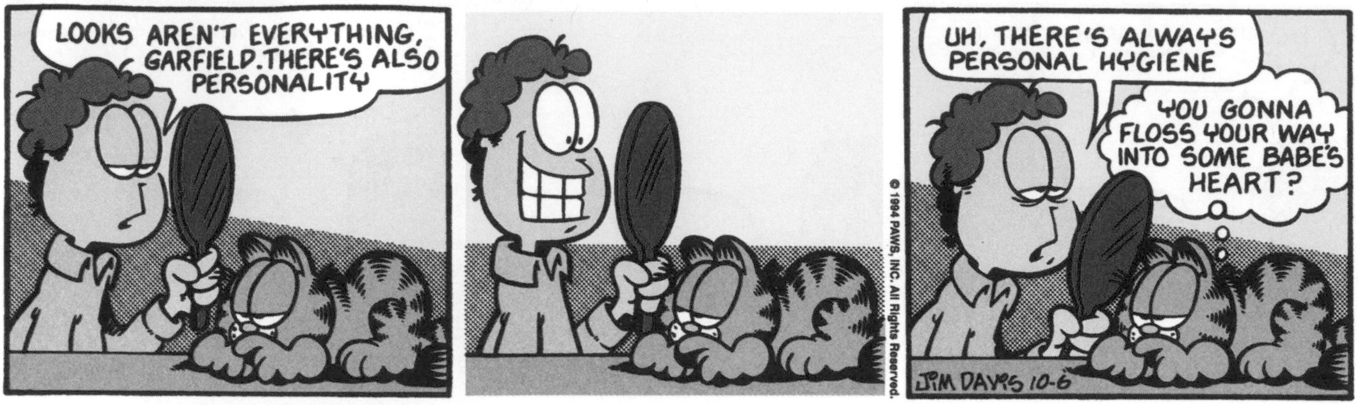
LOOKS AREN'T EVERYTHING, GARFIELD. THERE'S ALSO PERSONALITY
UH, THERE'S ALWAYS PERSONAL HYGIENE
YOU GONNA FLOSS YOUR WAY INTO SOME BABE'S HEART?
JIM DAVIS 10-6
© 1994 PAWS, INC. All Rights Reserved.

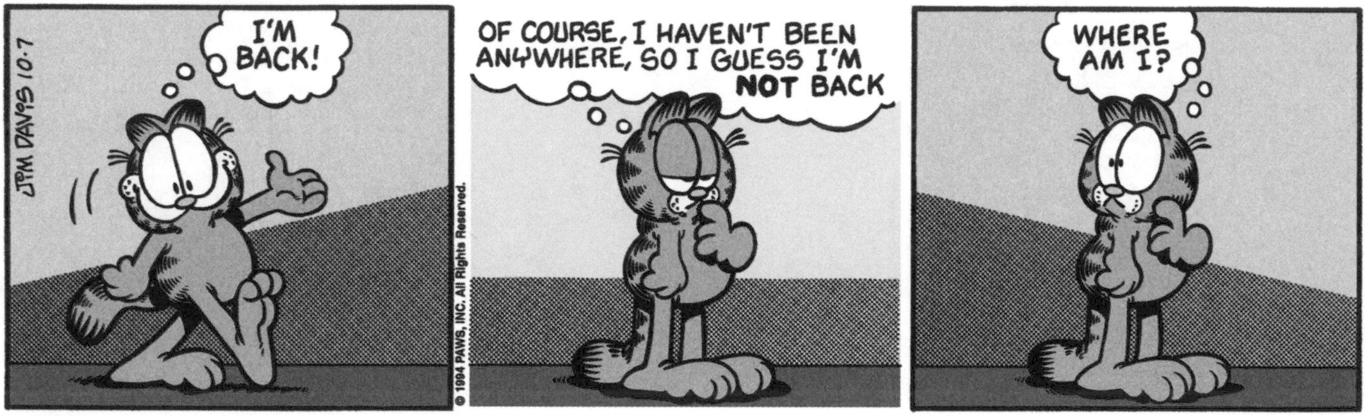
JIM DAVIS 10-7
I'M BACK!
OF COURSE, I HAVEN'T BEEN ANYWHERE, SO I GUESS I'M **NOT** BACK
WHERE AM I?
© 1994 PAWS, INC. All Rights Reserved.

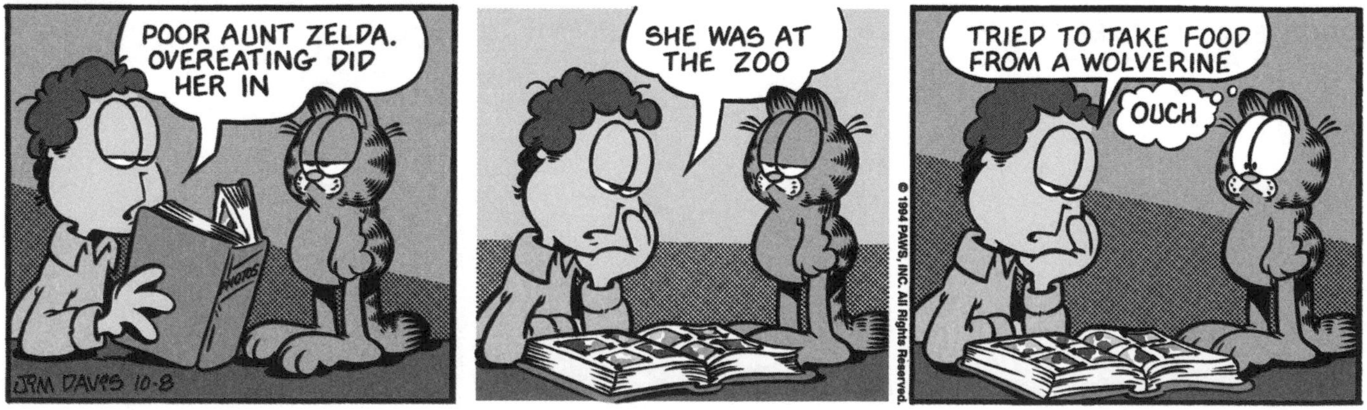
POOR AUNT ZELDA. OVEREATING DID HER IN
SHE WAS AT THE ZOO
TRIED TO TAKE FOOD FROM A WOLVERINE
OUCH
JIM DAVIS 10-8
© 1994 PAWS, INC. All Rights Reserved.

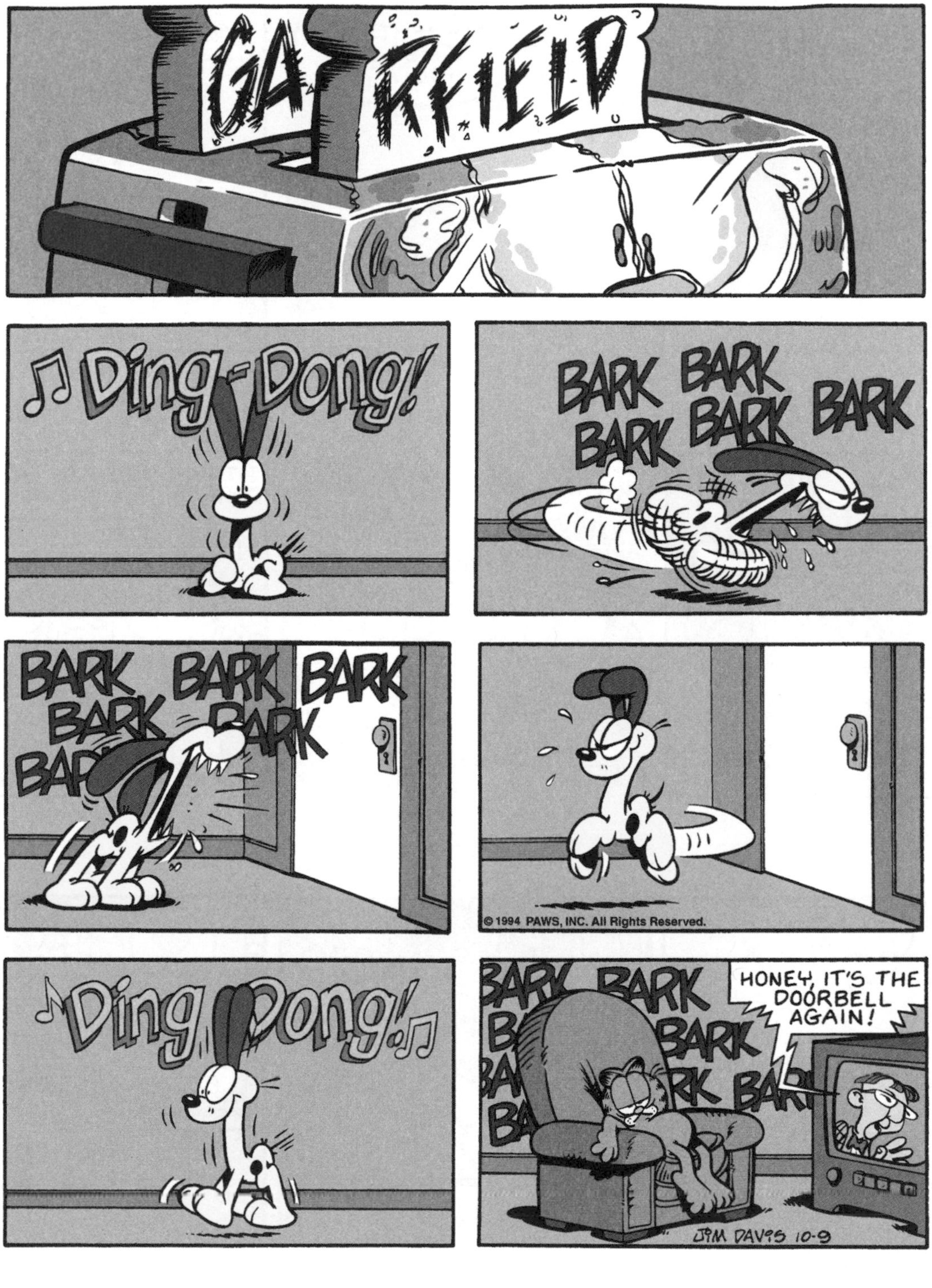
GARFIELD
♫ Ding-Dong!
BARK BARK
BARK BARK BARK BARK
BARK BARK BARK
BARK BARK
© 1994 PAWS, INC. All Rights Reserved.
♪ Ding Dong! ♫
HONEY, IT'S THE DOORBELL AGAIN!
JIM DAVIS 10-9

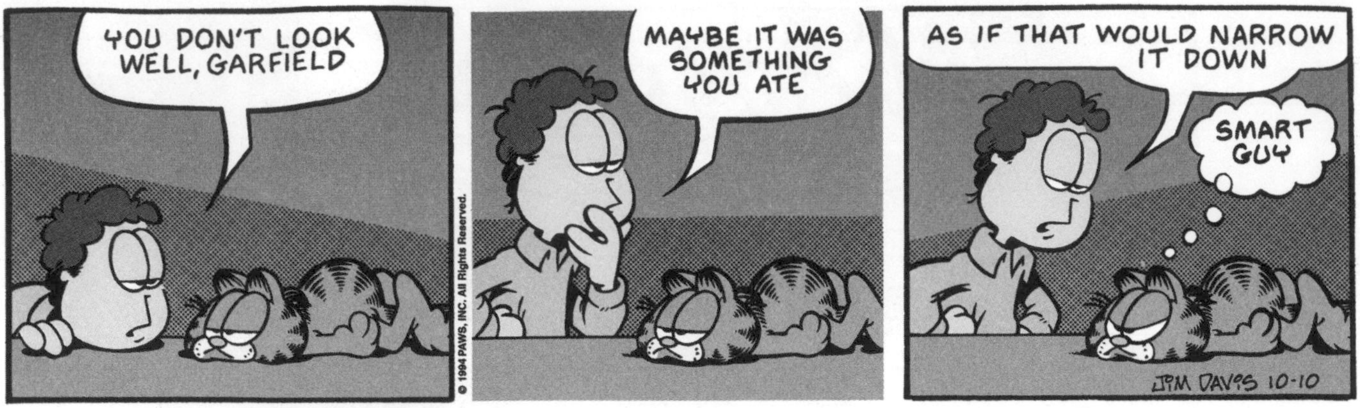
YOU DON'T LOOK WELL, GARFIELD
MAYBE IT WAS SOMETHING YOU ATE
AS IF THAT WOULD NARROW IT DOWN
SMART GUY
© 1994 PAWS, INC. All Rights Reserved.
JIM DAVIS 10-10

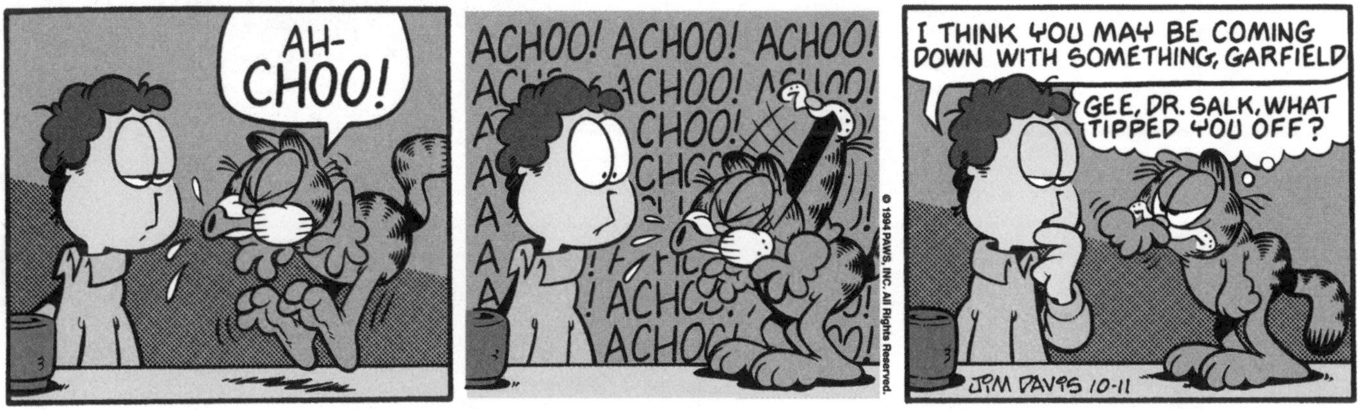
AH-CHOO!
ACHOO! ACHOO! ACHOO!
I THINK YOU MAY BE COMING DOWN WITH SOMETHING, GARFIELD
GEE, DR. SALK, WHAT TIPPED YOU OFF?
© 1994 PAWS, INC. All Rights Reserved.
JIM DAVIS 10-11

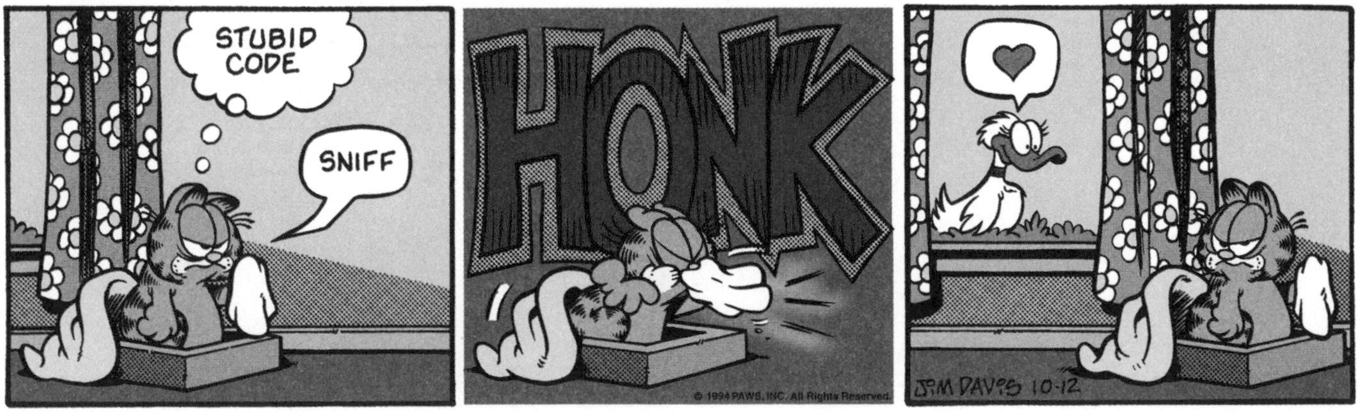
STUBID CODE
SNIFF
HONK
© 1994 PAWS, INC. All Rights Reserved.
JIM DAVIS 10-12

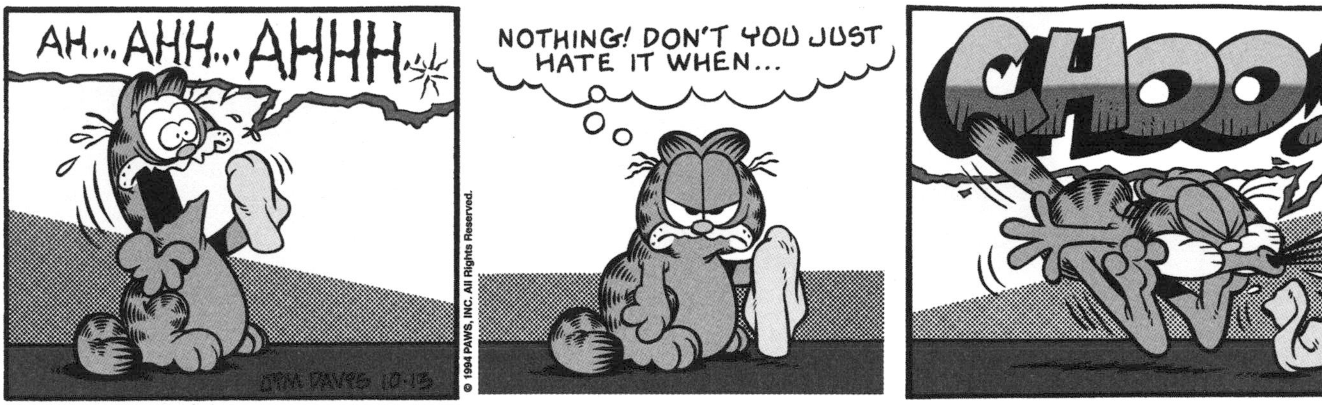
AH... AHH... AHHH
JIM DAVIS 10-13
© 1994 PAWS, INC. All Rights Reserved.
NOTHING! DON'T YOU JUST HATE IT WHEN...
CHOO!

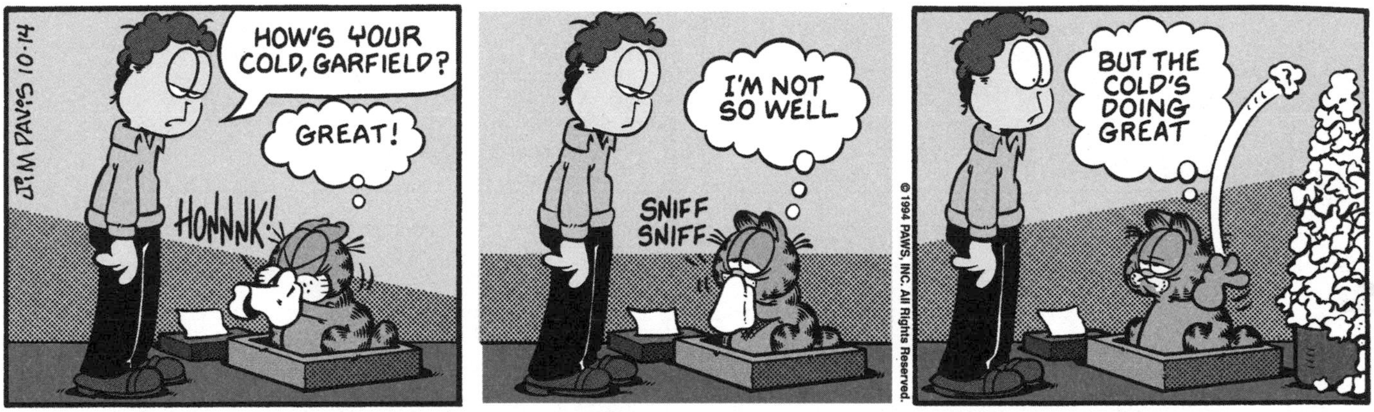
JIM DAVIS 10-14
HOW'S YOUR COLD, GARFIELD?
GREAT!
HONNNK!
I'M NOT SO WELL
SNIFF SNIFF
© 1994 PAWS, INC. All Rights Reserved.
BUT THE COLD'S DOING GREAT

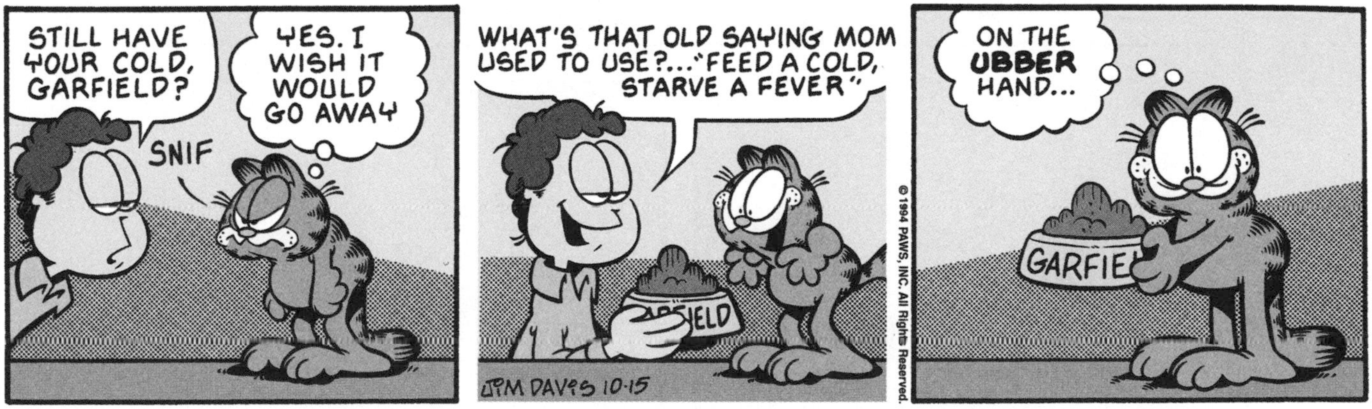
STILL HAVE YOUR COLD, GARFIELD?
YES. I WISH IT WOULD GO AWAY
SNIF
WHAT'S THAT OLD SAYING MOM USED TO USE?... "FEED A COLD, STARVE A FEVER"
JIM DAVIS 10-15
© 1994 PAWS, INC. All Rights Reserved.
ON THE UBBER HAND...
GARFIE

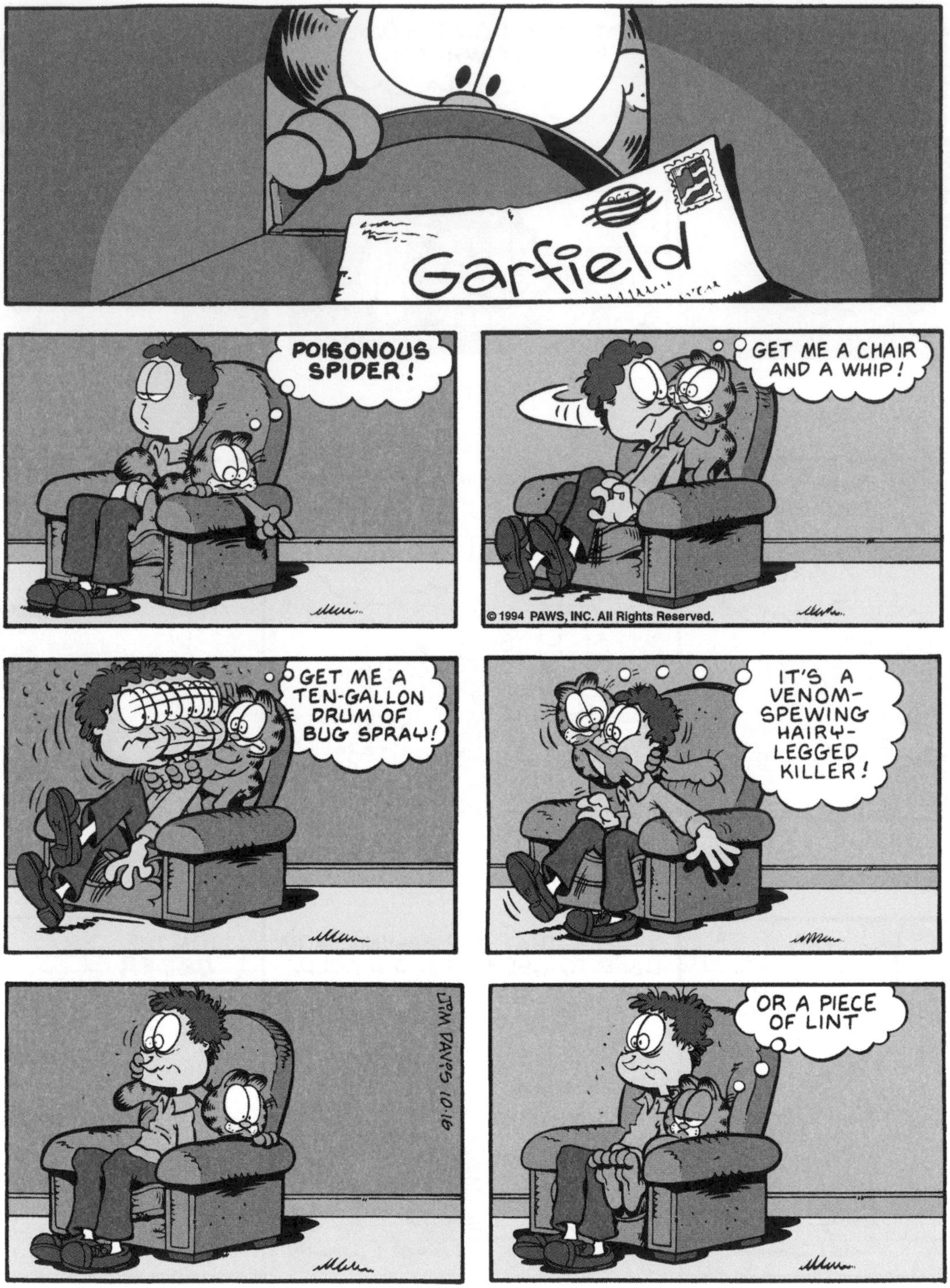
Garfield
POISONOUS SPIDER!
GET ME A CHAIR AND A WHIP!
© 1994 PAWS, INC. All Rights Reserved.
GET ME A TEN-GALLON DRUM OF BUG SPRAY!
IT'S A VENOM-SPEWING HAIRY-LEGGED KILLER!
JIM DAVIS 10-16
OR A PIECE OF LINT

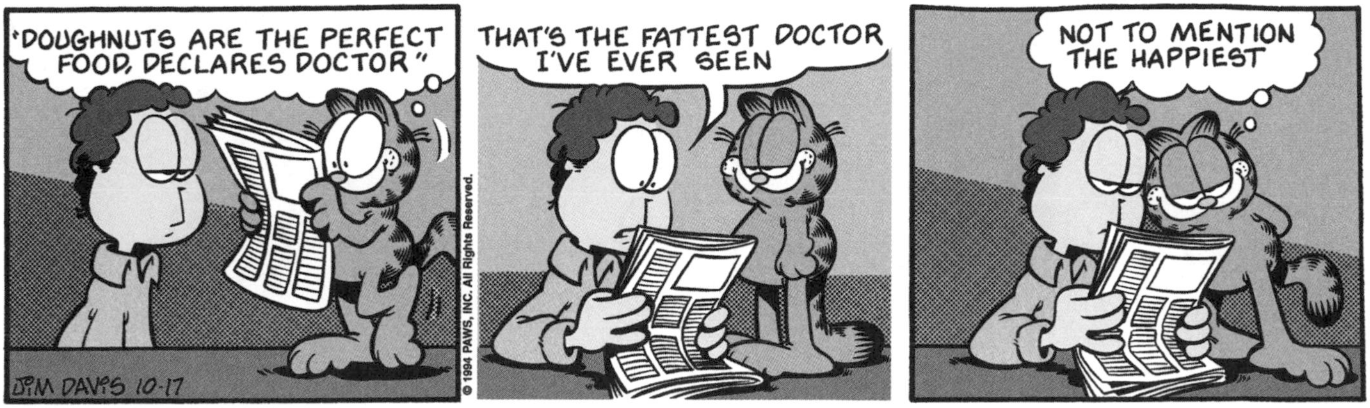
"DOUGHNUTS ARE THE PERFECT FOOD, DECLARES DOCTOR"
JIM DAVIS 10-17
© 1994 PAWS, INC. All Rights Reserved.
THAT'S THE FATTEST DOCTOR I'VE EVER SEEN
NOT TO MENTION THE HAPPIEST

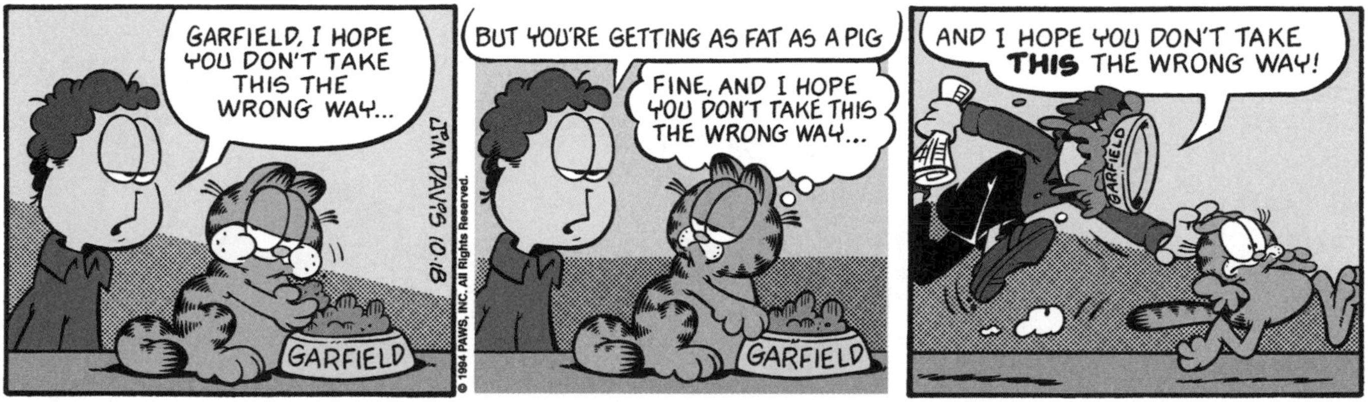
GARFIELD, I HOPE YOU DON'T TAKE THIS THE WRONG WAY...
GARFIELD
JIM DAVIS 10-18
© 1994 PAWS, INC. All Rights Reserved.
BUT YOU'RE GETTING AS FAT AS A PIG
FINE, AND I HOPE YOU DON'T TAKE THIS THE WRONG WAY...
GARFIELD
AND I HOPE YOU DON'T TAKE **THIS** THE WRONG WAY!
GARFIELD

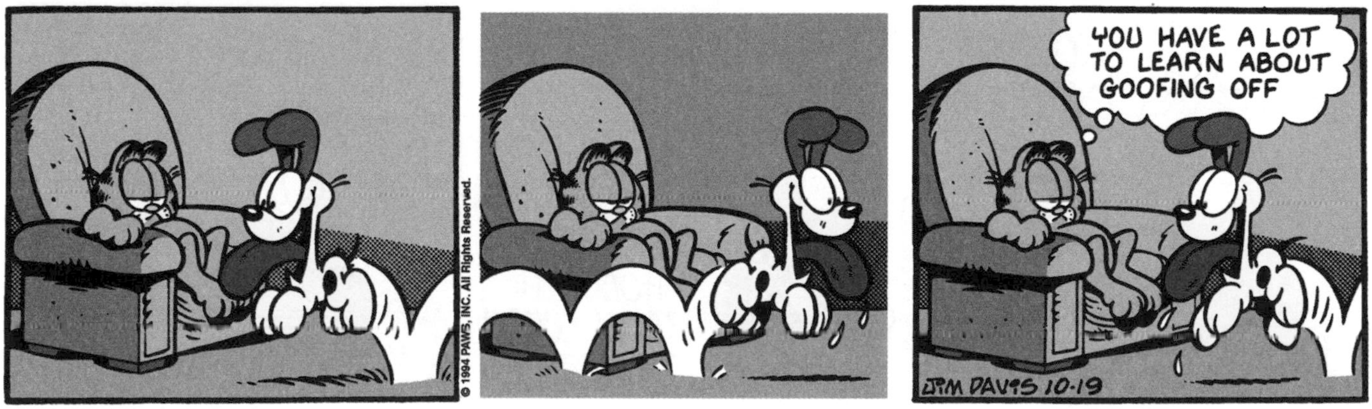
© 1994 PAWS, INC. All Rights Reserved.
YOU HAVE A LOT TO LEARN ABOUT GOOFING OFF
JIM DAVIS 10-19

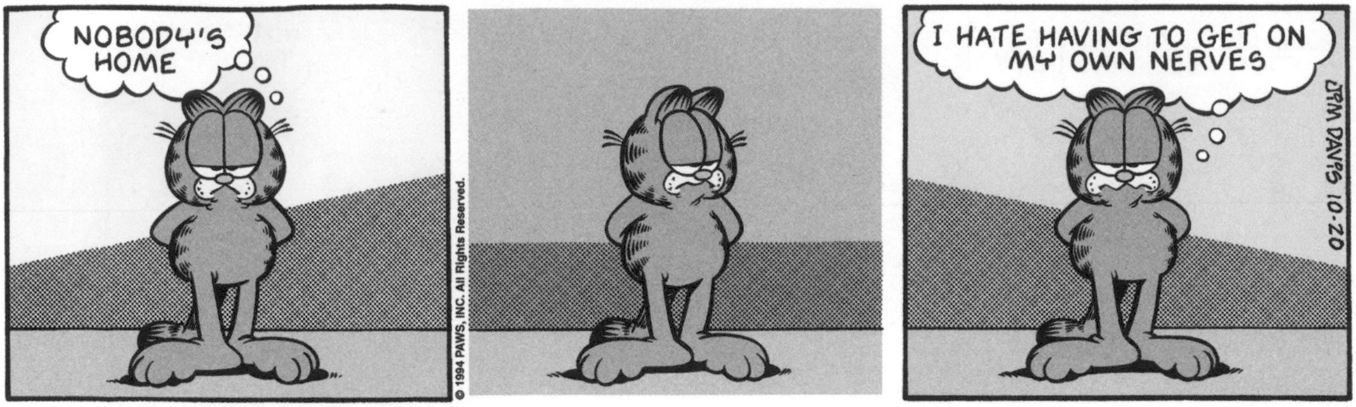

NOBODY'S HOME
I HATE HAVING TO GET ON MY OWN NERVES
JIM DAVIS 10-20
© 1994 PAWS, INC. All Rights Reserved.

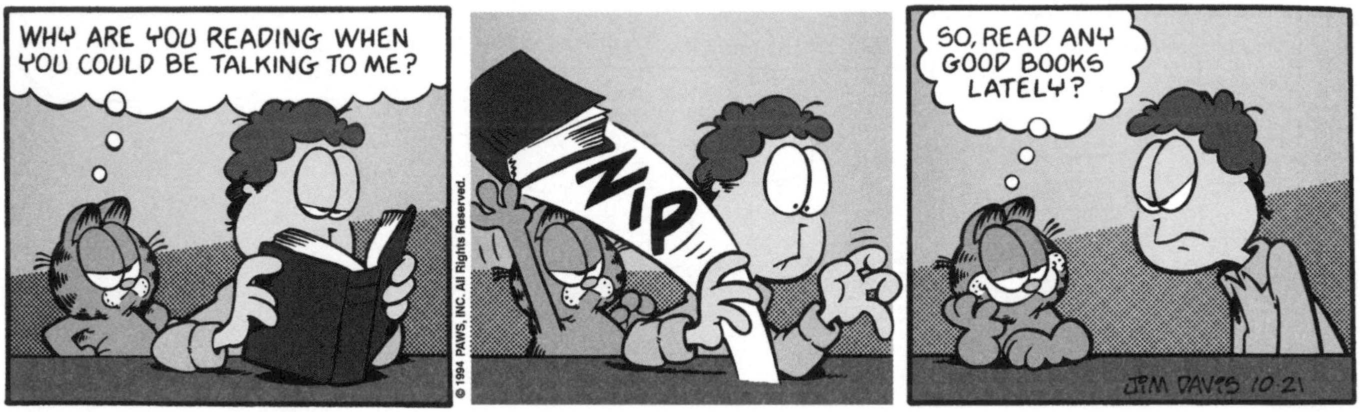

WHY ARE YOU READING WHEN YOU COULD BE TALKING TO ME?
RIP
SO, READ ANY GOOD BOOKS LATELY?
JIM DAVIS 10-21
© 1994 PAWS, INC. All Rights Reserved.

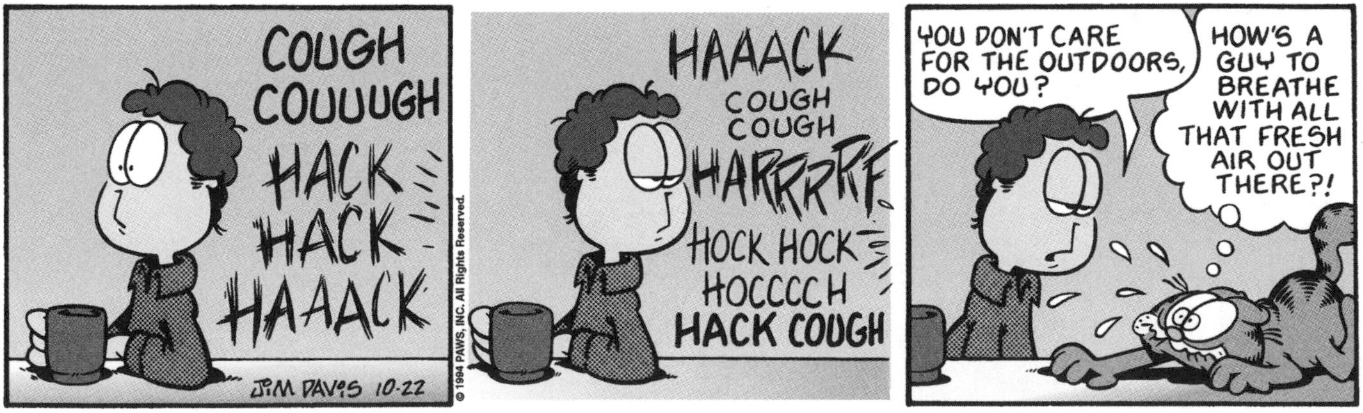

COUGH COUUUGH
HACK HACK HAAACK
JIM DAVIS 10-22
© 1994 PAWS, INC. All Rights Reserved.
HAAACK
COUGH COUGH
HARRRRF
HOCK HOCK HOCCCCH
HACK COUGH
YOU DON'T CARE FOR THE OUTDOORS, DO YOU?
HOW'S A GUY TO BREATHE WITH ALL THAT FRESH AIR OUT THERE?!

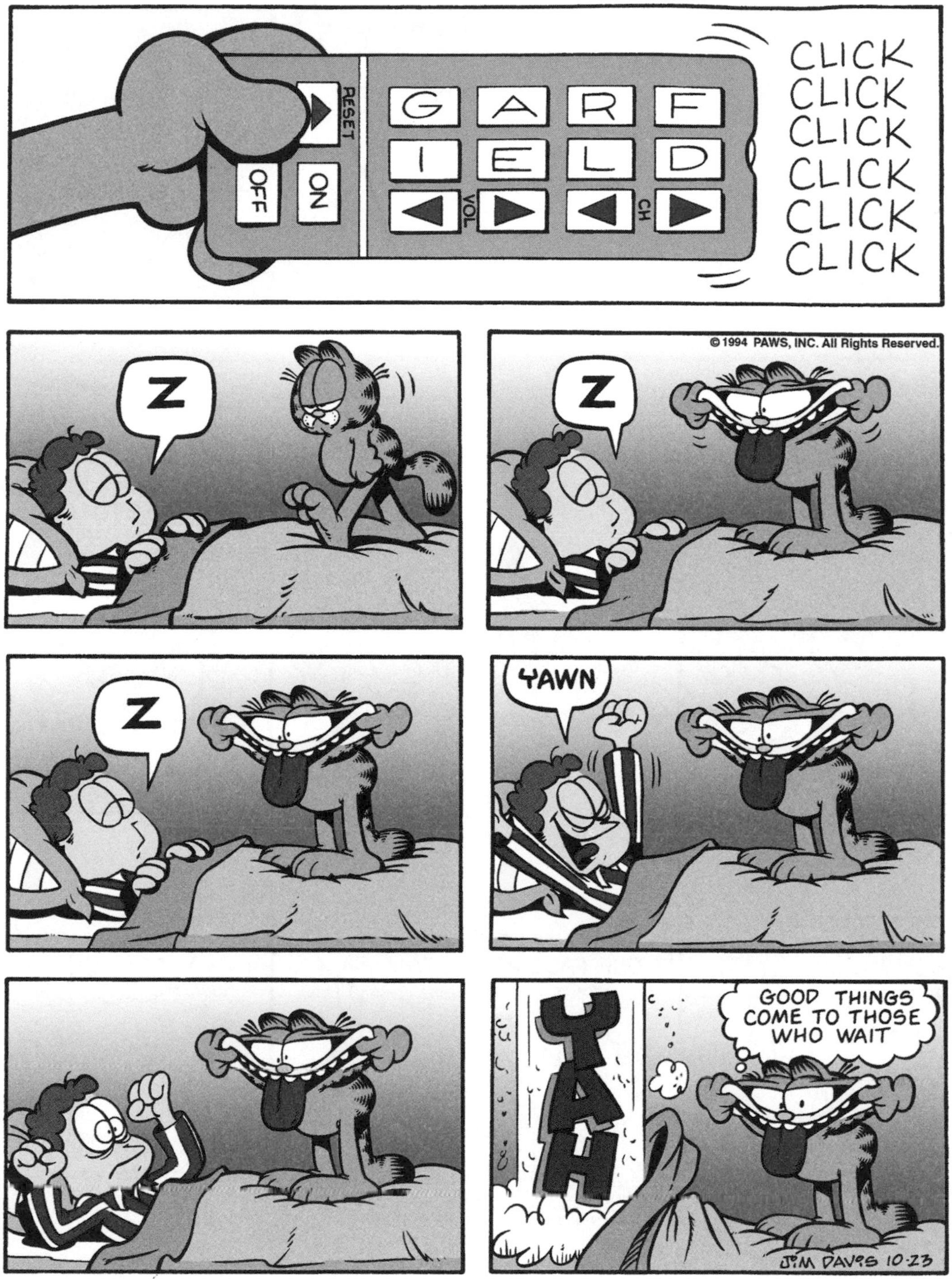
RESET
G A R F
I E L D
OFF
ON
VOL
CH
CLICK
CLICK
CLICK
CLICK
CLICK
CLICK
© 1994 PAWS, INC. All Rights Reserved.
Z
Z
Z
YAWN
YAH
GOOD THINGS COME TO THOSE WHO WAIT
JIM DAVIS 10-23

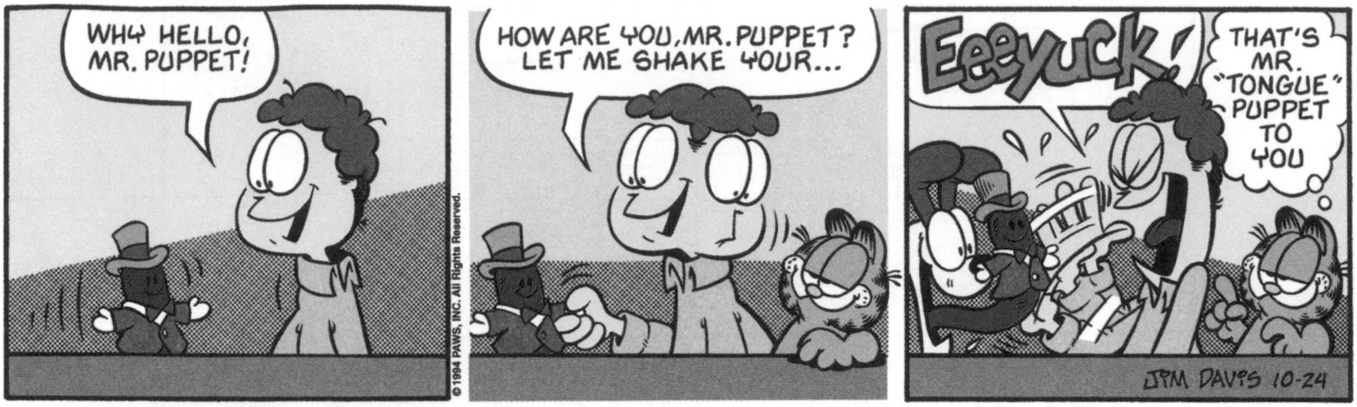
WHY HELLO, MR. PUPPET!
HOW ARE YOU, MR. PUPPET? LET ME SHAKE YOUR...
EEEYUCK!
THAT'S MR. "TONGUE" PUPPET TO YOU
JIM DAVIS 10-24
© 1994 PAWS, INC. All Rights Reserved.

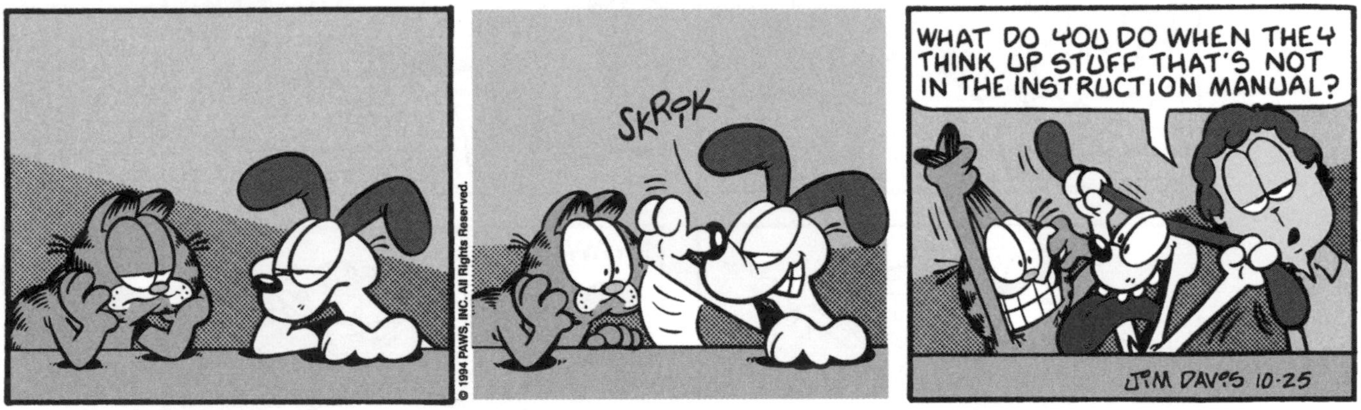
SKROK
WHAT DO YOU DO WHEN THEY THINK UP STUFF THAT'S NOT IN THE INSTRUCTION MANUAL?
JIM DAVIS 10-25
© 1994 PAWS, INC. All Rights Reserved.

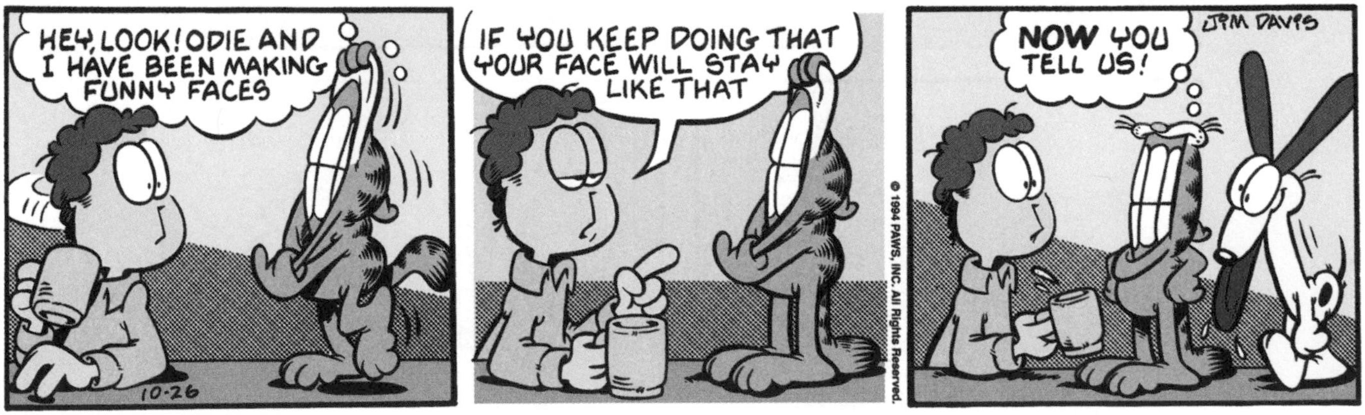
HEY, LOOK! ODIE AND I HAVE BEEN MAKING FUNNY FACES
10-26
IF YOU KEEP DOING THAT YOUR FACE WILL STAY LIKE THAT
NOW YOU TELL US!
JIM DAVIS
© 1994 PAWS, INC. All Rights Reserved.

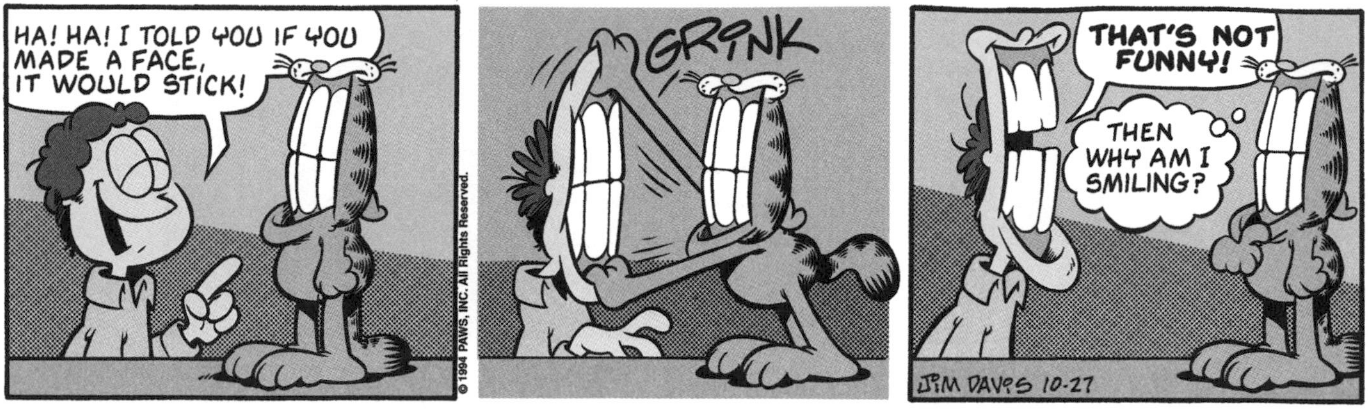
HA! HA! I TOLD YOU IF YOU MADE A FACE, IT WOULD STICK!
© 1994 PAWS, INC. All Rights Reserved.
GRINK
THAT'S NOT FUNNY!
THEN WHY AM I SMILING?
JIM DAVIS 10-27

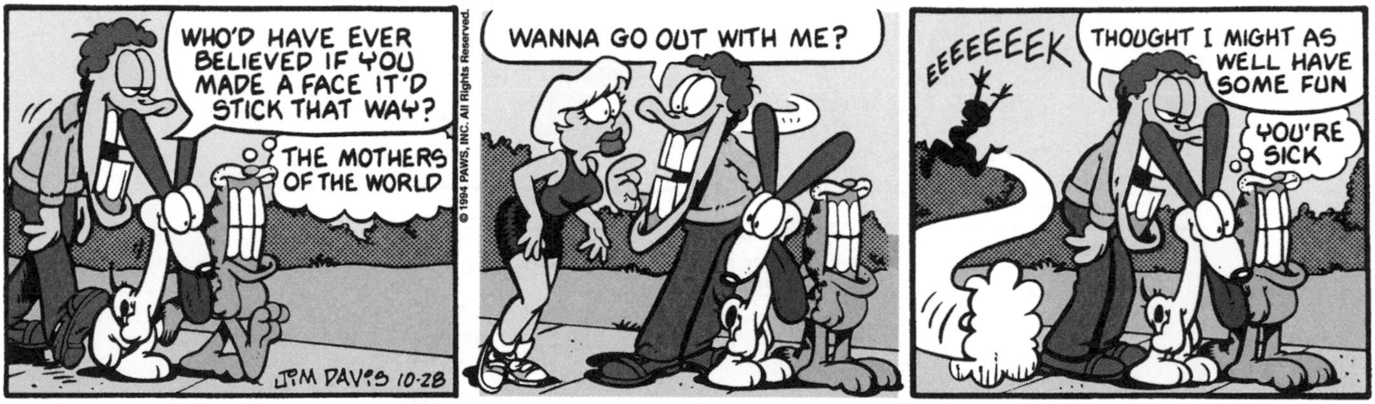
WHO'D HAVE EVER BELIEVED IF YOU MADE A FACE IT'D STICK THAT WAY?
THE MOTHERS OF THE WORLD
JIM DAVIS 10-28
© 1994 PAWS, INC. All Rights Reserved.
WANNA GO OUT WITH ME?
EEEEEEEK
THOUGHT I MIGHT AS WELL HAVE SOME FUN
YOU'RE SICK

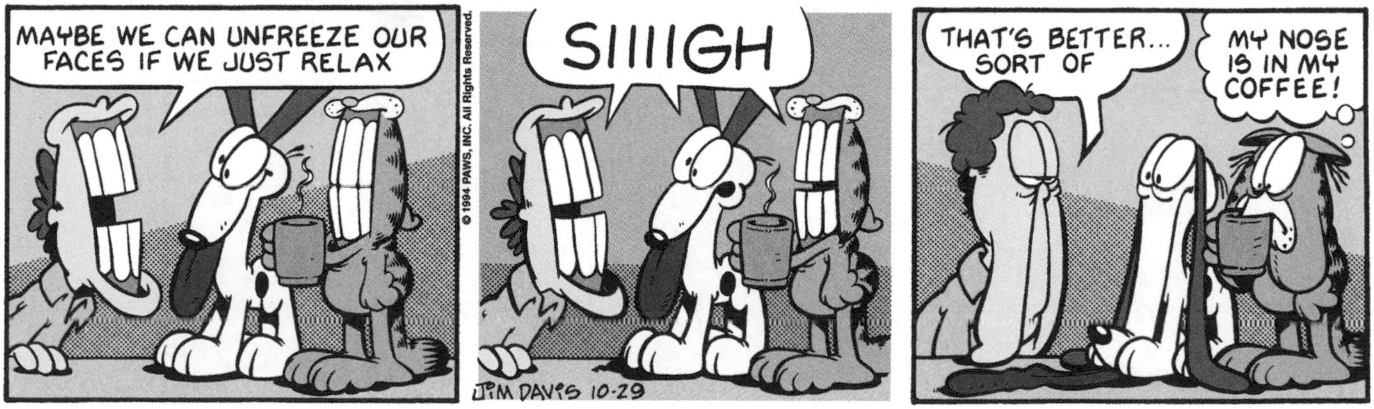
MAYBE WE CAN UNFREEZE OUR FACES IF WE JUST RELAX
© 1994 PAWS, INC. All Rights Reserved.
SIIIIGH
JIM DAVIS 10-29
THAT'S BETTER... SORT OF
MY NOSE IS IN MY COFFEE!

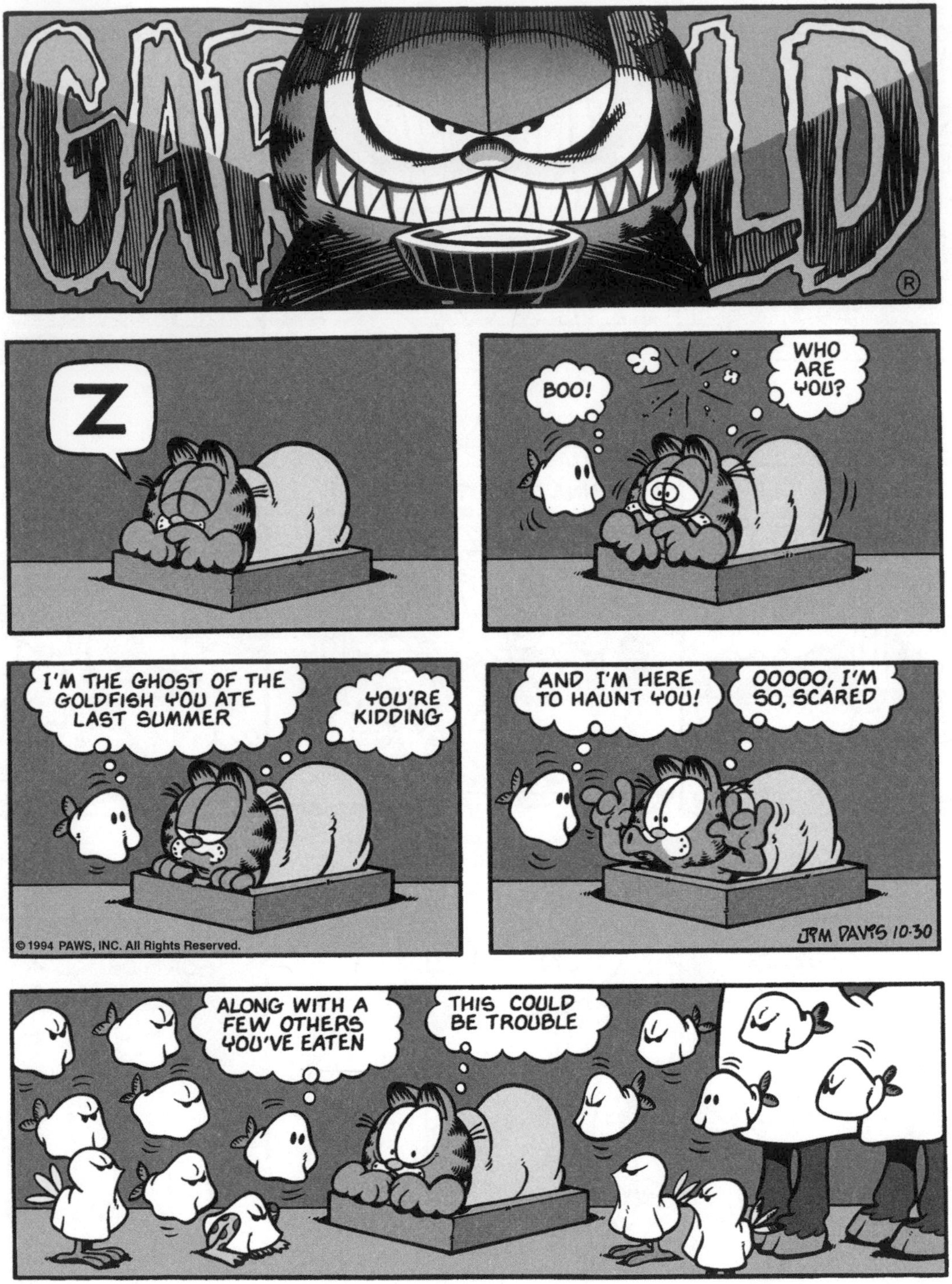
GARFIELD
Z
BOO!
WHO ARE YOU?
I'M THE GHOST OF THE GOLDFISH YOU ATE LAST SUMMER
YOU'RE KIDDING
AND I'M HERE TO HAUNT YOU!
OOOOO, I'M SO, SCARED
ALONG WITH A FEW OTHERS YOU'VE EATEN
THIS COULD BE TROUBLE
JIM DAVIS 10-30

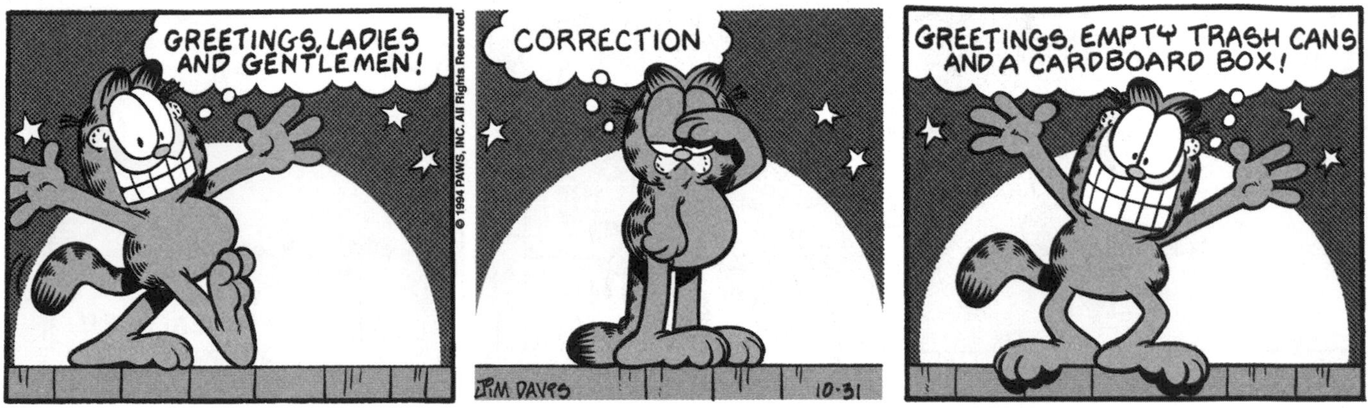
GREETINGS, LADIES AND GENTLEMEN!
© 1994 PAWS, INC. All Rights Reserved.
CORRECTION
JIM DAVIS 10-31
GREETINGS, EMPTY TRASH CANS AND A CARDBOARD BOX!

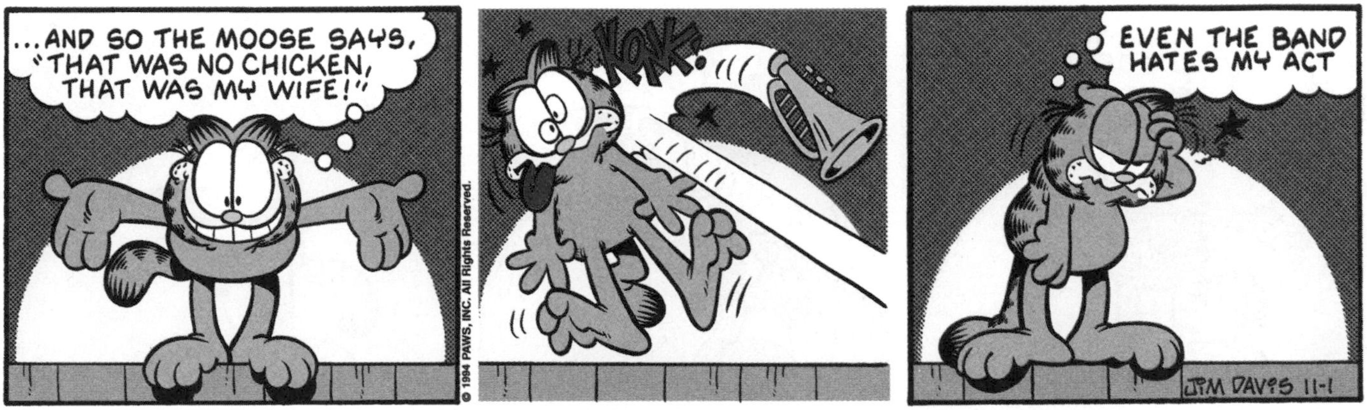
...AND SO THE MOOSE SAYS, "THAT WAS NO CHICKEN, THAT WAS MY WIFE!"
© 1994 PAWS, INC. All Rights Reserved.
EVEN THE BAND HATES MY ACT
JIM DAVIS 11-1

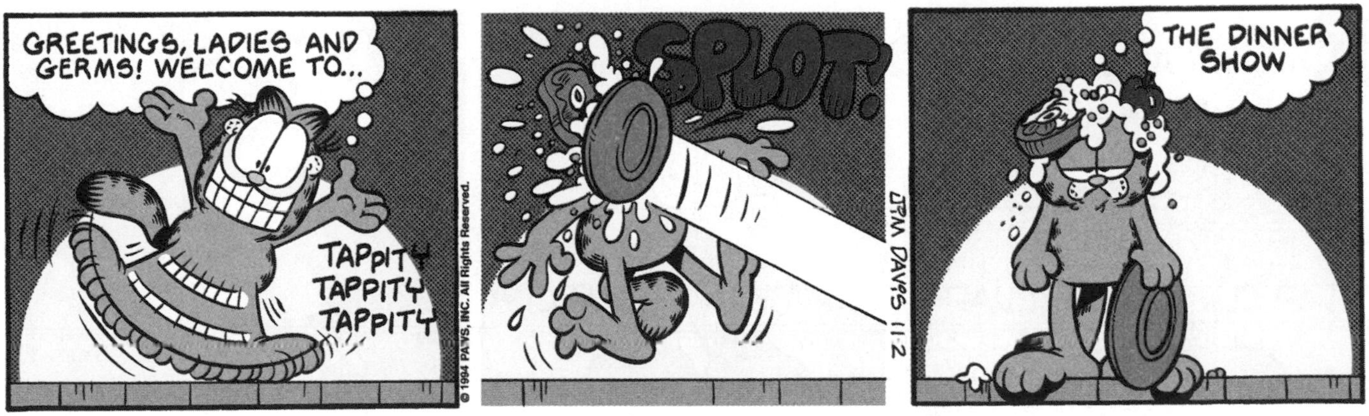
GREETINGS, LADIES AND GERMS! WELCOME TO...
TAPPITY
TAPPITY
TAPPITY
© 1994 PAWS, INC. All Rights Reserved.
SPLOT!
JIM DAVIS 11-2
THE DINNER SHOW

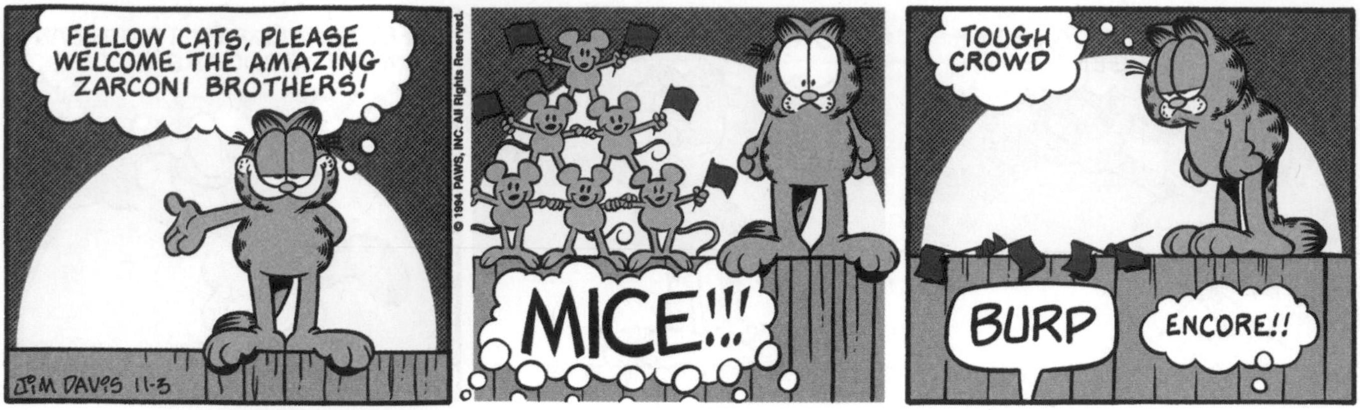
FELLOW CATS, PLEASE WELCOME THE AMAZING ZARCONI BROTHERS!
JIM DAVIS 11-3
© 1994 PAWS, INC. All Rights Reserved.
MICE!!!
TOUGH CROWD
BURP
ENCORE!!

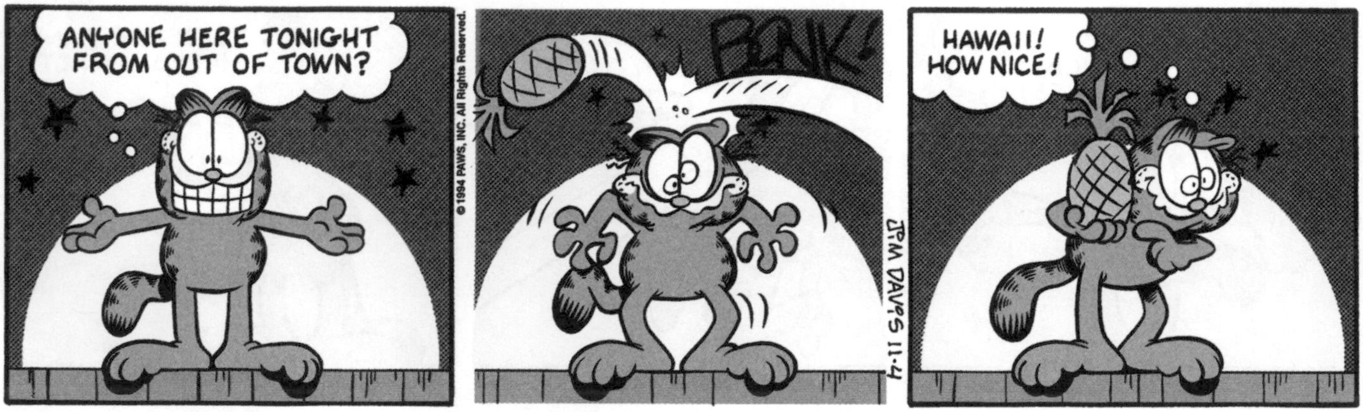
ANYONE HERE TONIGHT FROM OUT OF TOWN?
© 1994 PAWS, INC. All Rights Reserved.
BONK!
JIM DAVIS 11-4
HAWAII! HOW NICE!

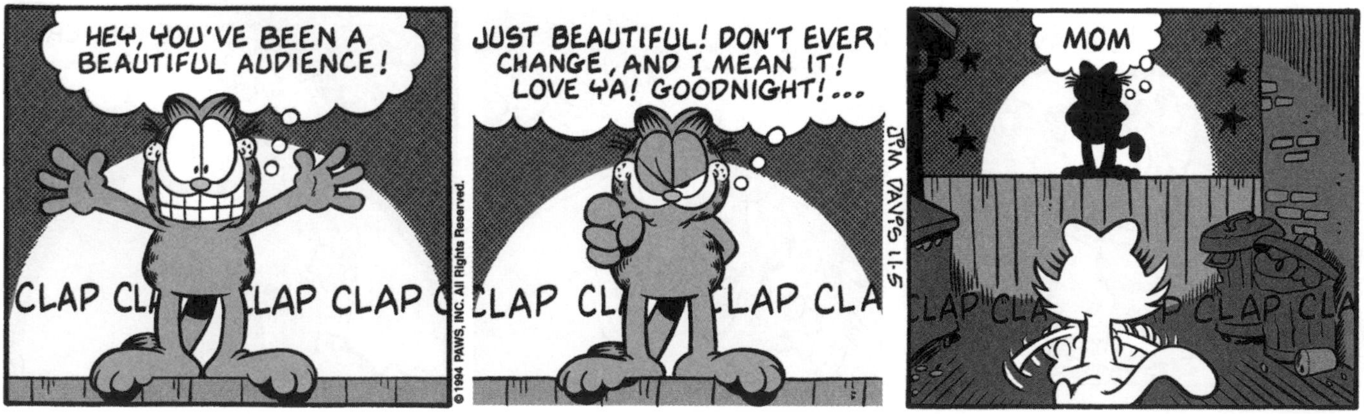
HEY, YOU'VE BEEN A BEAUTIFUL AUDIENCE!
CLAP CLA CLAP CLAP C
© 1994 PAWS, INC. All Rights Reserved.
JUST BEAUTIFUL! DON'T EVER CHANGE, AND I MEAN IT! LOVE YA! GOODNIGHT!...
CLAP CL CLAP CLA
JIM DAVIS 11-5
MOM
CLAP CLA P CLAP CLA

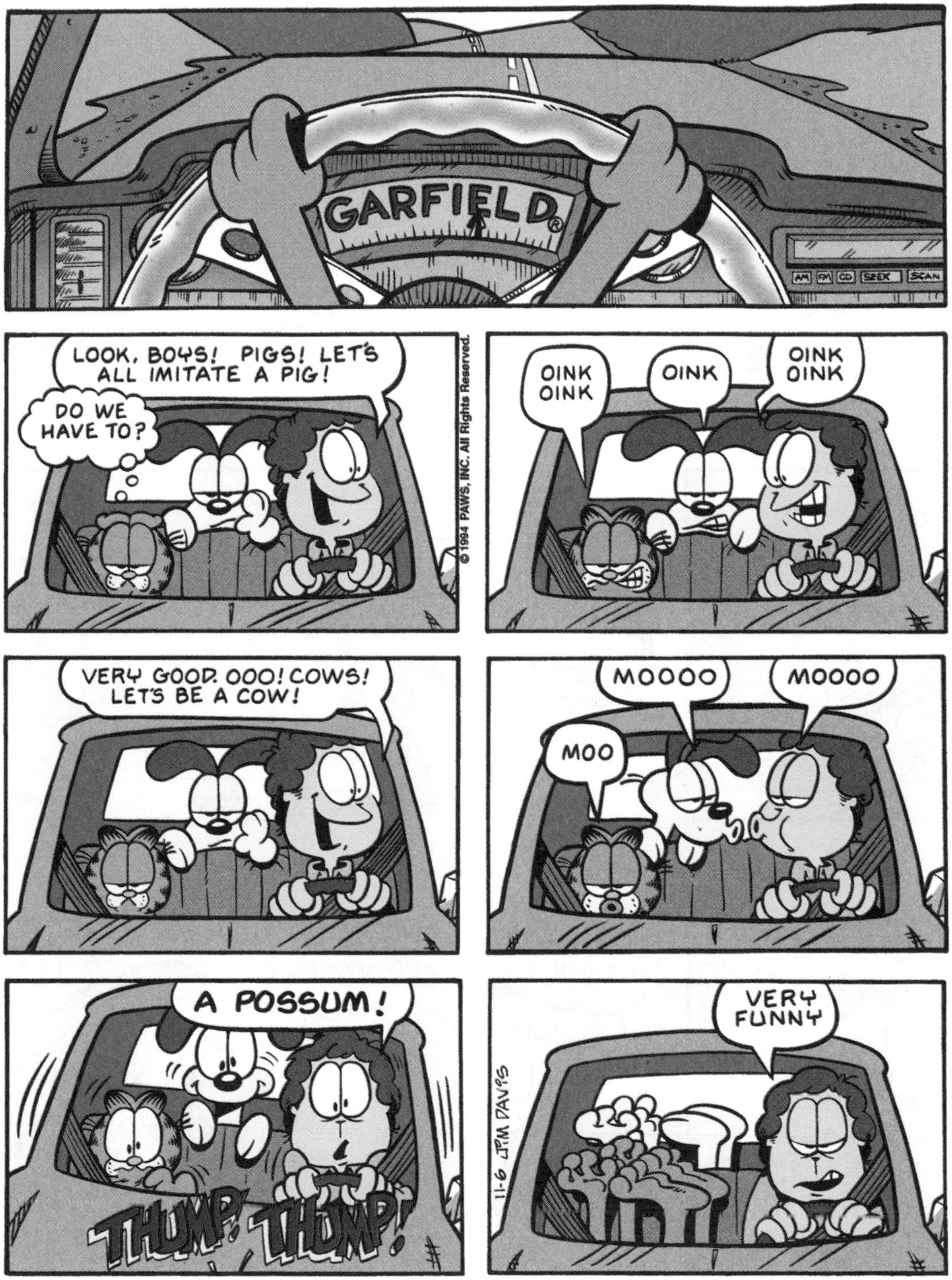
GARFIELD®
AM FM CD SEEK SCAN
LOOK, BOYS! PIGS! LET'S ALL IMITATE A PIG!
DO WE HAVE TO?
© 1994 PAWS, INC. All Rights Reserved.
OINK OINK
OINK
OINK OINK
VERY GOOD. OOO! COWS! LET'S BE A COW!
MOOO
MOOOO
MOOOO
A POSSUM!
THUMP! THUMP!
11-6 JPM DAVIS
VERY FUNNY

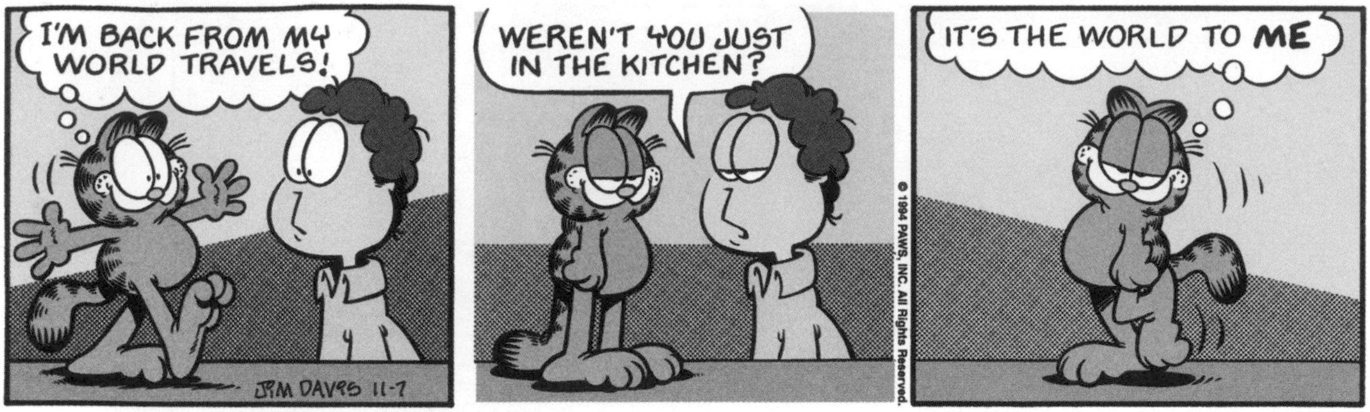
I'M BACK FROM MY WORLD TRAVELS!
JIM DAVIS 11-7
WEREN'T YOU JUST IN THE KITCHEN?
© 1994 PAWS, INC. All Rights Reserved.
IT'S THE WORLD TO **ME**

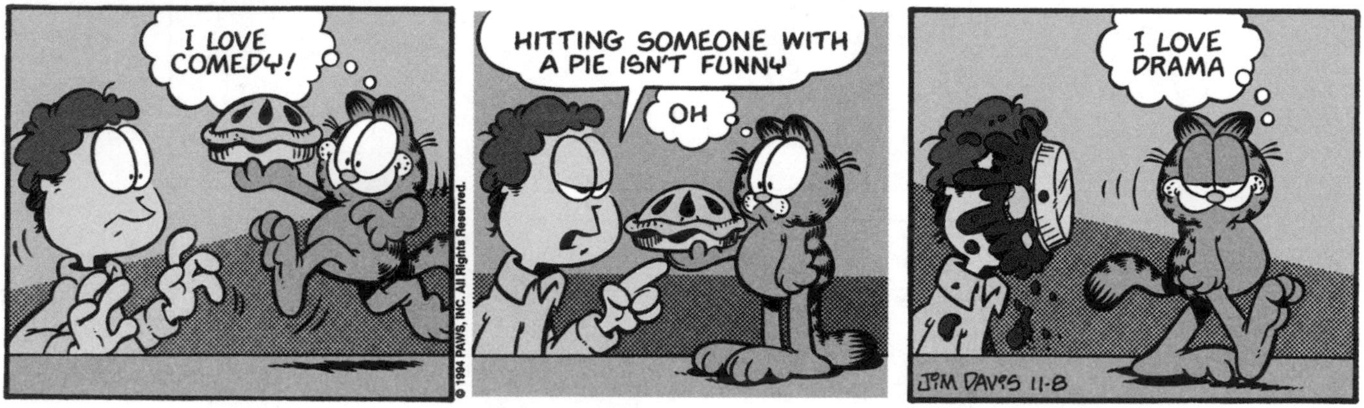
I LOVE COMEDY!
© 1994 PAWS, INC. All Rights Reserved.
HITTING SOMEONE WITH A PIE ISN'T FUNNY
OH
I LOVE DRAMA
JIM DAVIS 11-8

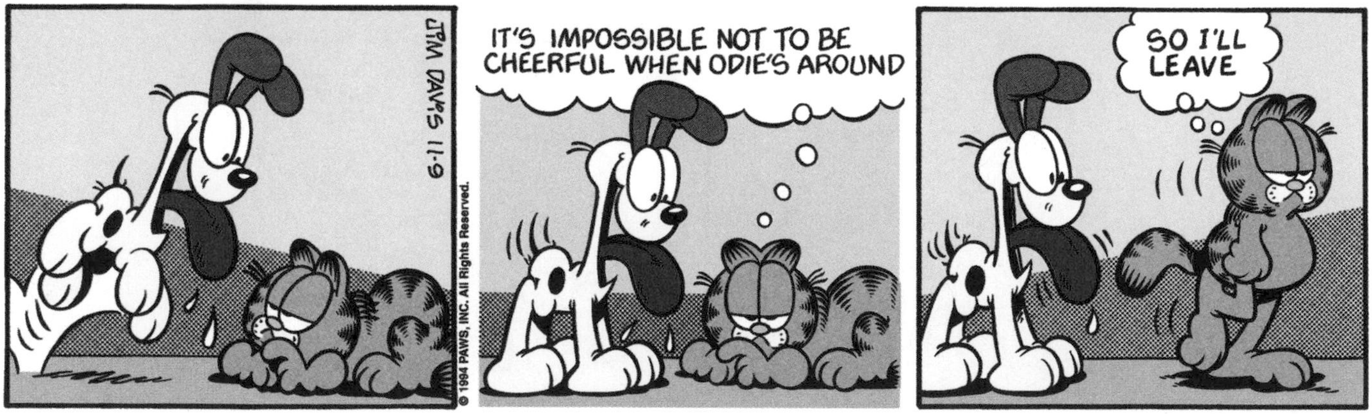
JIM DAVIS 11-9
© 1994 PAWS, INC. All Rights Reserved.
IT'S IMPOSSIBLE NOT TO BE CHEERFUL WHEN ODIE'S AROUND
SO I'LL LEAVE

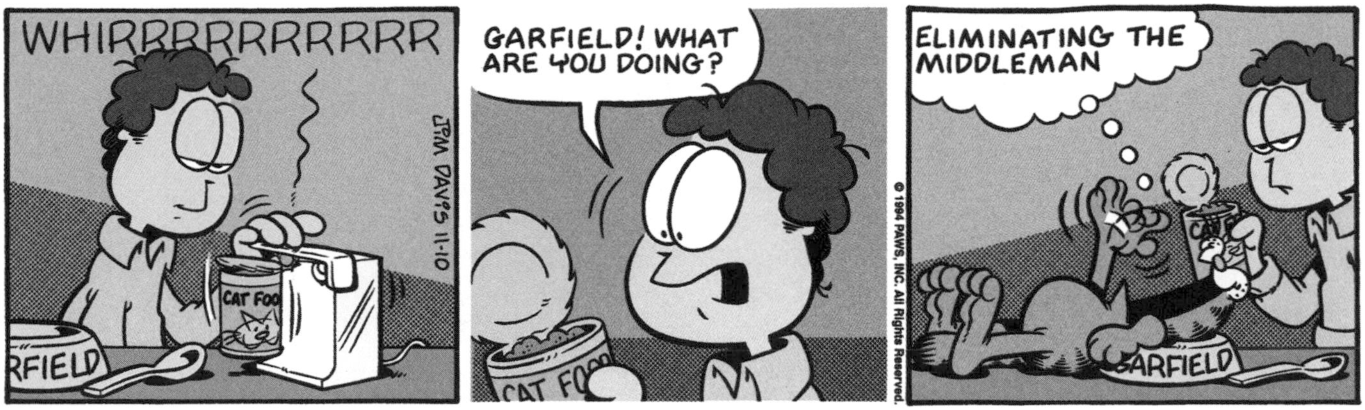
WHIRRRRRRRRRRR
JIM DAVIS 11-10
CAT FOOD
GARFIELD! WHAT ARE YOU DOING?
© 1994 PAWS, INC. All Rights Reserved.
ELIMINATING THE MIDDLEMAN
GARFIELD

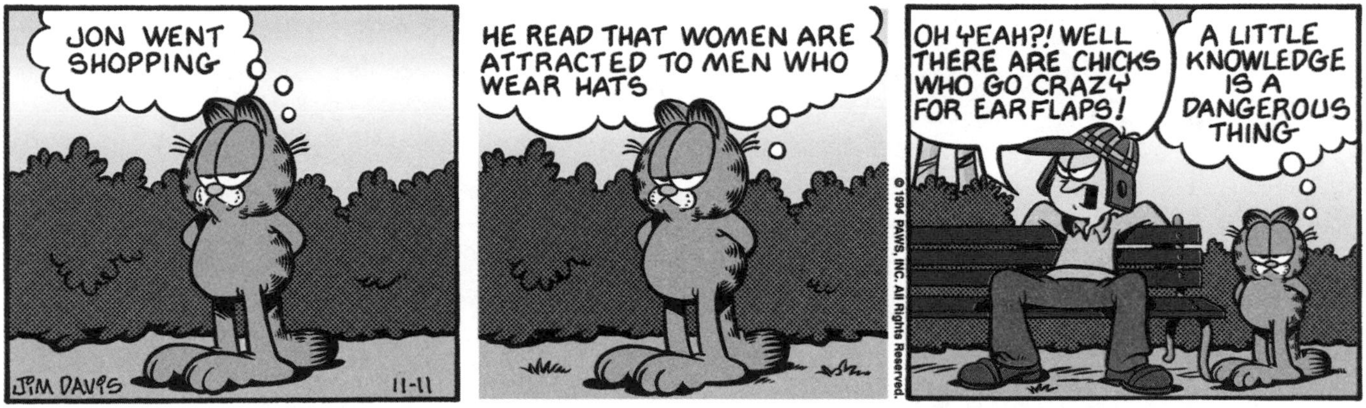
JON WENT SHOPPING
JIM DAVIS
11-11
HE READ THAT WOMEN ARE ATTRACTED TO MEN WHO WEAR HATS
© 1994 PAWS, INC. All Rights Reserved.
OH YEAH?! WELL THERE ARE CHICKS WHO GO CRAZY FOR EARFLAPS!
A LITTLE KNOWLEDGE IS A DANGEROUS THING

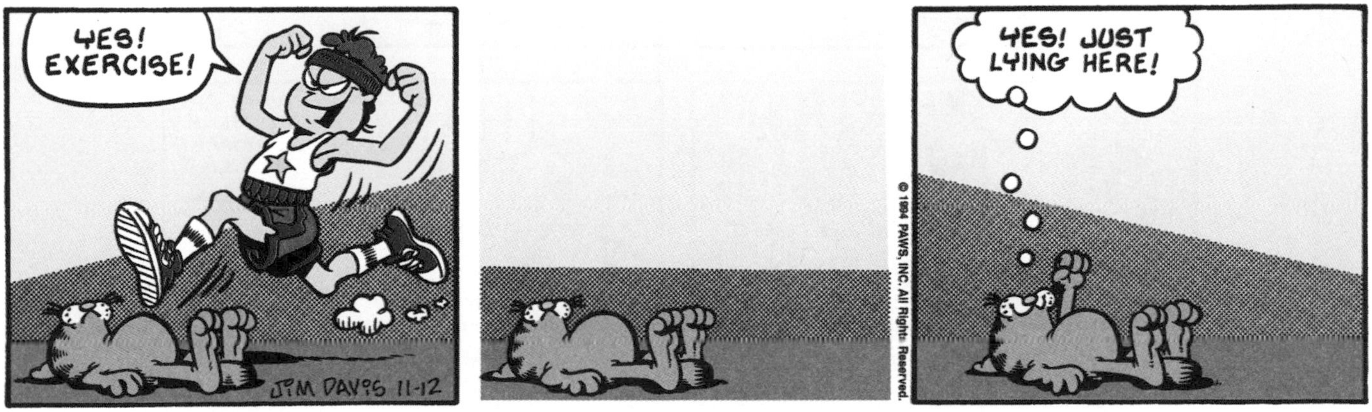
YES! EXERCISE!
JIM DAVIS 11-12
© 1994 PAWS, INC. All Rights Reserved.
YES! JUST LYING HERE!

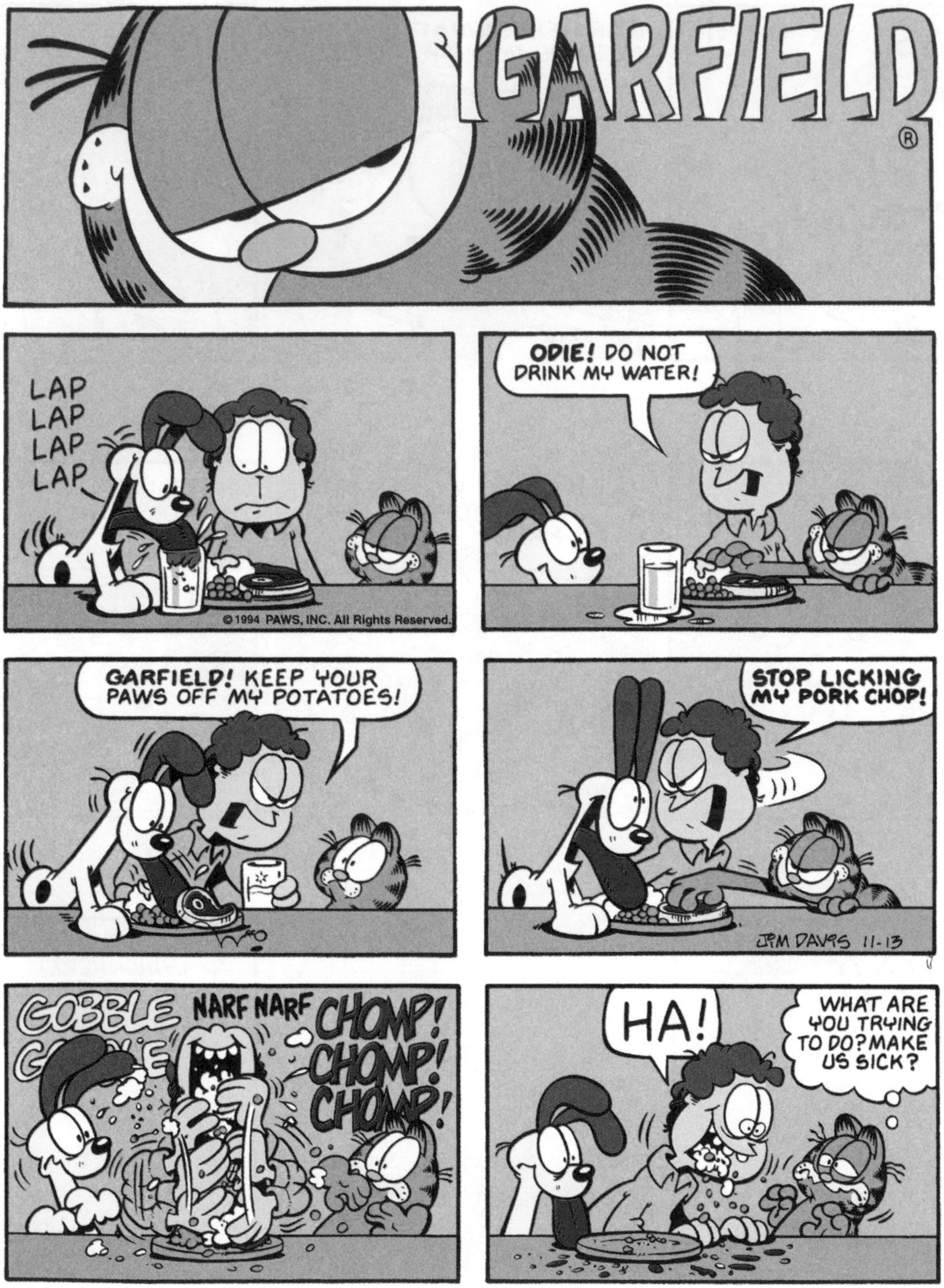
GARFIELD
®
LAP
LAP
LAP
LAP
© 1994 PAWS, INC. All Rights Reserved.
ODIE! DO NOT DRINK MY WATER!
GARFIELD! KEEP YOUR PAWS OFF MY POTATOES!
STOP LICKING MY PORK CHOP!
JIM DAVIS 11-13
GOBBLE GOBBLE
NARF NARF
CHOMP! CHOMP! CHOMP!
HA!
WHAT ARE YOU TRYING TO DO? MAKE US SICK?

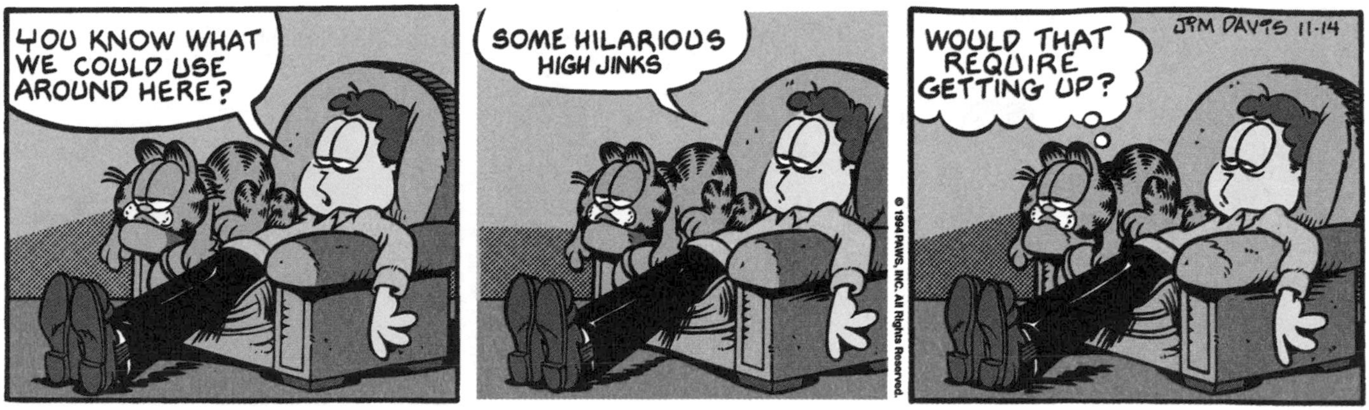
YOU KNOW WHAT WE COULD USE AROUND HERE?
SOME HILARIOUS HIGH JINKS
WOULD THAT REQUIRE GETTING UP?
JIM DAVIS 11-14
© 1994 PAWS, INC. All Rights Reserved.

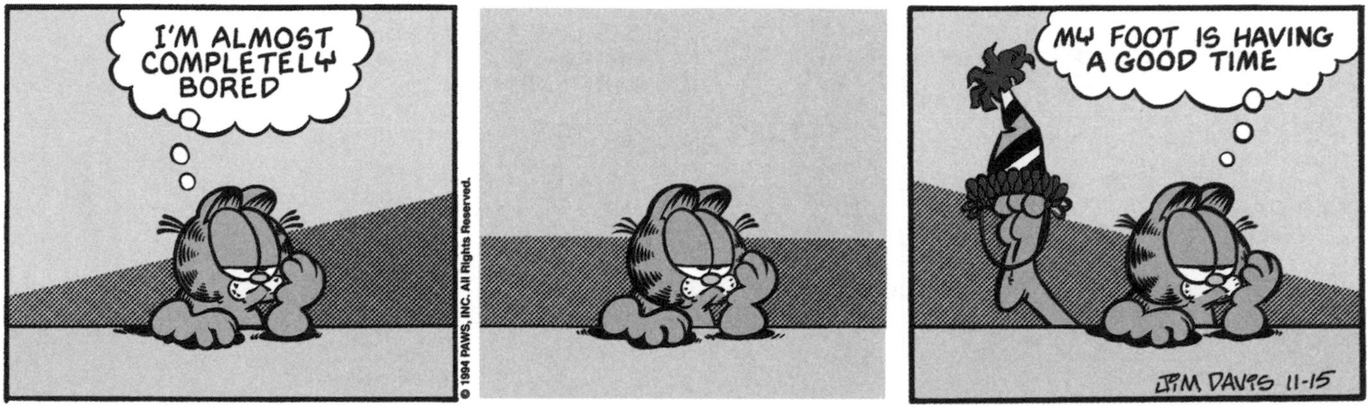
I'M ALMOST COMPLETELY BORED
MY FOOT IS HAVING A GOOD TIME
JIM DAVIS 11-15
© 1994 PAWS, INC. All Rights Reserved.

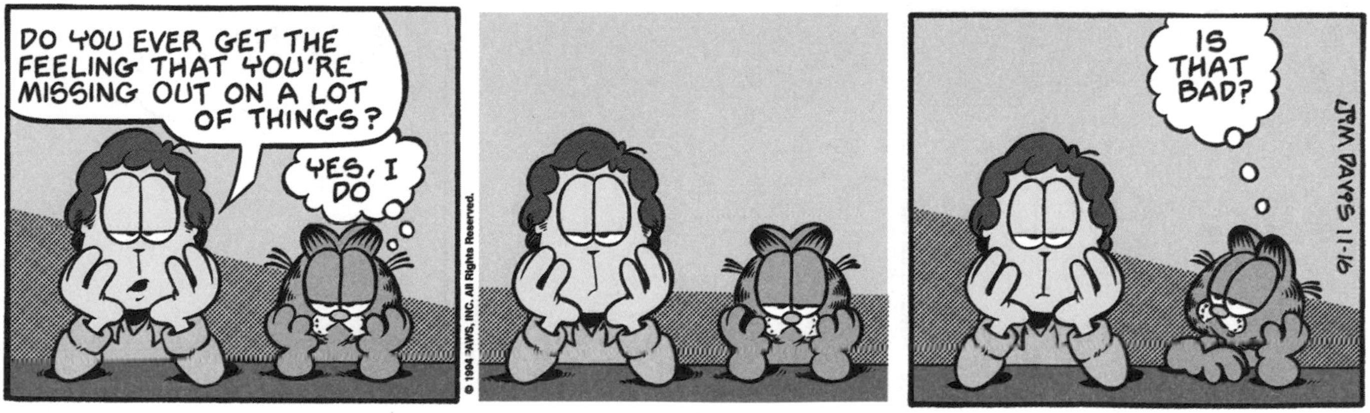
DO YOU EVER GET THE FEELING THAT YOU'RE MISSING OUT ON A LOT OF THINGS?
YES, I DO
IS THAT BAD?
JIM DAVIS 11-16
© 1994 PAWS, INC. All Rights Reserved.

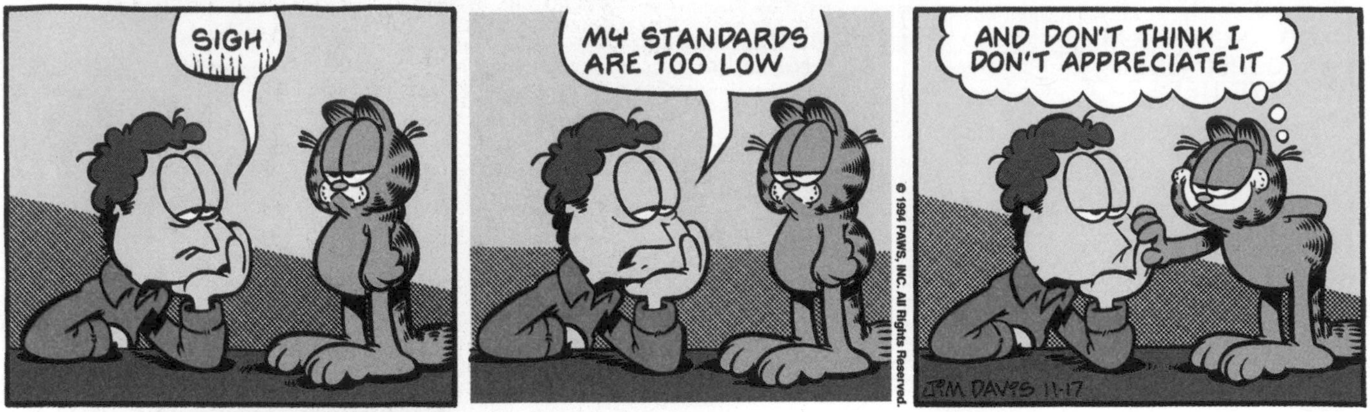
SIGH
MY STANDARDS ARE TOO LOW
© 1994 PAWS, INC. All Rights Reserved.
AND DON'T THINK I DON'T APPRECIATE IT
JIM DAVIS 11-17

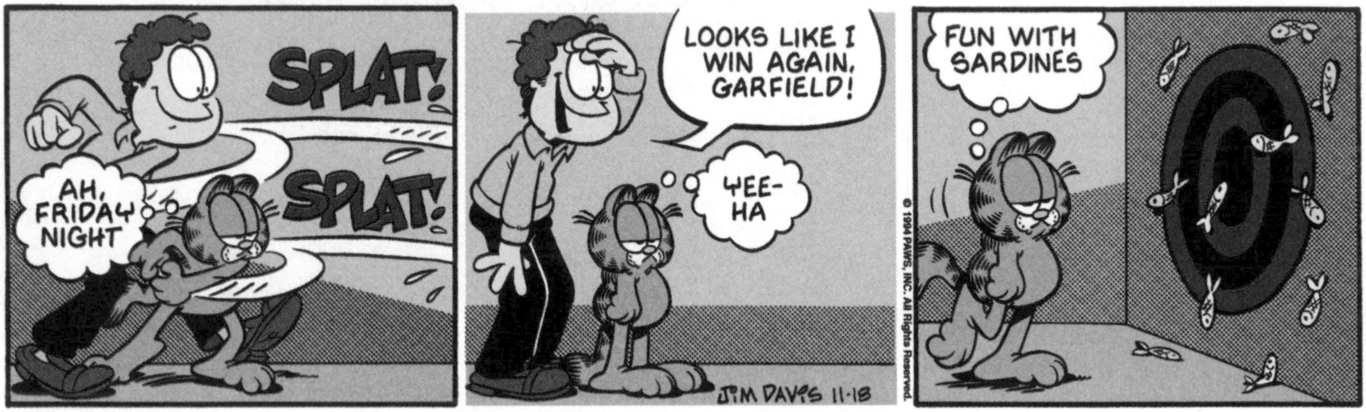
SPLAT!
SPLAT!
AH, FRIDAY NIGHT
LOOKS LIKE I WIN AGAIN, GARFIELD!
YEE-HA
JIM DAVIS 11-18
© 1994 PAWS, INC. All Rights Reserved.
FUN WITH SARDINES

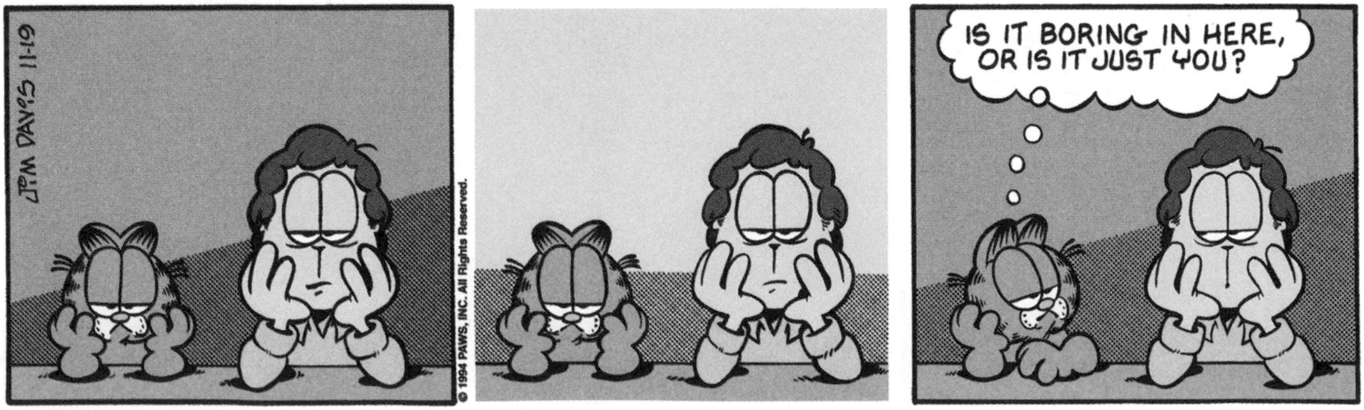
JIM DAVIS 11-19
© 1994 PAWS, INC. All Rights Reserved.
IS IT BORING IN HERE, OR IS IT JUST YOU?

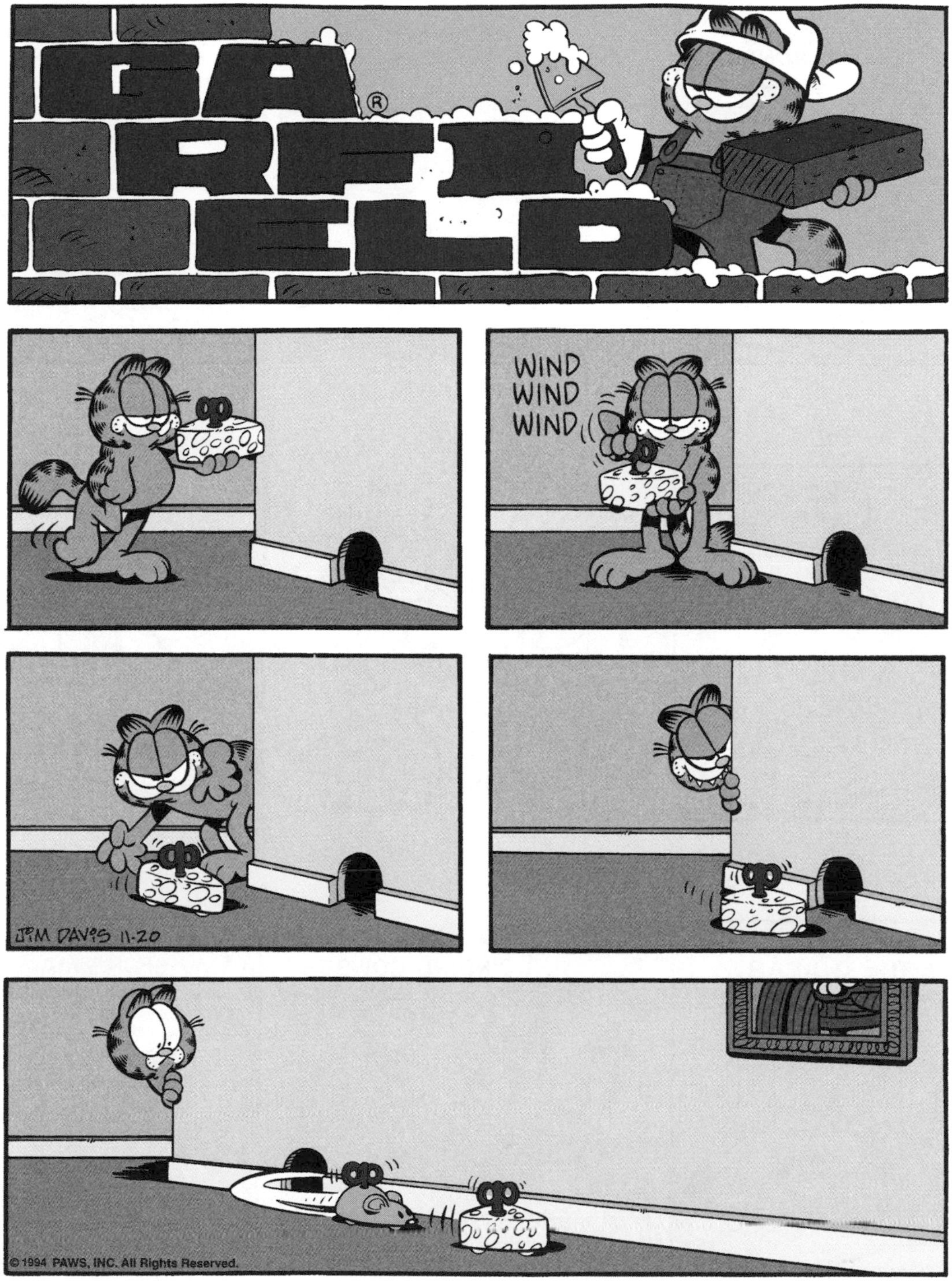
GARFIELD®
WIND
WIND
WIND
JIM DAVIS 11-20
© 1994 PAWS, INC. All Rights Reserved.

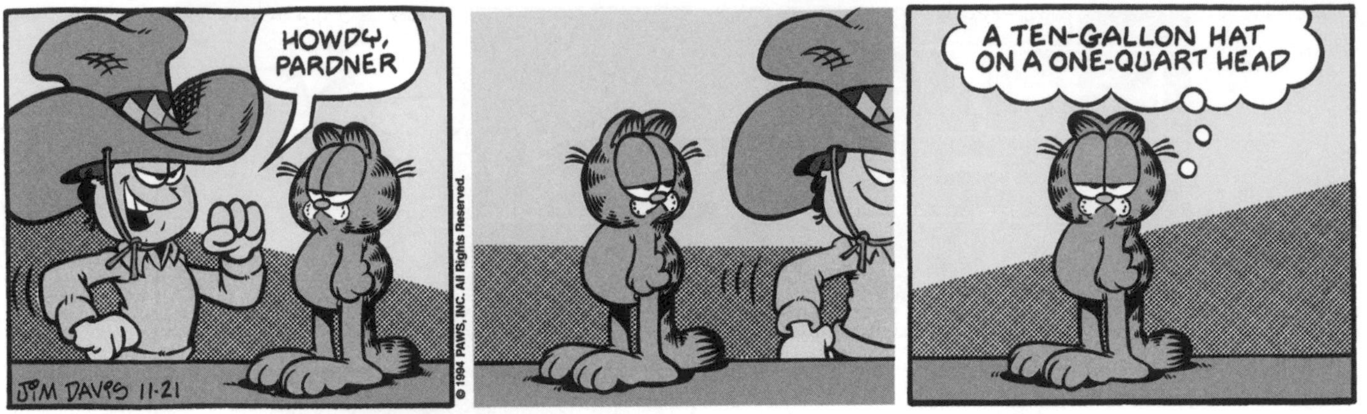
HOWDY, PARDNER
A TEN-GALLON HAT ON A ONE-QUART HEAD
JIM DAVIS 11-21
© 1994 PAWS, INC. All Rights Reserved.

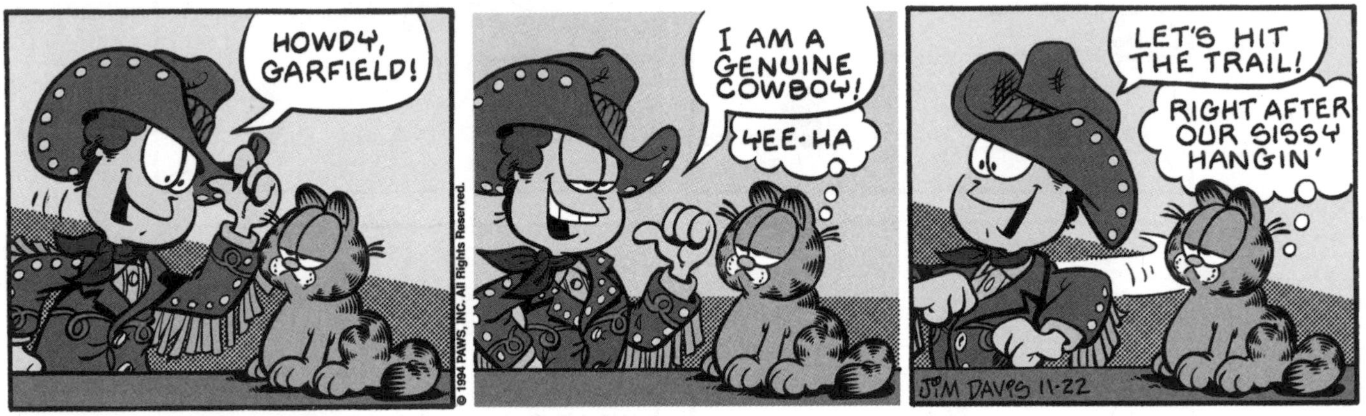
HOWDY, GARFIELD!
I AM A GENUINE COWBOY!
YEE-HA
LET'S HIT THE TRAIL!
RIGHT AFTER OUR SISSY HANGIN'
JIM DAVIS 11-22
© 1994 PAWS, INC. All Rights Reserved.

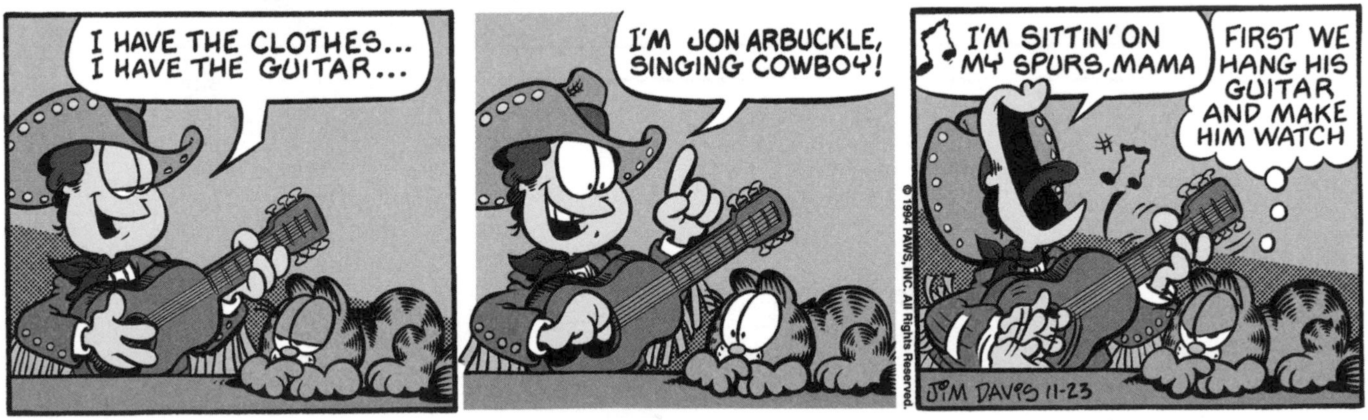
I HAVE THE CLOTHES... I HAVE THE GUITAR...
I'M JON ARBUCKLE, SINGING COWBOY!
I'M SITTIN' ON MY SPURS, MAMA
FIRST WE HANG HIS GUITAR AND MAKE HIM WATCH
JIM DAVIS 11-23
© 1994 PAWS, INC. All Rights Reserved.

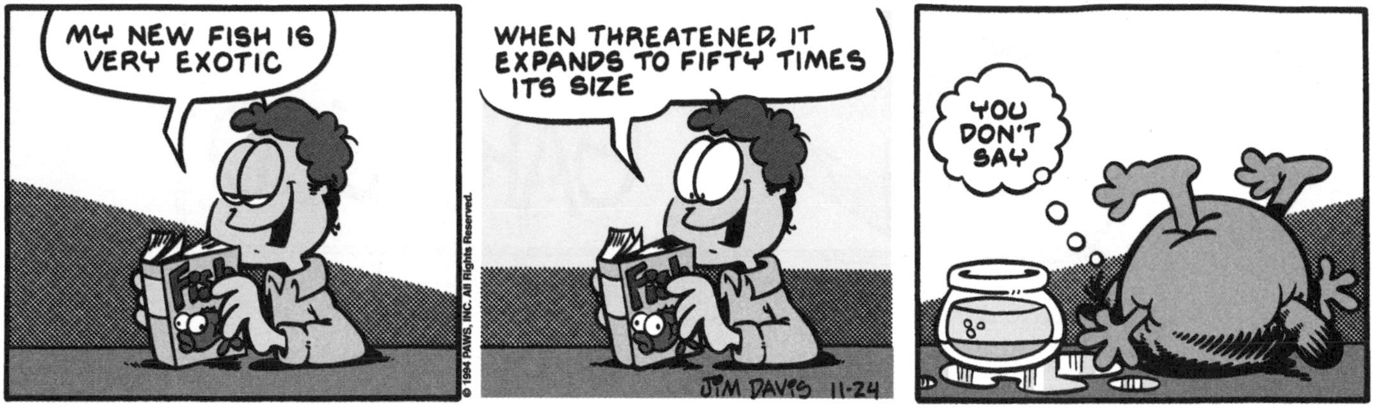
MY NEW FISH IS VERY EXOTIC
© 1994 PAWS, INC. All Rights Reserved.
WHEN THREATENED, IT EXPANDS TO FIFTY TIMES ITS SIZE
JIM DAVIS 11-24
YOU DON'T SAY

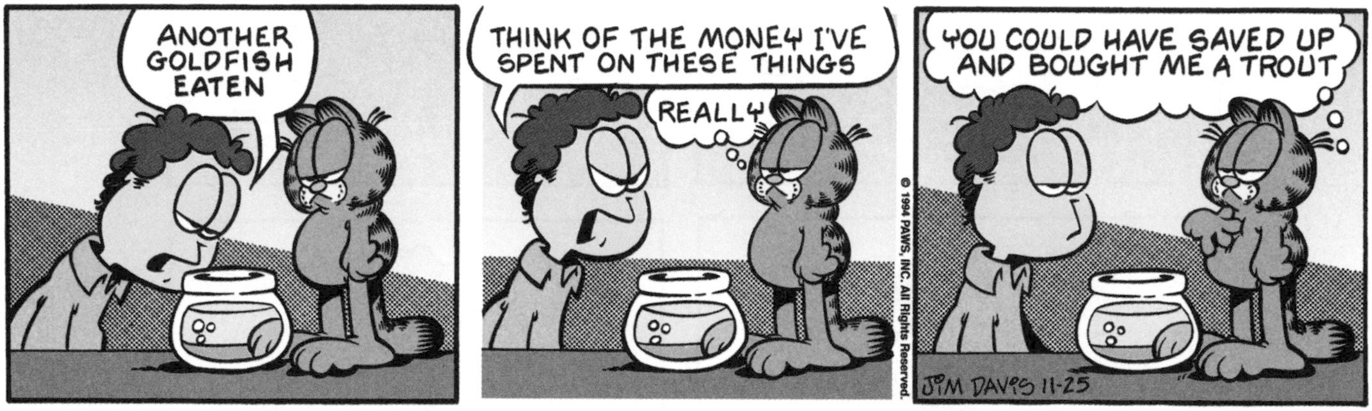
ANOTHER GOLDFISH EATEN
THINK OF THE MONEY I'VE SPENT ON THESE THINGS
REALLY
YOU COULD HAVE SAVED UP AND BOUGHT ME A TROUT
© 1994 PAWS, INC. All Rights Reserved.
JIM DAVIS 11-25

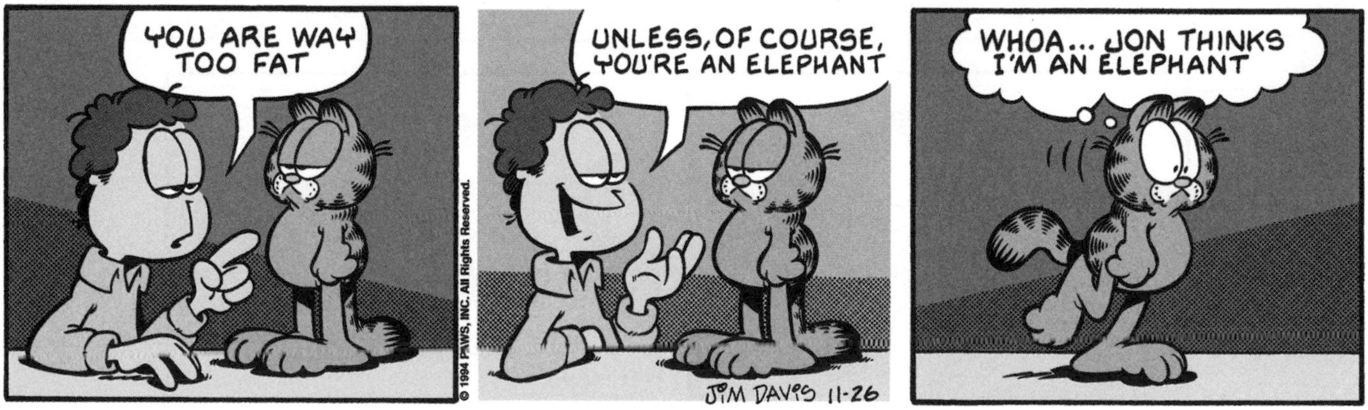
YOU ARE WAY TOO FAT
© 1994 PAWS, INC. All Rights Reserved.
UNLESS, OF COURSE, YOU'RE AN ELEPHANT
JIM DAVIS 11-26
WHOA... JON THINKS I'M AN ELEPHANT

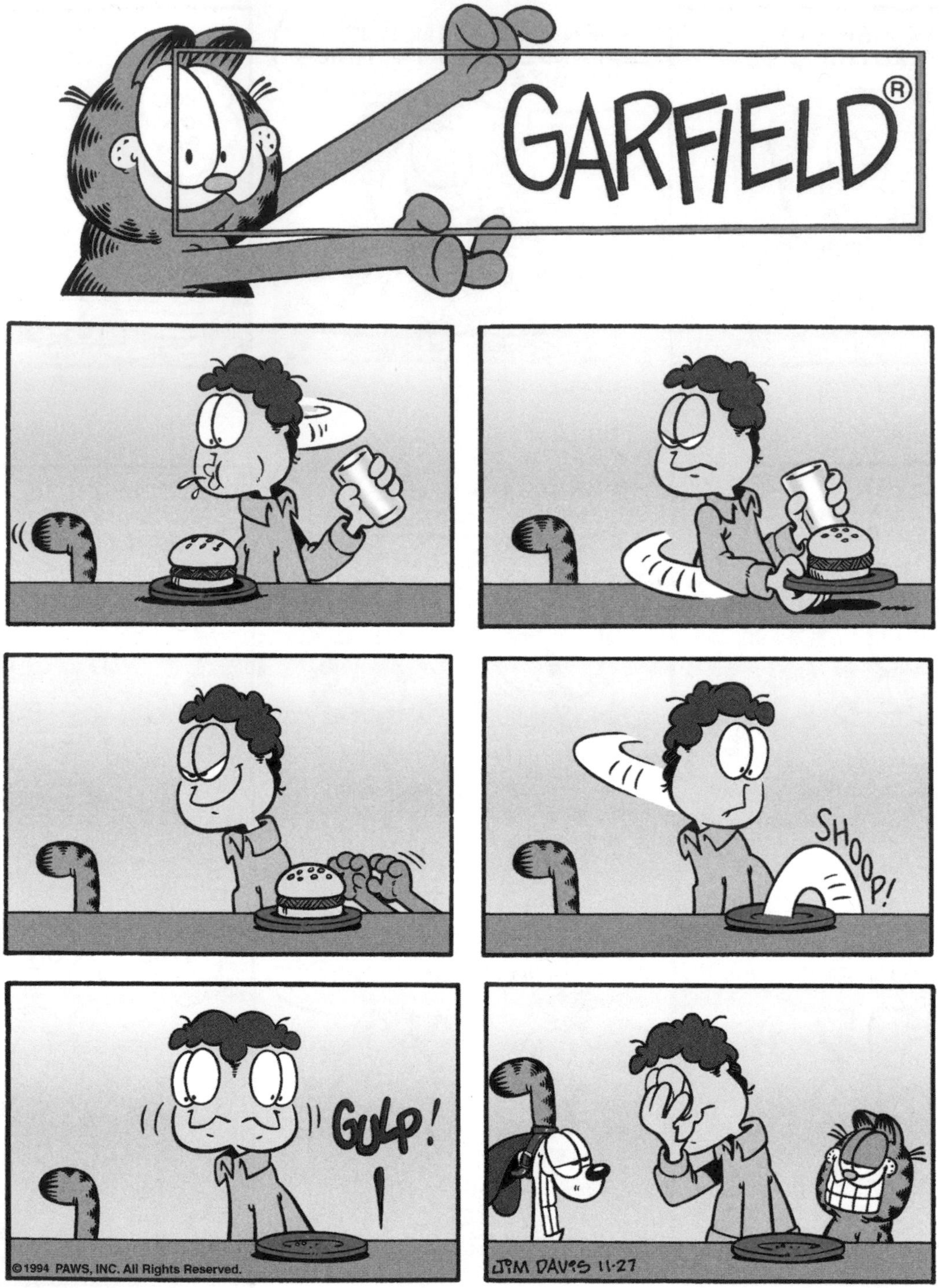
GARFIELD®
SHOOOP!
GULP!
©1994 PAWS, INC. All Rights Reserved.
JIM DAVIS 11-27

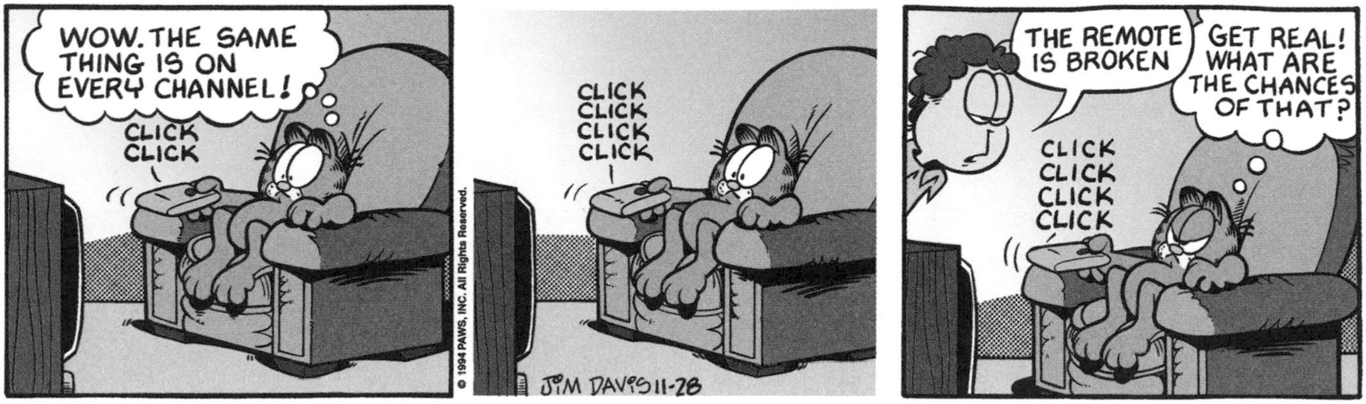
WOW. THE SAME THING IS ON EVERY CHANNEL!
CLICK CLICK
© 1994 PAWS, INC. All Rights Reserved.
CLICK CLICK CLICK CLICK
JIM DAVIS 11-28
THE REMOTE IS BROKEN
GET REAL! WHAT ARE THE CHANCES OF THAT?
CLICK CLICK CLICK CLICK

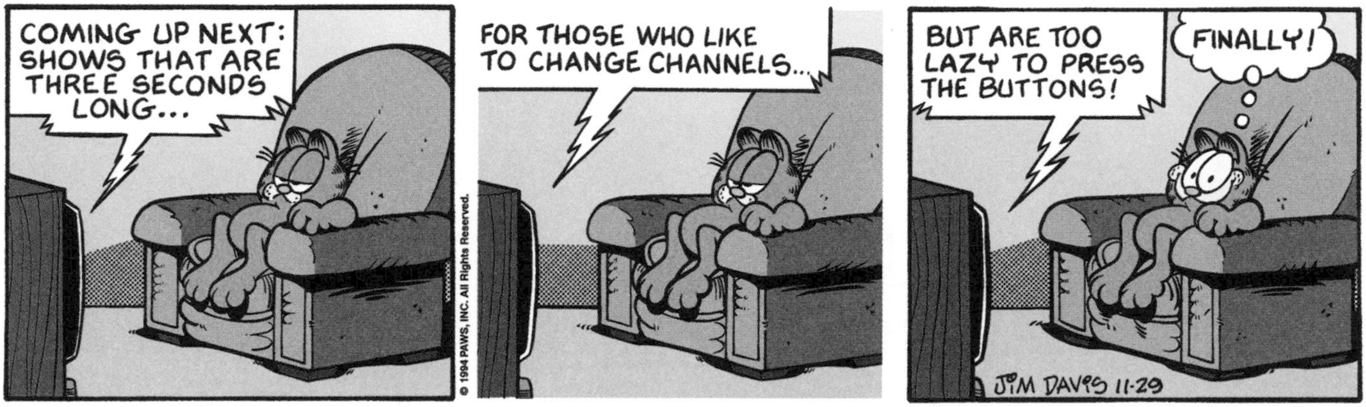
COMING UP NEXT: SHOWS THAT ARE THREE SECONDS LONG...
© 1994 PAWS, INC. All Rights Reserved.
FOR THOSE WHO LIKE TO CHANGE CHANNELS...
BUT ARE TOO LAZY TO PRESS THE BUTTONS!
FINALLY!
JIM DAVIS 11-29

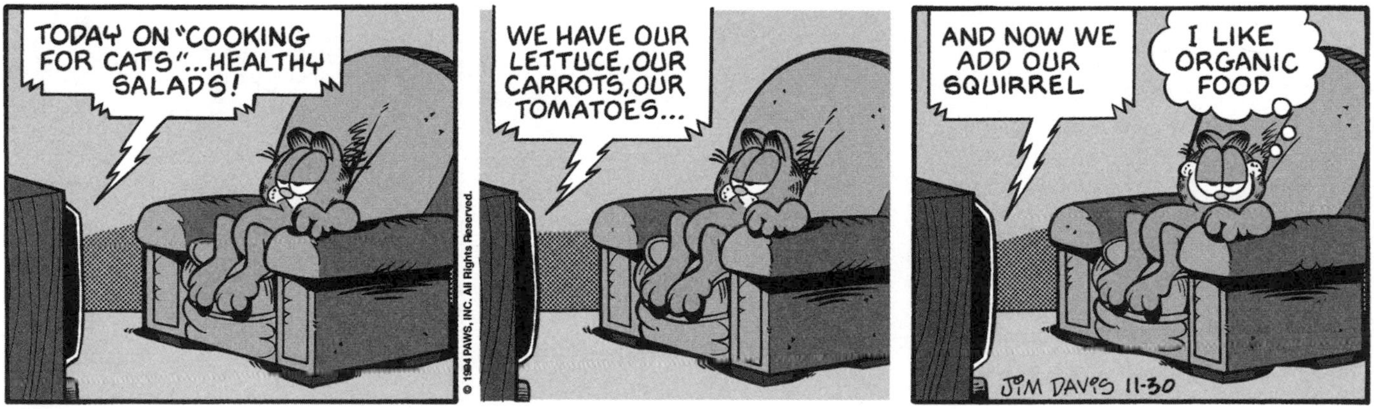
TODAY ON "COOKING FOR CATS"...HEALTHY SALADS!
© 1994 PAWS, INC. All Rights Reserved.
WE HAVE OUR LETTUCE, OUR CARROTS, OUR TOMATOES...
AND NOW WE ADD OUR SQUIRREL
I LIKE ORGANIC FOOD
JIM DAVIS 11-30

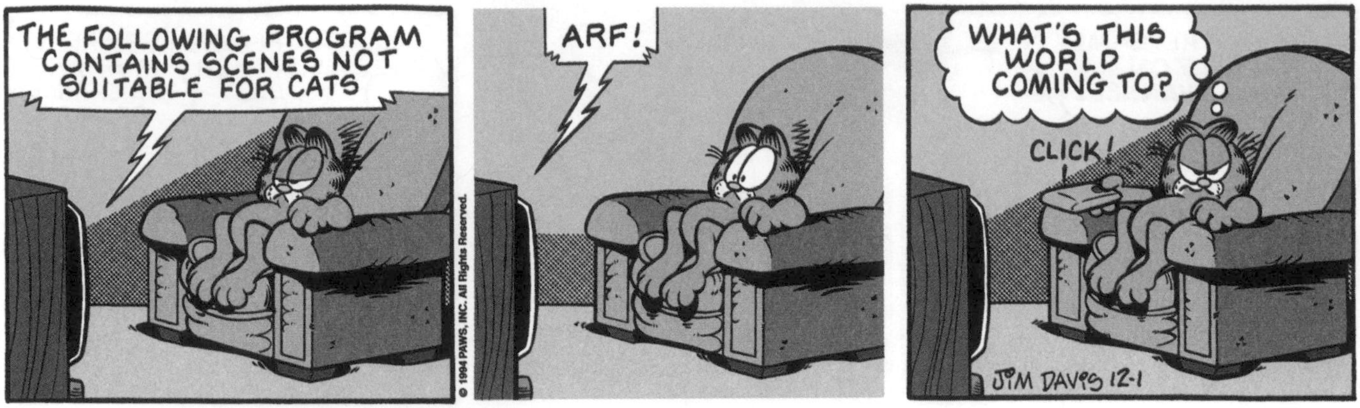
THE FOLLOWING PROGRAM CONTAINS SCENES NOT SUITABLE FOR CATS
© 1994 PAWS, INC. All Rights Reserved.
ARF!
WHAT'S THIS WORLD COMING TO?
CLICK!
JIM DAVIS 12-1

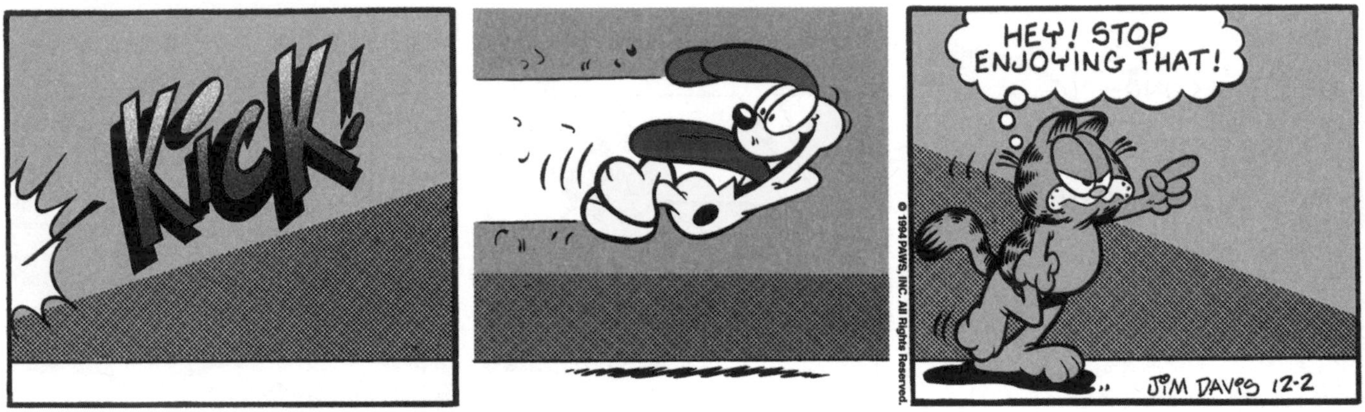
KICK!
© 1994 PAWS, INC. All Rights Reserved.
HEY! STOP ENJOYING THAT!
JIM DAVIS 12-2

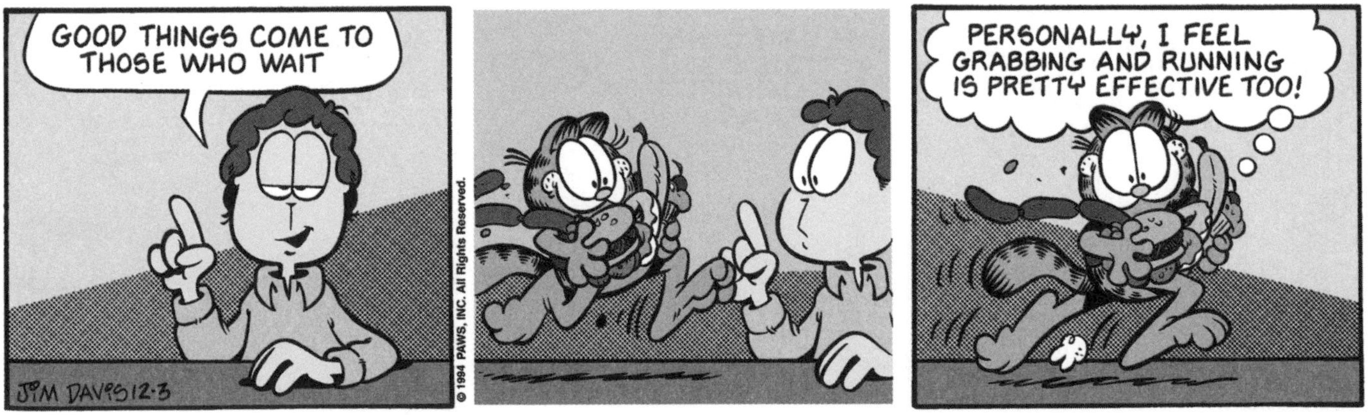
GOOD THINGS COME TO THOSE WHO WAIT
JIM DAVIS 12-3
© 1994 PAWS, INC. All Rights Reserved.
PERSONALLY, I FEEL GRABBING AND RUNNING IS PRETTY EFFECTIVE TOO!

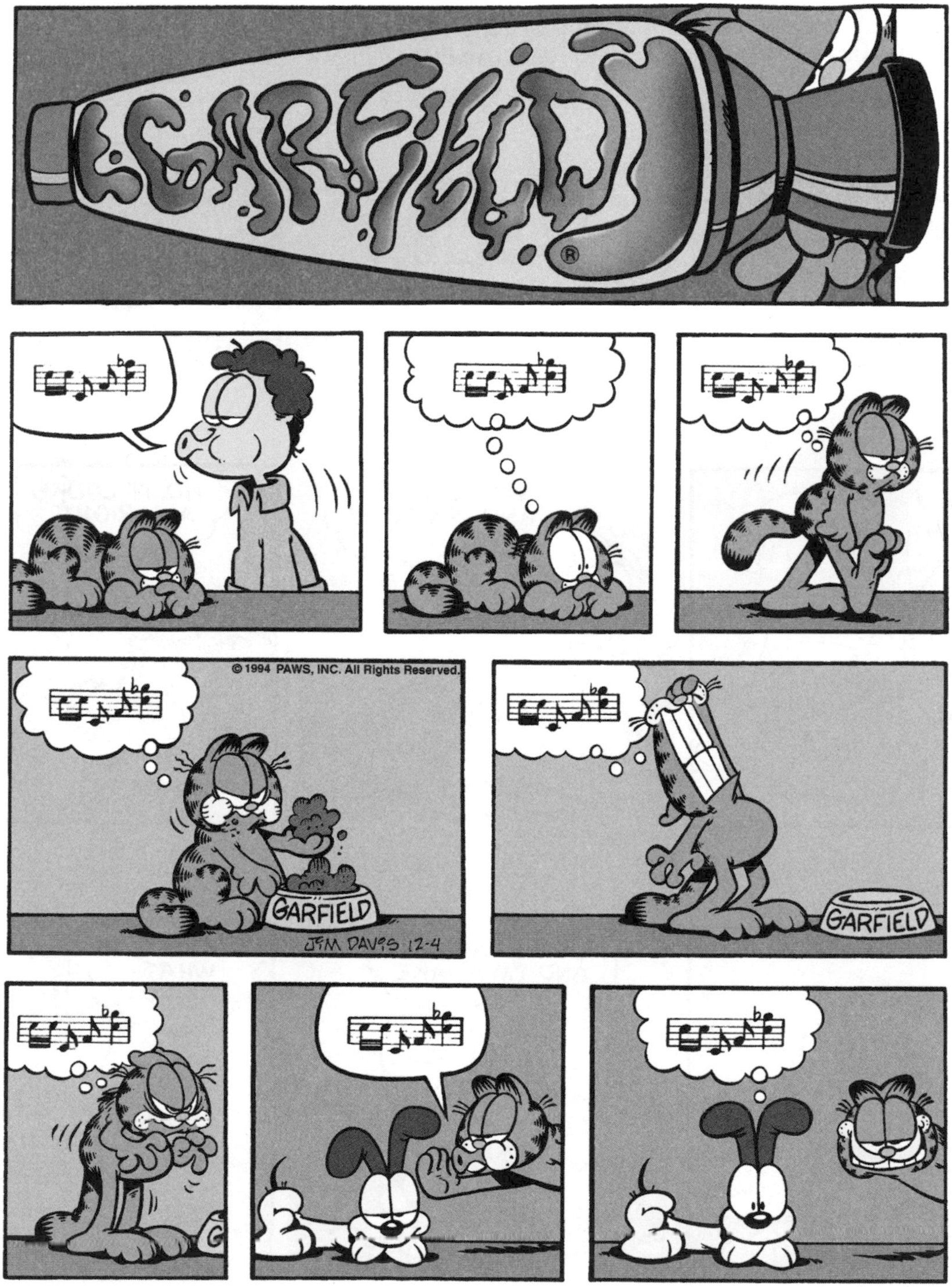
GARFIELD®
© 1994 PAWS, INC. All Rights Reserved.
GARFIELD
JIM DAVIS 12-4
GARFIELD

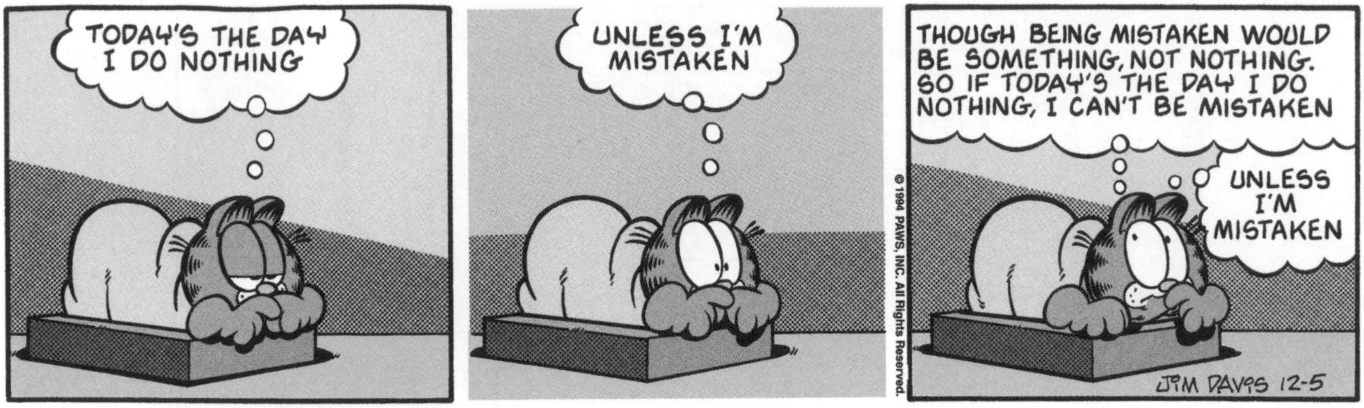
TODAY'S THE DAY I DO NOTHING
UNLESS I'M MISTAKEN
THOUGH BEING MISTAKEN WOULD BE SOMETHING, NOT NOTHING. SO IF TODAY'S THE DAY I DO NOTHING, I CAN'T BE MISTAKEN
UNLESS I'M MISTAKEN
© 1994 PAWS, INC. All Rights Reserved.
JIM DAVIS 12-5

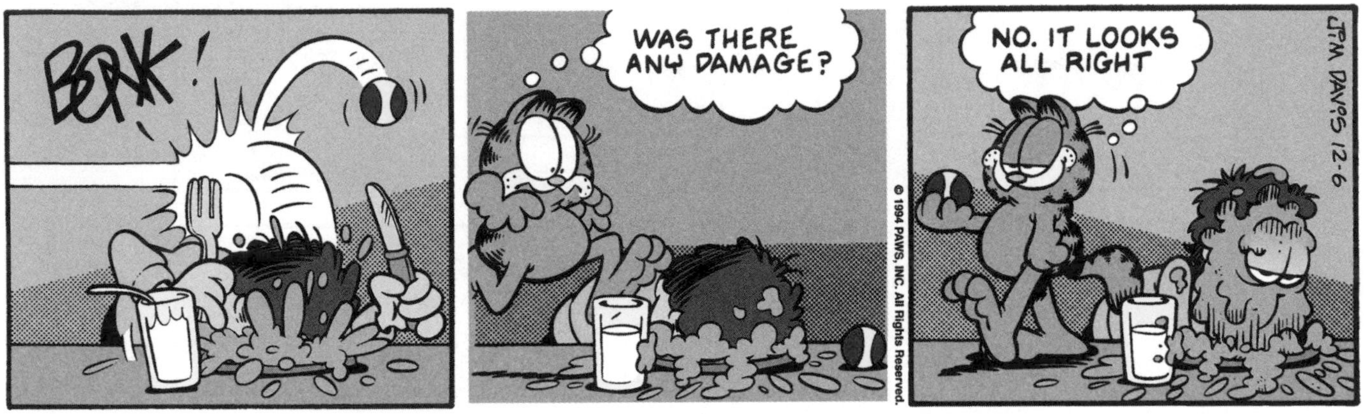
BONK!
WAS THERE ANY DAMAGE?
NO. IT LOOKS ALL RIGHT
© 1994 PAWS, INC. All Rights Reserved.
JIM DAVIS 12-6

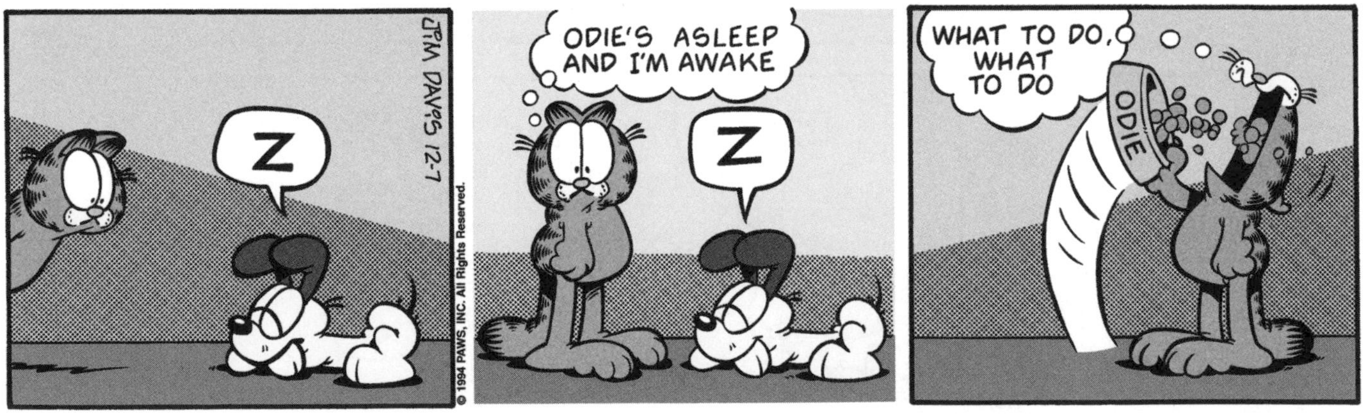
Z
JIM DAVIS 12-7
© 1994 PAWS, INC. All Rights Reserved.
ODIE'S ASLEEP AND I'M AWAKE
Z
WHAT TO DO, WHAT TO DO
ODIE

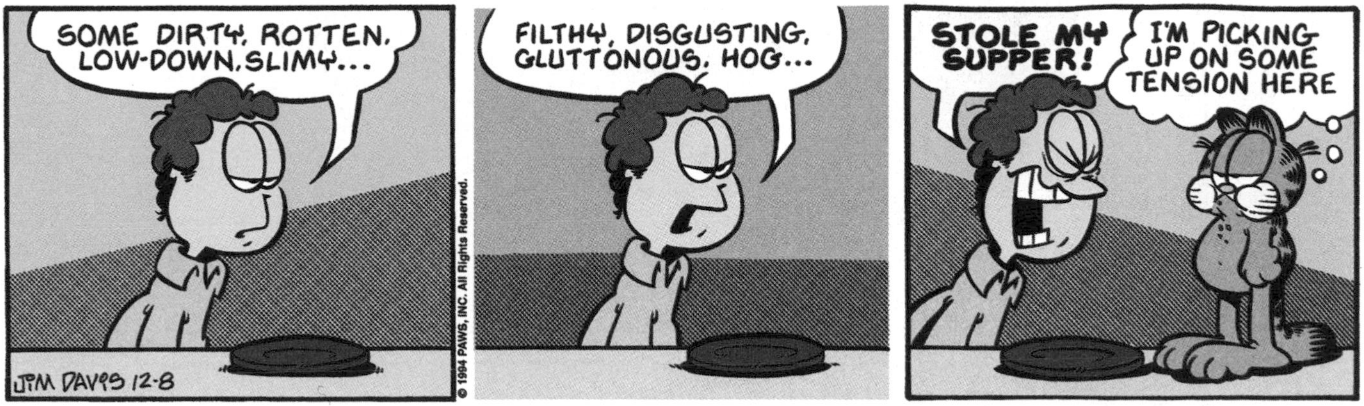
SOME DIRTY, ROTTEN, LOW-DOWN, SLIMY...
JIM DAVIS 12-8
© 1994 PAWS, INC. All Rights Reserved.
FILTHY, DISGUSTING, GLUTTONOUS, HOG...
STOLE MY SUPPER!
I'M PICKING UP ON SOME TENSION HERE

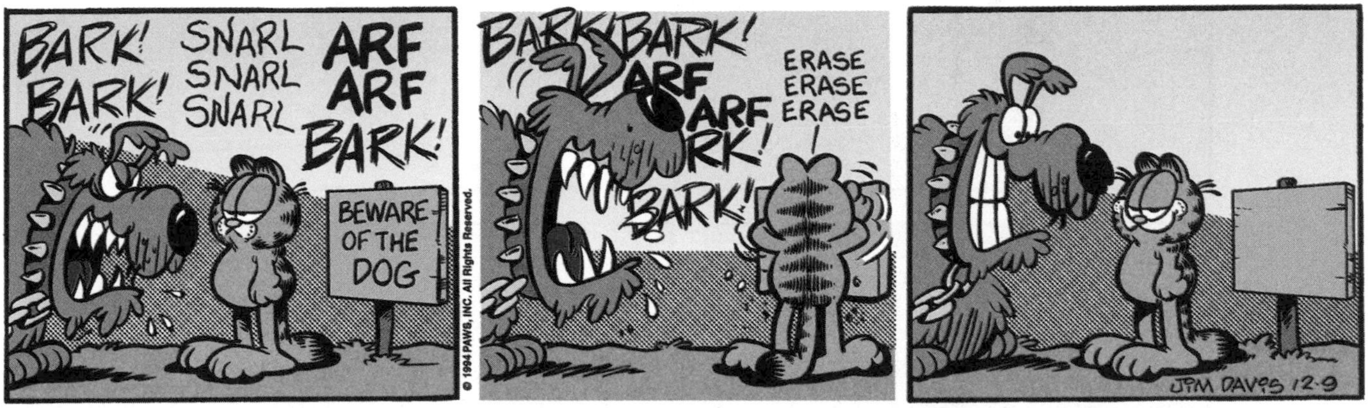
BARK! BARK!
SNARL SNARL SNARL
ARF ARF BARK!
BEWARE OF THE DOG
© 1994 PAWS, INC. All Rights Reserved.
BARK! BARK!
ARF
ARF
BARK!
ERASE ERASE ERASE
JIM DAVIS 12-9

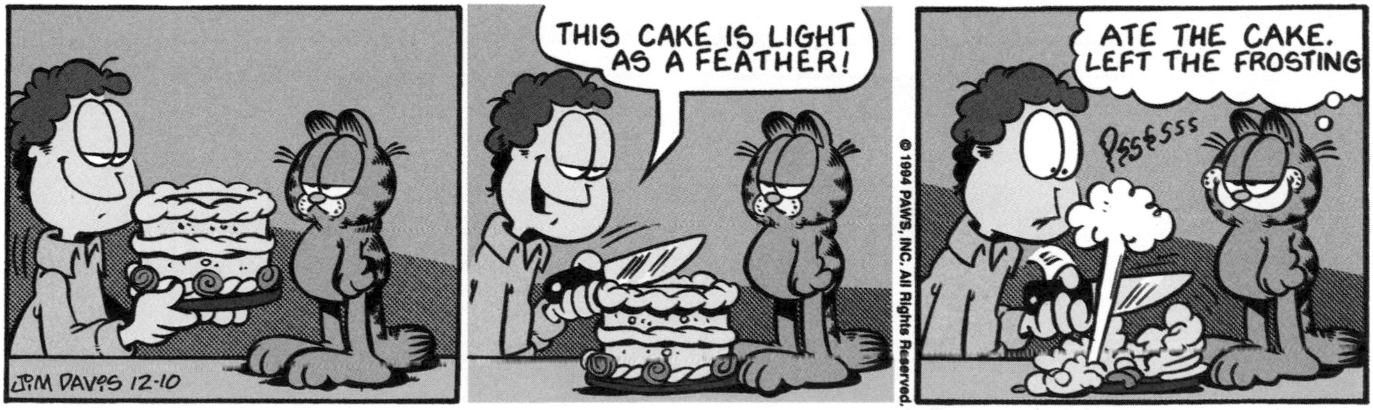
JIM DAVIS 12-10
THIS CAKE IS LIGHT AS A FEATHER!
© 1994 PAWS, INC. All Rights Reserved.
ATE THE CAKE. LEFT THE FROSTING

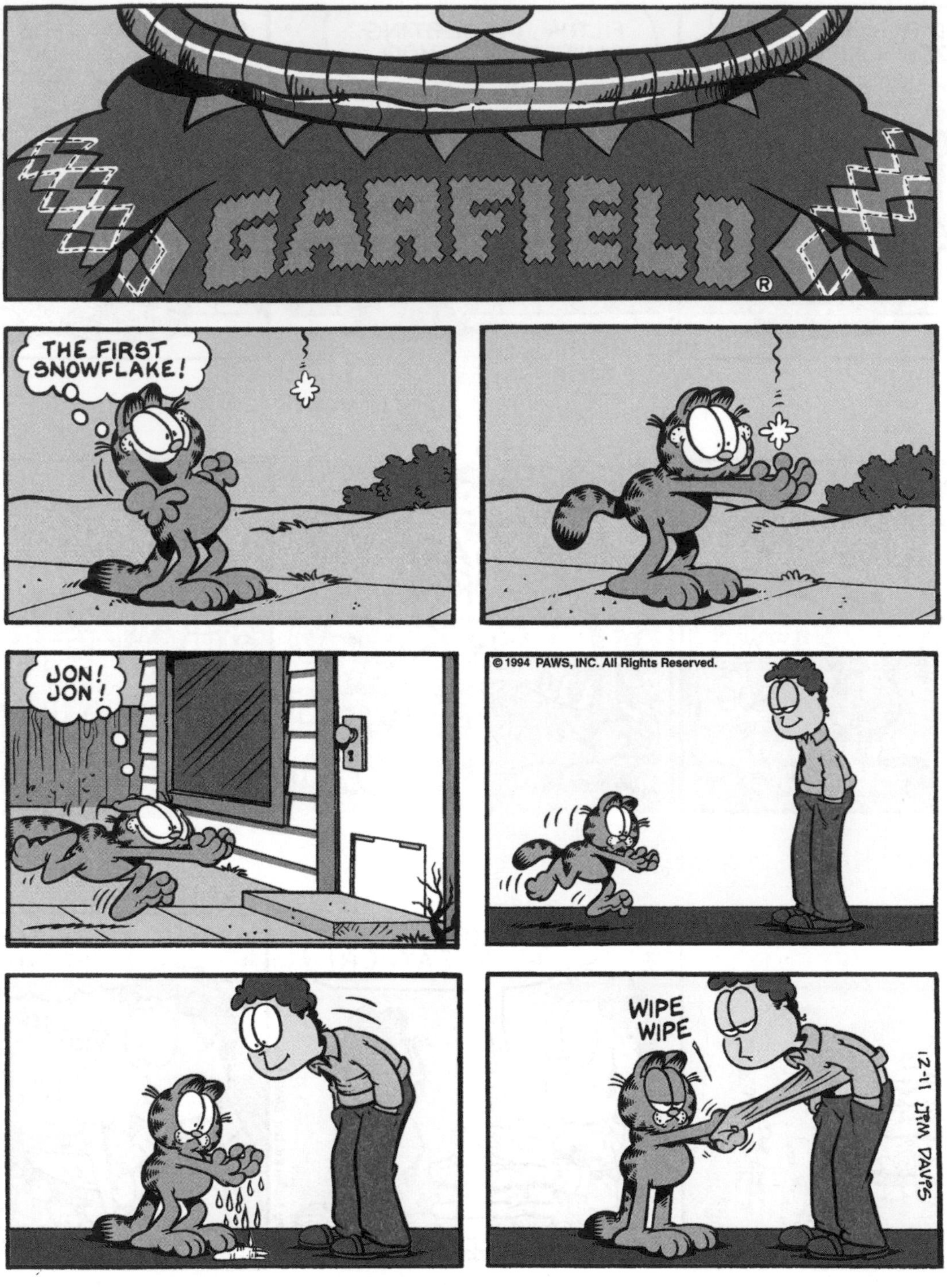
GARFIELD®
THE FIRST SNOWFLAKE!
JON! JON!
© 1994 PAWS, INC. All Rights Reserved.
WIPE WIPE
12-11 JIM DAVIS

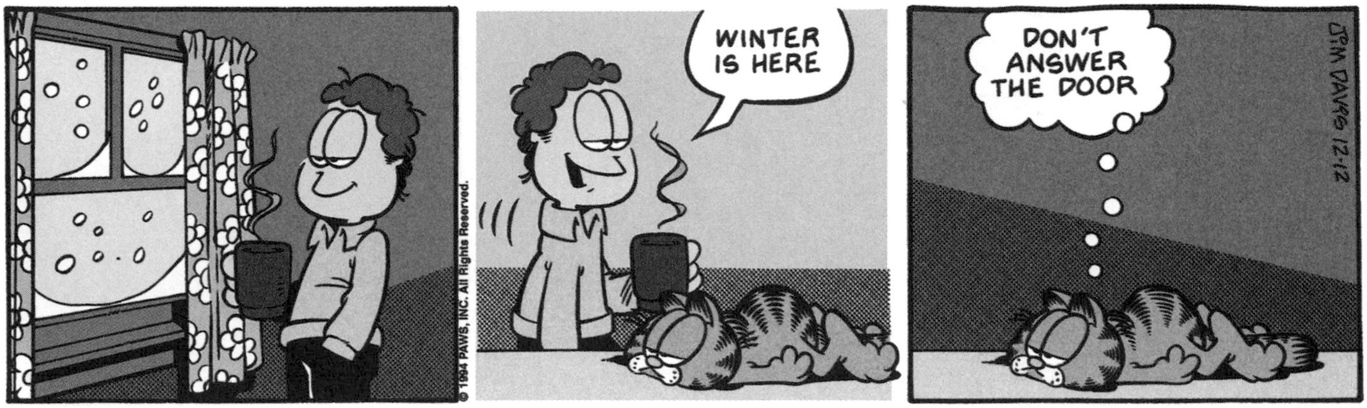
© 1994 PAWS, INC. All Rights Reserved.
WINTER IS HERE
DON'T ANSWER THE DOOR
JIM DAVIS 12-12

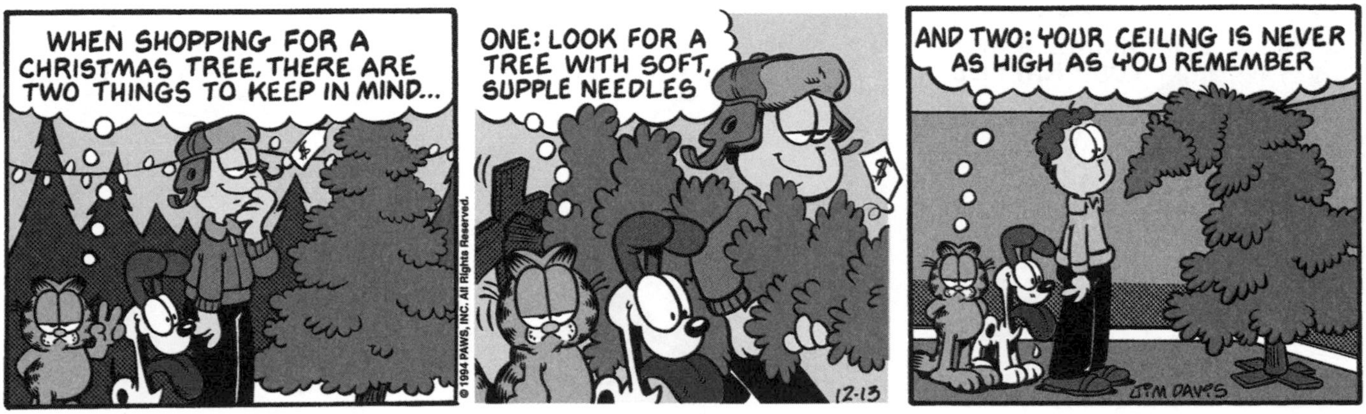
WHEN SHOPPING FOR A CHRISTMAS TREE, THERE ARE TWO THINGS TO KEEP IN MIND...
© 1994 PAWS, INC. All Rights Reserved.
ONE: LOOK FOR A TREE WITH SOFT, SUPPLE NEEDLES
12-13
AND TWO: YOUR CEILING IS NEVER AS HIGH AS YOU REMEMBER
JIM DAVIS

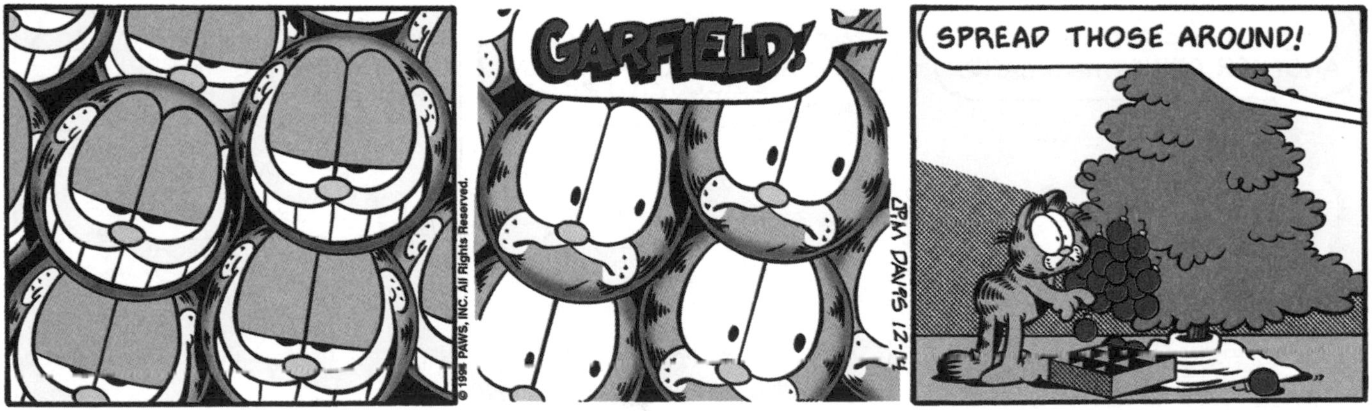
© 1996 PAWS, INC. All Rights Reserved.
GARFIELD!
JIM DAVIS 12-14
SPREAD THOSE AROUND!

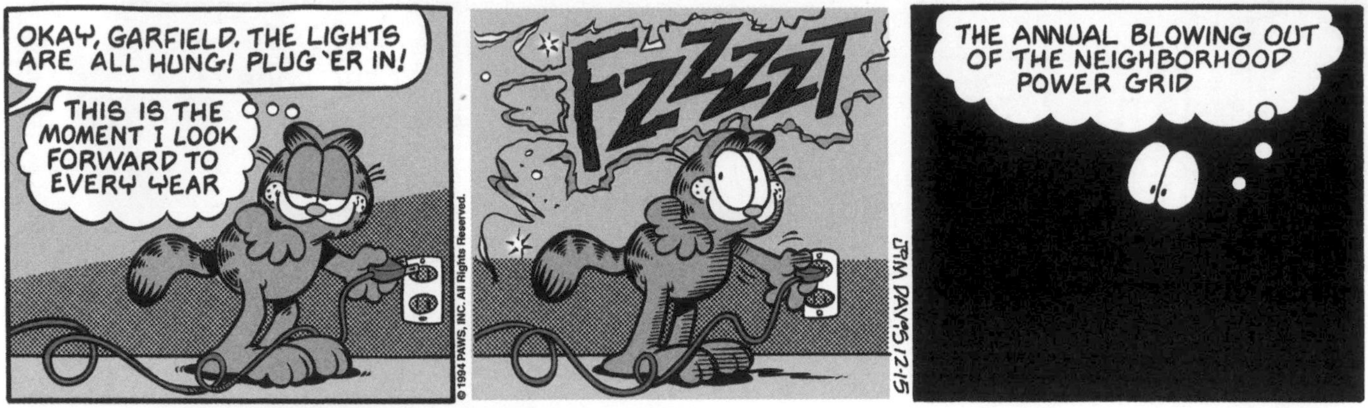
OKAY, GARFIELD. THE LIGHTS ARE ALL HUNG! PLUG 'ER IN!
THIS IS THE MOMENT I LOOK FORWARD TO EVERY YEAR
FZZZZZT
THE ANNUAL BLOWING OUT OF THE NEIGHBORHOOD POWER GRID
© 1994 PAWS, INC. All Rights Reserved.
JIM DAVIS 12-15

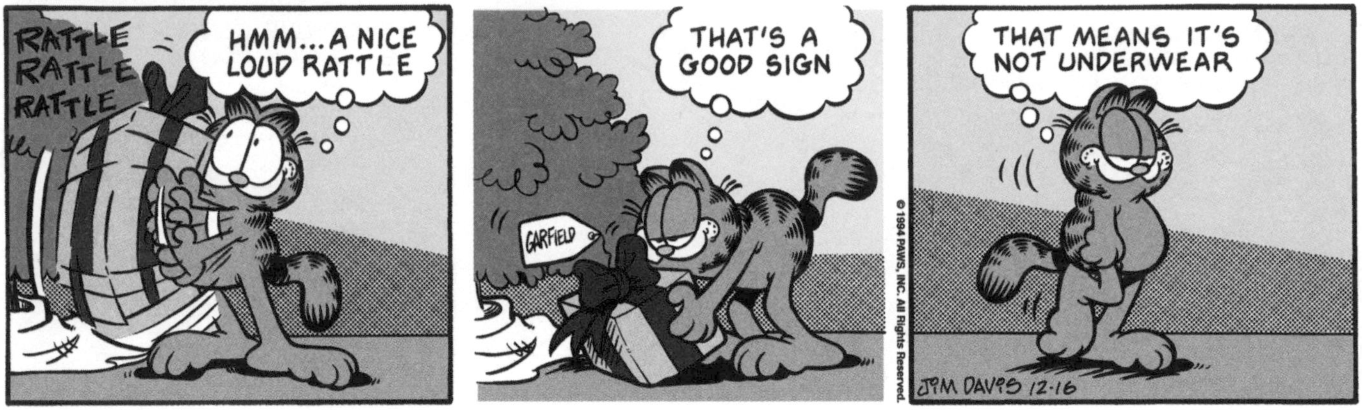
RATTLE RATTLE RATTLE
HMM... A NICE LOUD RATTLE
GARFIELD
THAT'S A GOOD SIGN
THAT MEANS IT'S NOT UNDERWEAR
© 1994 PAWS, INC. All Rights Reserved.
JIM DAVIS 12-16

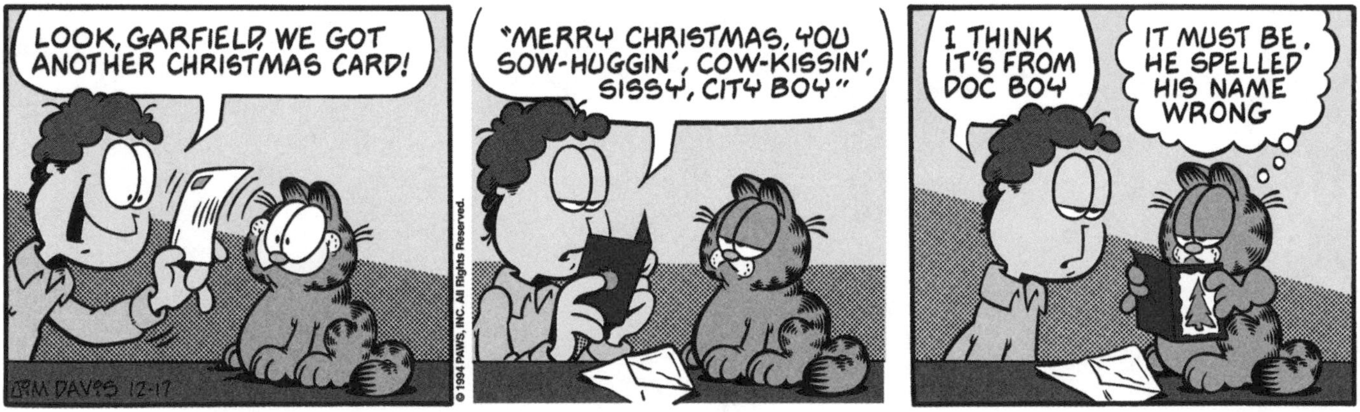
LOOK, GARFIELD. WE GOT ANOTHER CHRISTMAS CARD!
"MERRY CHRISTMAS, YOU SOW-HUGGIN', COW-KISSIN', SISSY, CITY BOY"
I THINK IT'S FROM DOC BOY
IT MUST BE. HE SPELLED HIS NAME WRONG
© 1994 PAWS, INC. All Rights Reserved.
JIM DAVIS 12-17

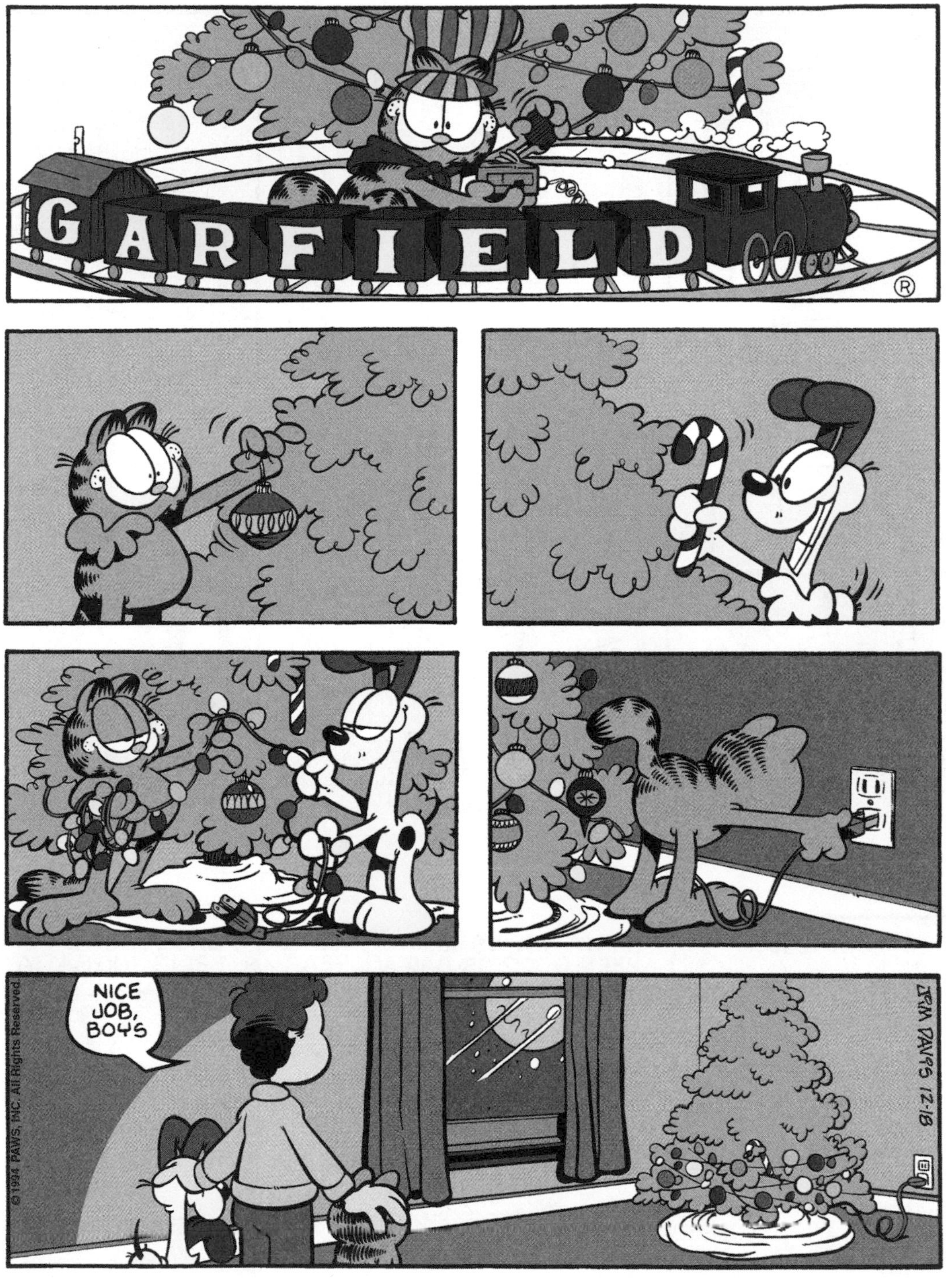
GARFIELD
NICE JOB, BOYS
JIM DAVIS 12-18

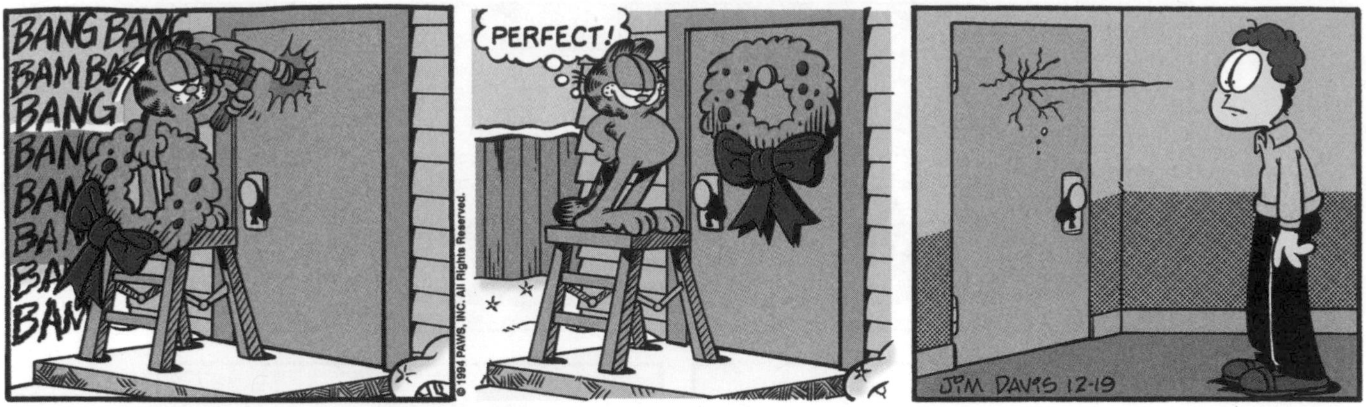
BANG BANG
BAM BA
BANG
BANG
BAM
BA
BA
BAM
© 1994 PAWS, INC. All Rights Reserved.
PERFECT!
JIM DAVIS 12-19

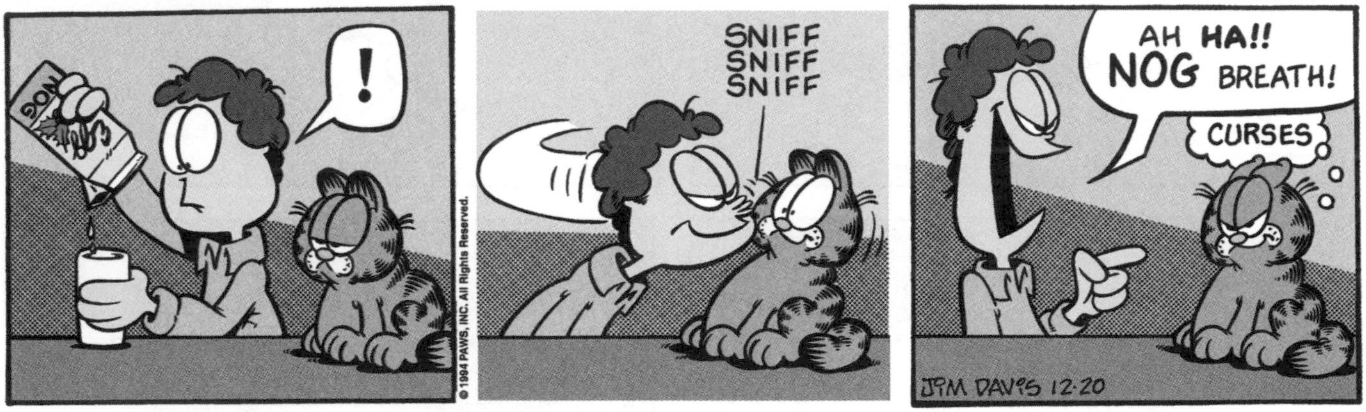
!
© 1994 PAWS, INC. All Rights Reserved.
SNIFF
SNIFF
SNIFF
AH HA!! NOG BREATH!
CURSES
JIM DAVIS 12-20

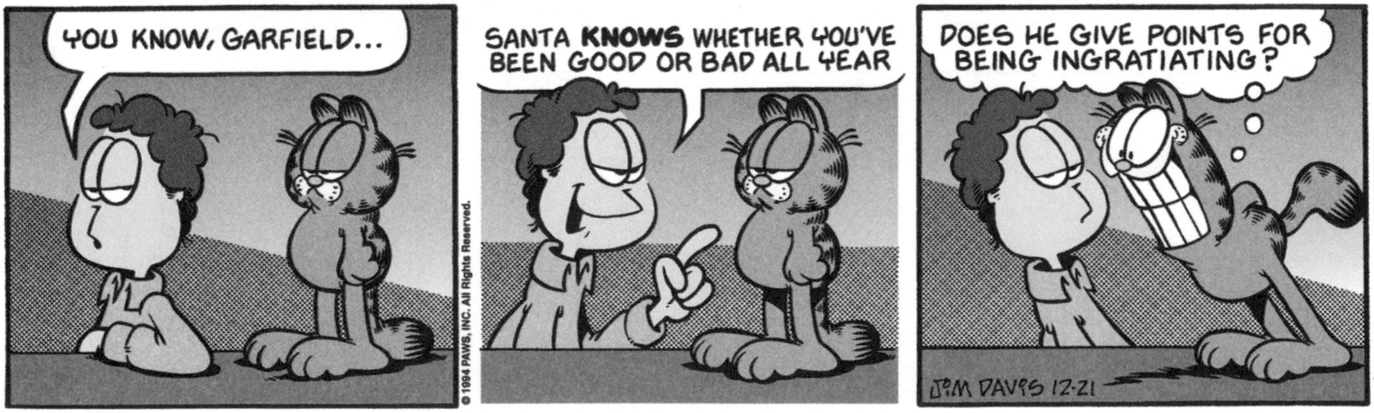
YOU KNOW, GARFIELD...
© 1994 PAWS, INC. All Rights Reserved.
SANTA KNOWS WHETHER YOU'VE BEEN GOOD OR BAD ALL YEAR
DOES HE GIVE POINTS FOR BEING INGRATIATING?
JIM DAVIS 12-21

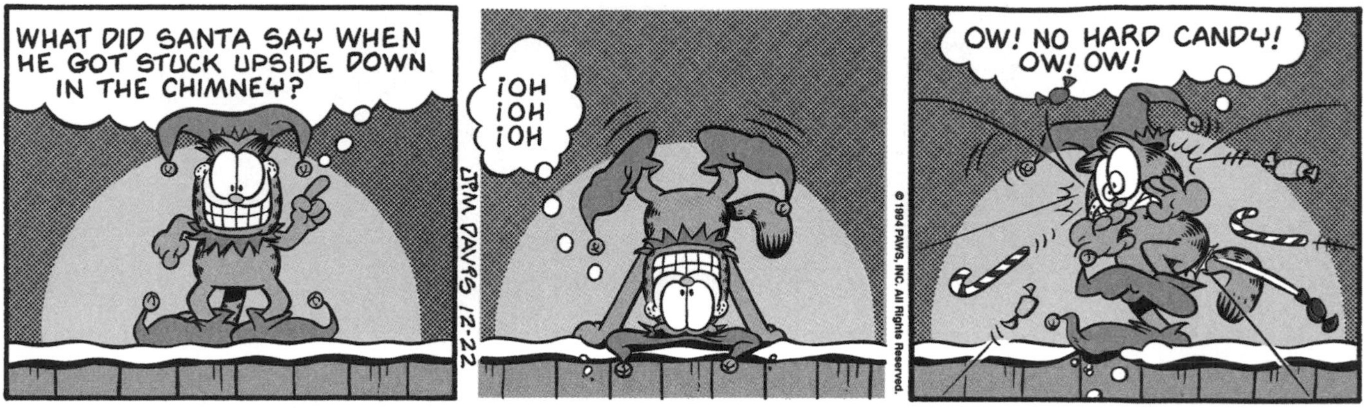
WHAT DID SANTA SAY WHEN HE GOT STUCK UPSIDE DOWN IN THE CHIMNEY?
¡OH
¡OH
¡OH
JIM DAVIS 12-22
OW! NO HARD CANDY! OW! OW!

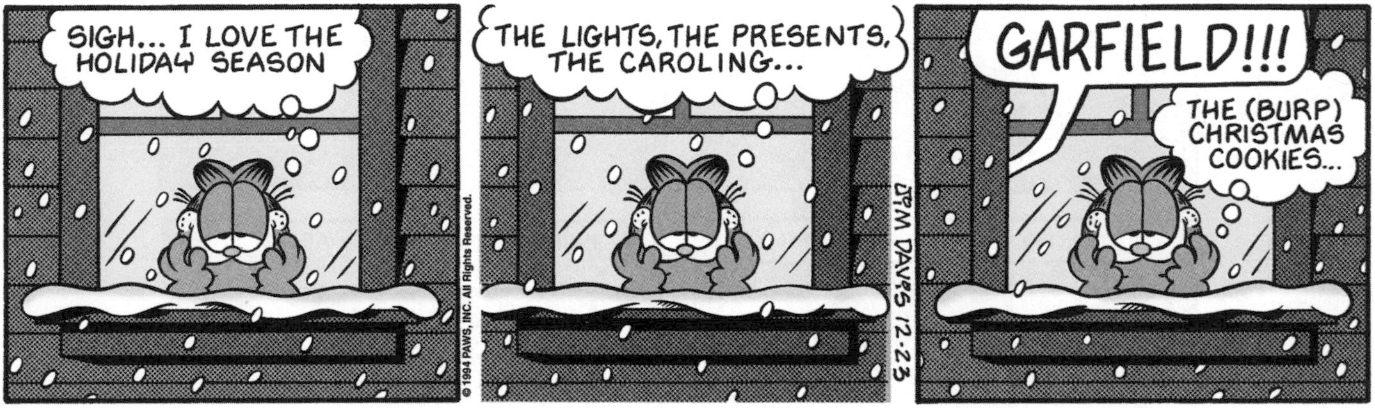
SIGH... I LOVE THE HOLIDAY SEASON
THE LIGHTS, THE PRESENTS, THE CAROLING...
JIM DAVIS 12-23
GARFIELD!!!
THE (BURP) CHRISTMAS COOKIES...

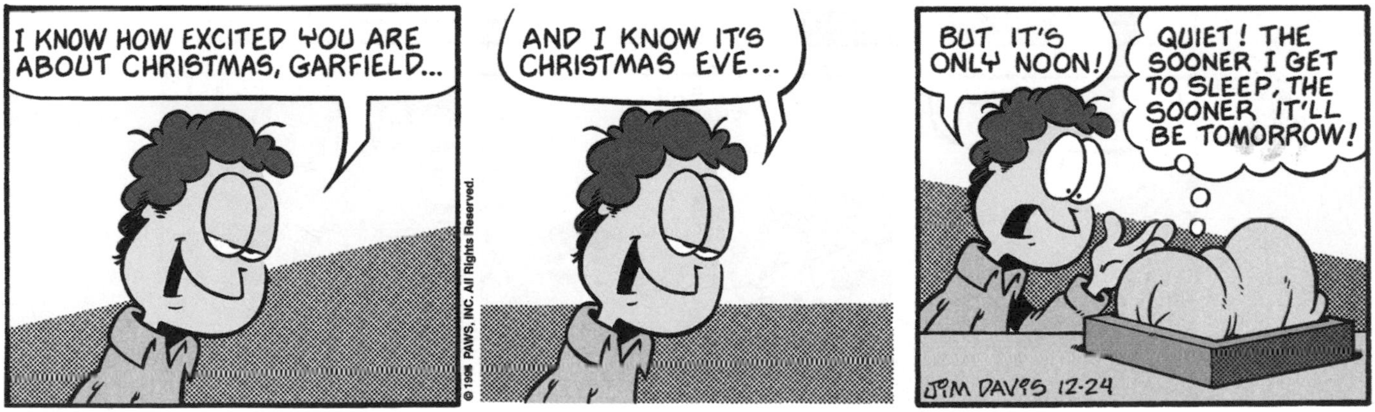
I KNOW HOW EXCITED YOU ARE ABOUT CHRISTMAS, GARFIELD...
AND I KNOW IT'S CHRISTMAS EVE...
BUT IT'S ONLY NOON!
QUIET! THE SOONER I GET TO SLEEP, THE SOONER IT'LL BE TOMORROW!
JIM DAVIS 12-24

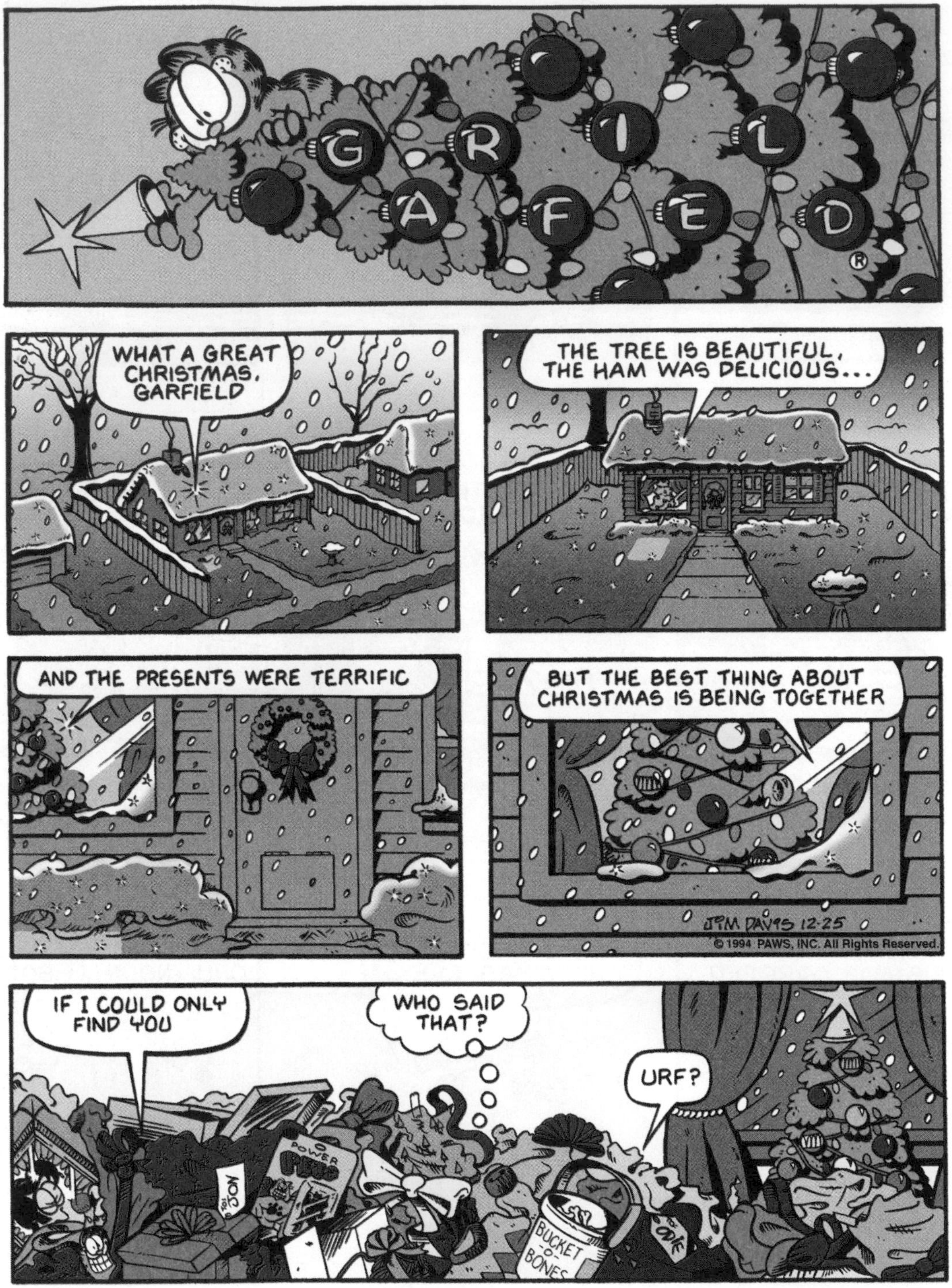
GARFIELD ®
WHAT A GREAT CHRISTMAS, GARFIELD
THE TREE IS BEAUTIFUL, THE HAM WAS DELICIOUS...
AND THE PRESENTS WERE TERRIFIC
BUT THE BEST THING ABOUT CHRISTMAS IS BEING TOGETHER
JIM DAVIS 12-25
© 1994 PAWS, INC. All Rights Reserved.
IF I COULD ONLY FIND YOU
WHO SAID THAT?
URF?
POWER
BUCKET -O- BONES

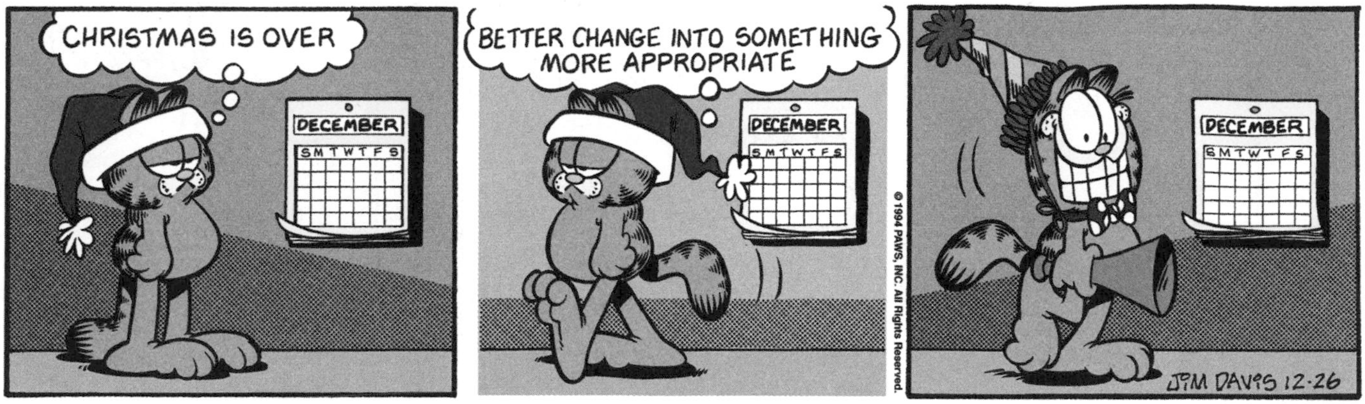
CHRISTMAS IS OVER
BETTER CHANGE INTO SOMETHING MORE APPROPRIATE
DECEMBER
S M T W T F S
© 1994 PAWS, INC. All Rights Reserved.
JIM DAVIS 12-26

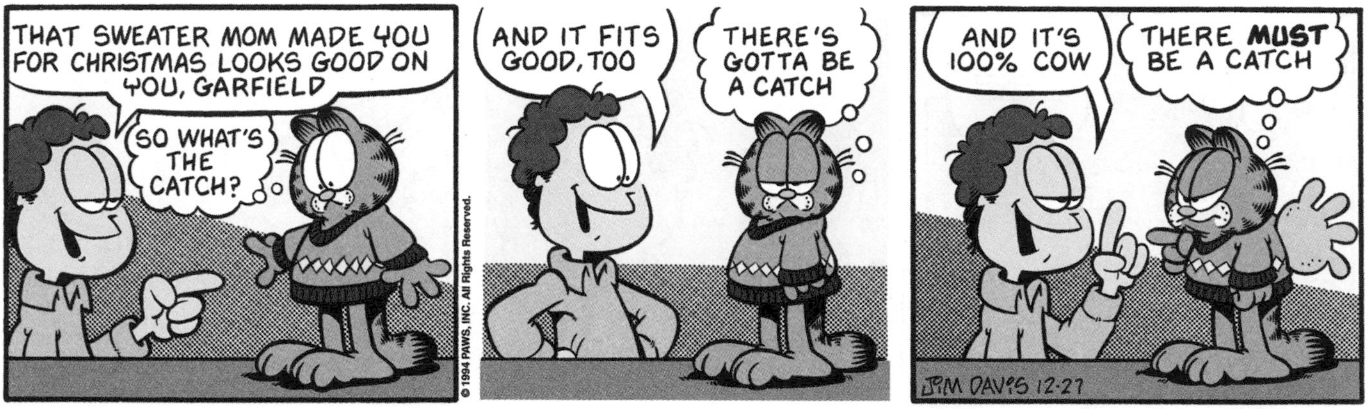
THAT SWEATER MOM MADE YOU FOR CHRISTMAS LOOKS GOOD ON YOU, GARFIELD
SO WHAT'S THE CATCH?
© 1994 PAWS, INC. All Rights Reserved.
AND IT FITS GOOD, TOO
THERE'S GOTTA BE A CATCH
AND IT'S 100% COW
THERE **MUST** BE A CATCH
JIM DAVIS 12-27

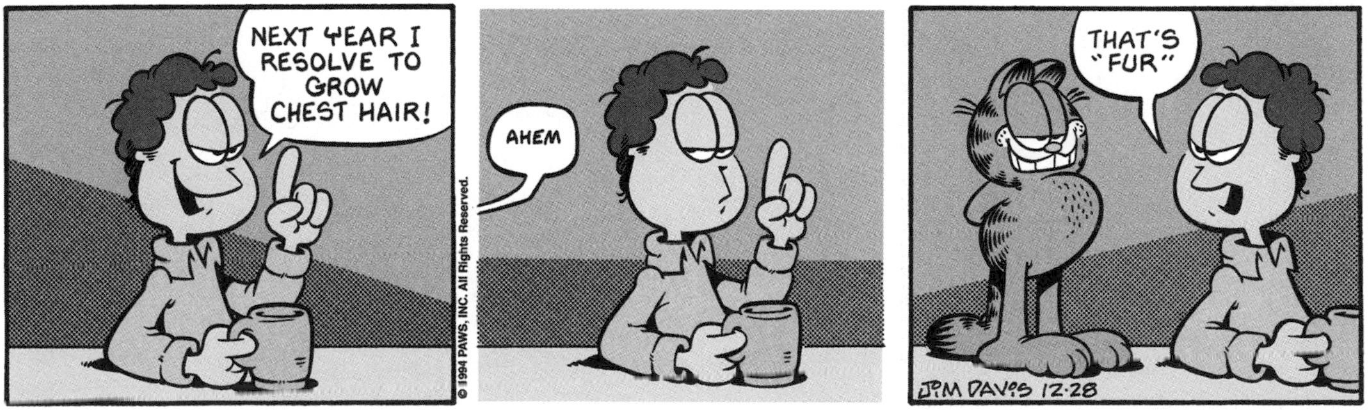
NEXT YEAR I RESOLVE TO GROW CHEST HAIR!
© 1994 PAWS, INC. All Rights Reserved.
AHEM
THAT'S "FUR"
JIM DAVIS 12-28

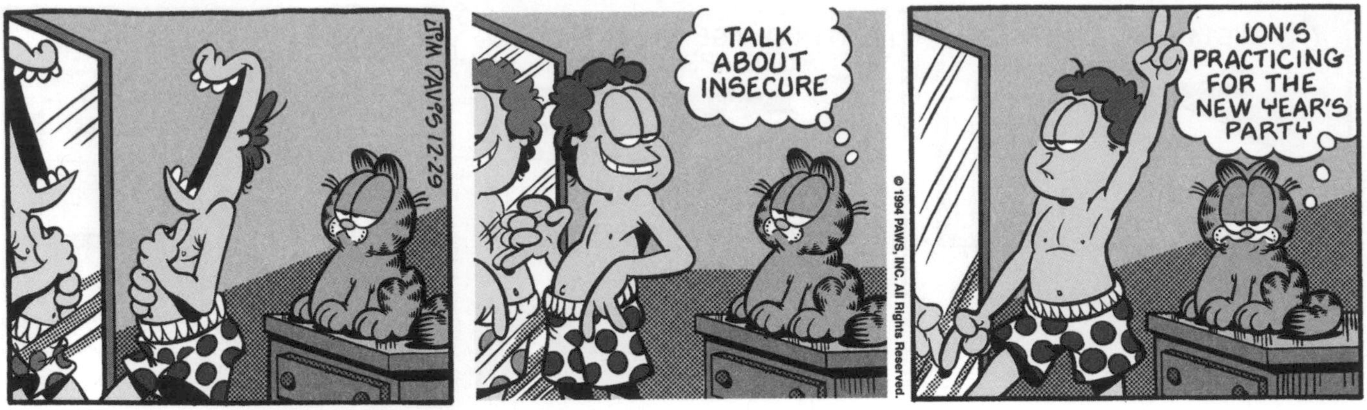
JIM DAVIS 12-29
TALK ABOUT INSECURE
© 1994 PAWS, INC. All Rights Reserved.
JON'S PRACTICING FOR THE NEW YEAR'S PARTY

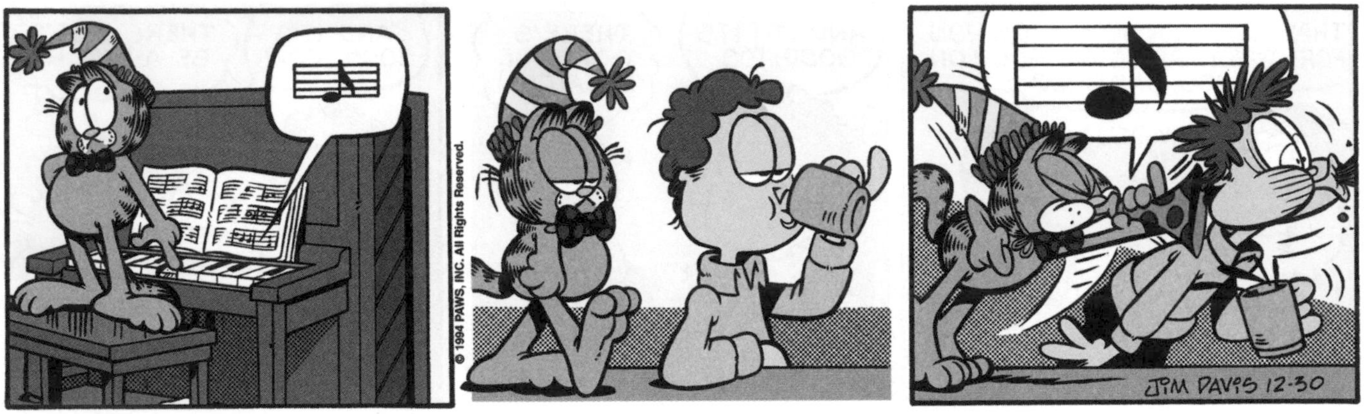
© 1994 PAWS, INC. All Rights Reserved.
JIM DAVIS 12-30

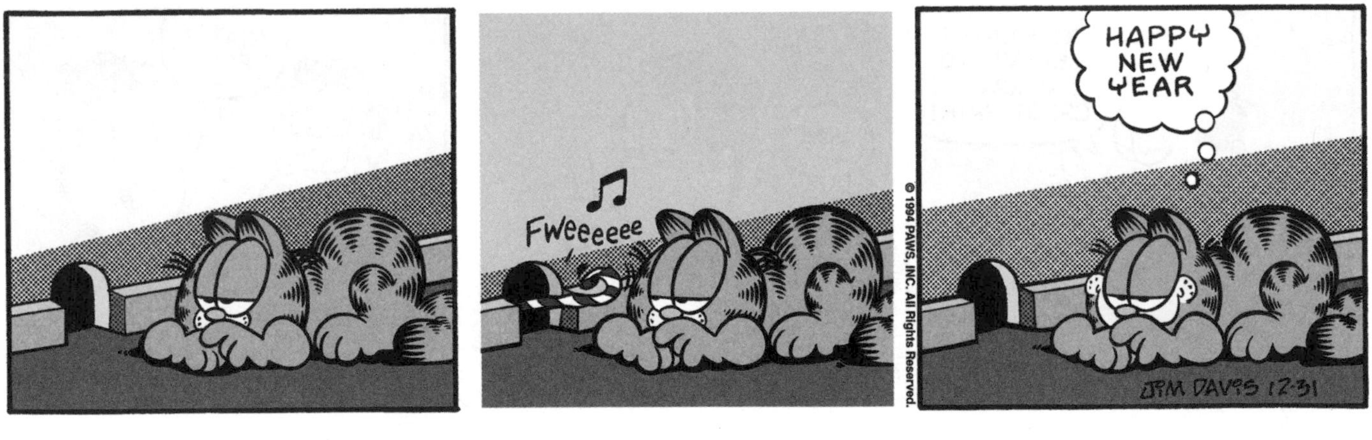
Fweeeeee
© 1994 PAWS, INC. All Rights Reserved.
HAPPY NEW YEAR
JIM DAVIS 12-31

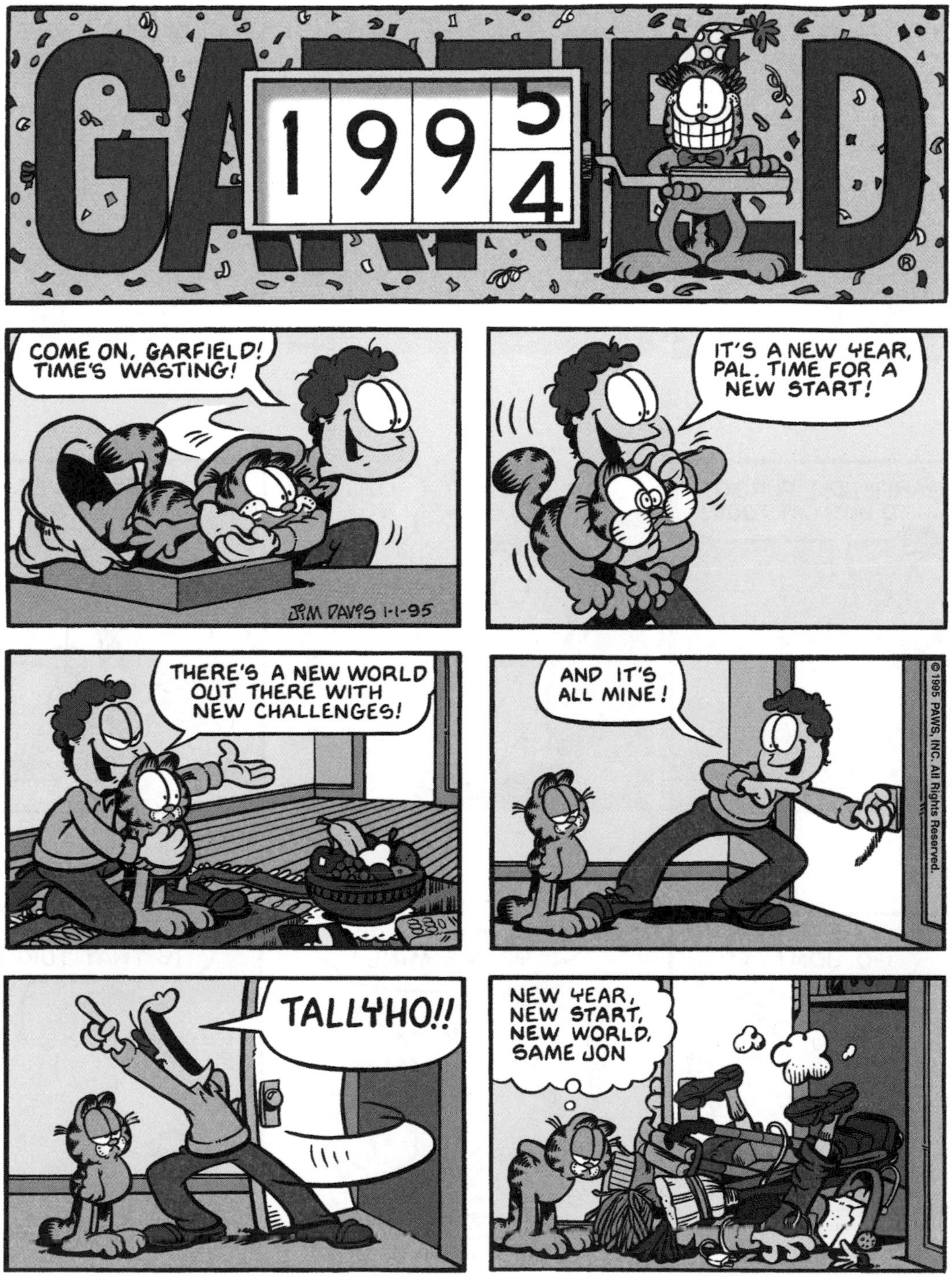

GARFIELD
1995
1994
COME ON, GARFIELD! TIME'S WASTING!
JIM DAVIS 1-1-95
IT'S A NEW YEAR, PAL. TIME FOR A NEW START!
THERE'S A NEW WORLD OUT THERE WITH NEW CHALLENGES!
AND IT'S ALL MINE!
© 1995 PAWS, INC. All Rights Reserved.
TALLYHO!!
NEW YEAR, NEW START, NEW WORLD, SAME JON

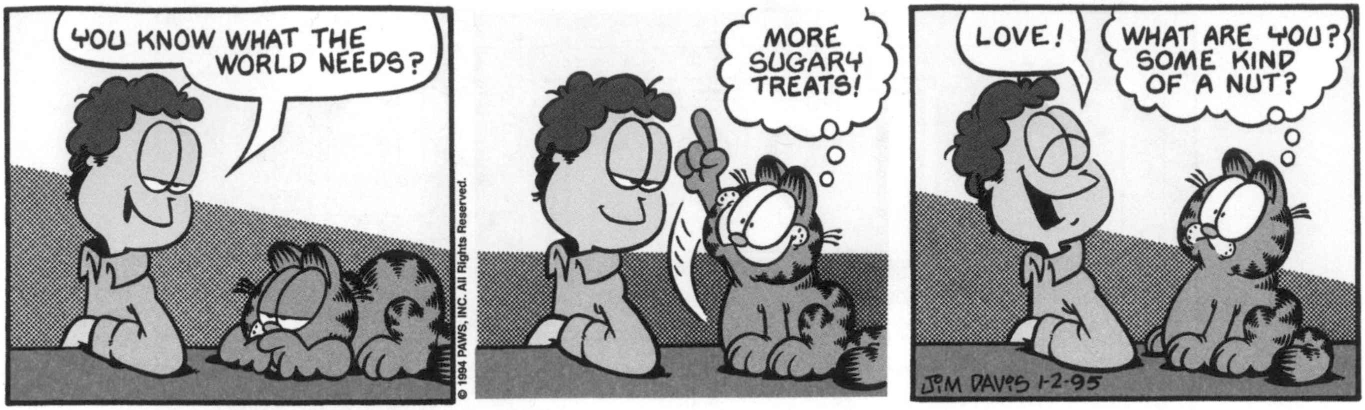
YOU KNOW WHAT THE WORLD NEEDS?
MORE SUGARY TREATS!
LOVE!
WHAT ARE YOU? SOME KIND OF A NUT?
JIM DAVIS 1-2-95

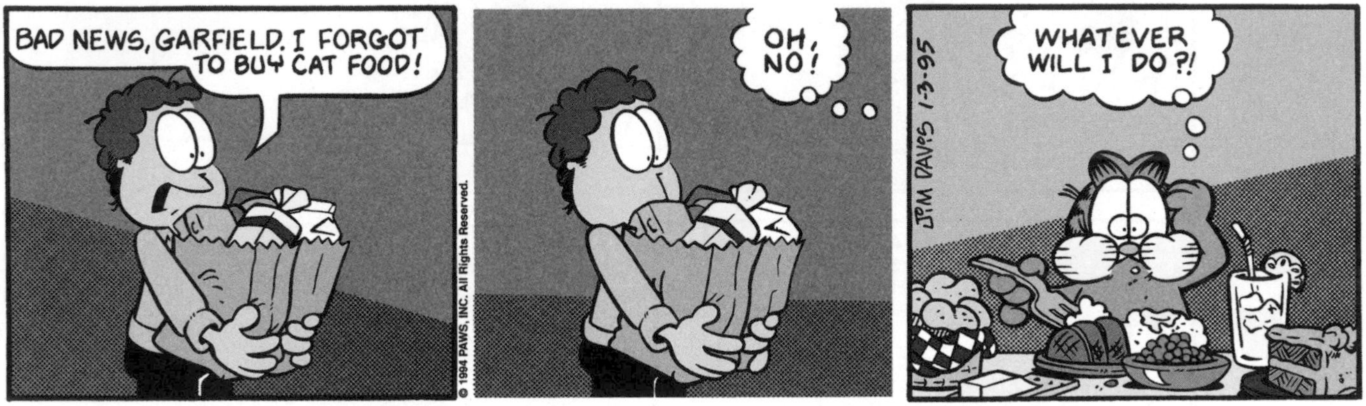
BAD NEWS, GARFIELD. I FORGOT TO BUY CAT FOOD!
OH, NO!
JIM DAVIS 1-3-95
WHATEVER WILL I DO?!

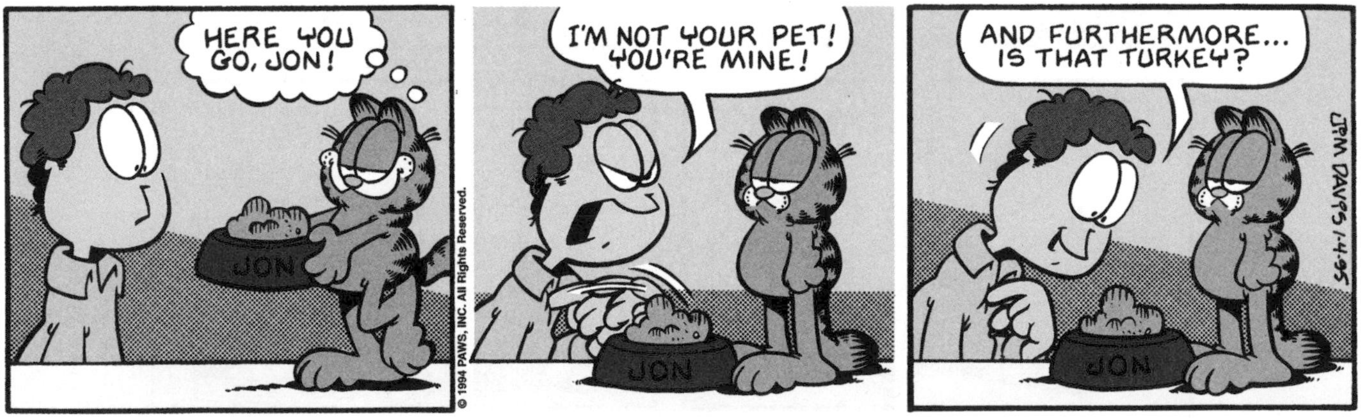
HERE YOU GO, JON!
JON
I'M NOT YOUR PET! YOU'RE MINE!
JON
AND FURTHERMORE... IS THAT TURKEY?
JON
JIM DAVIS 1-4-95

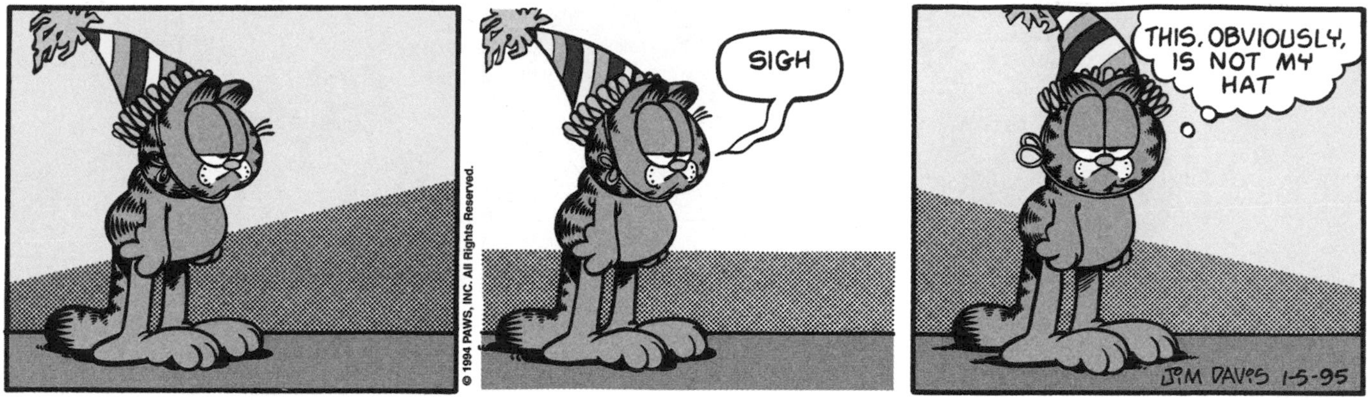
© 1994 PAWS, INC. All Rights Reserved.
SIGH
THIS, OBVIOUSLY, IS NOT MY HAT
JIM DAVIS 1-5-95

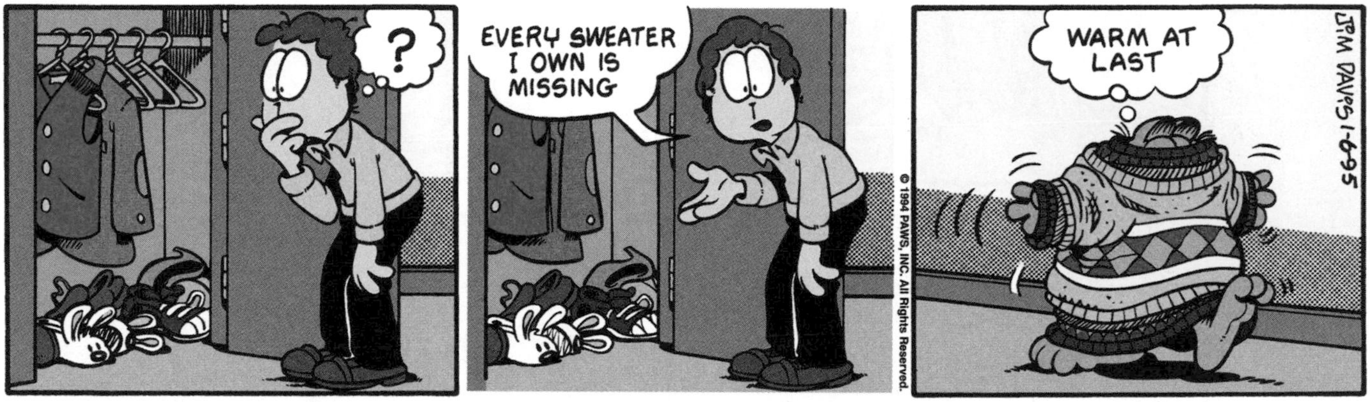
?
EVERY SWEATER I OWN IS MISSING
© 1994 PAWS, INC. All Rights Reserved.
WARM AT LAST
JIM DAVIS 1-6-95

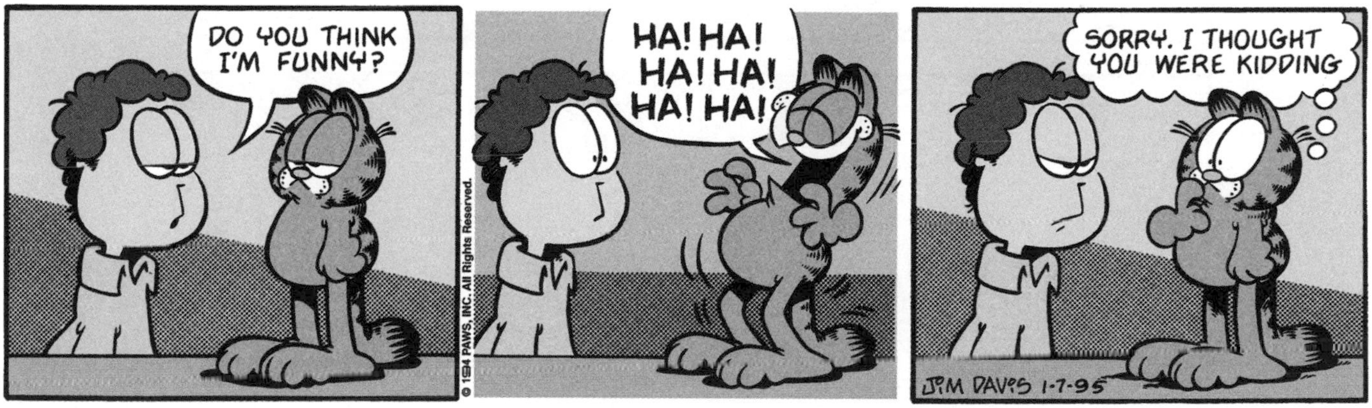
DO YOU THINK I'M FUNNY?
© 1994 PAWS, INC. All Rights Reserved.
HA! HA! HA! HA! HA! HA!
SORRY. I THOUGHT YOU WERE KIDDING
JIM DAVIS 1-7-95

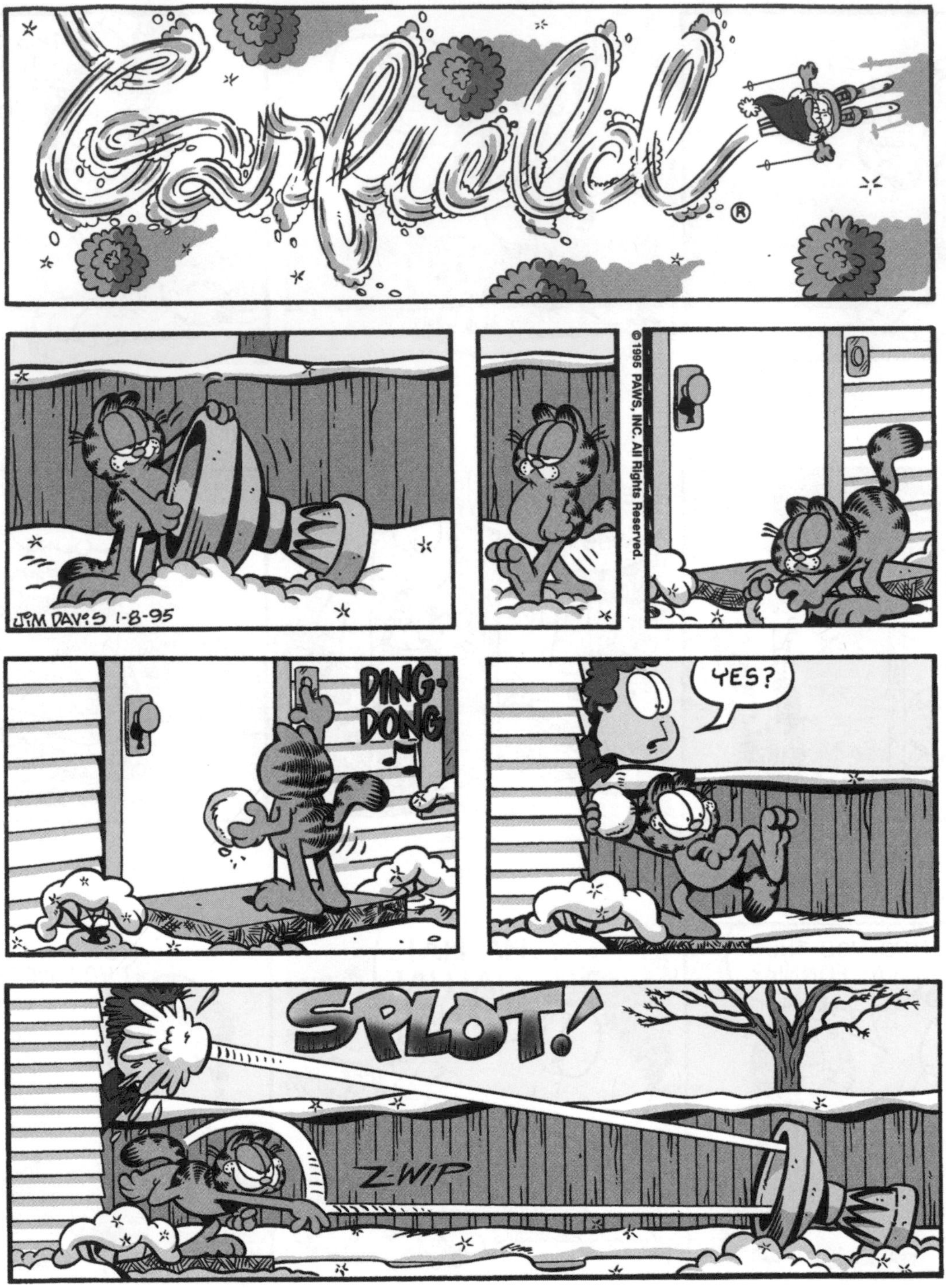
Garfield®
JIM DAVIS 1-8-95
© 1995 PAWS, INC. All Rights Reserved.
DING-DONG
YES?
SPLOT!
Z-WIP

FOUND A SPIDER IN THE FREEZER
© 1995 PAWS, INC. All Rights Reserved.
JIM DAVIS 1-9

SPIDER RACE!
© 1994 PAWS, INC. All Rights Reserved.
WHAP!
THE WINNER!
JIM DAVIS 1-10

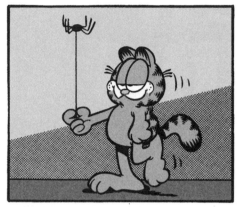

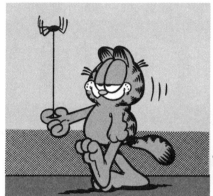

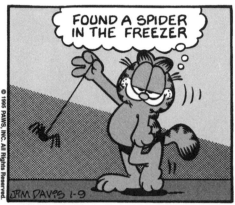

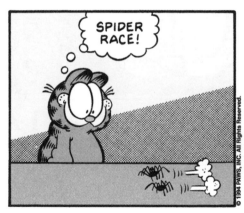

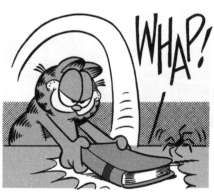

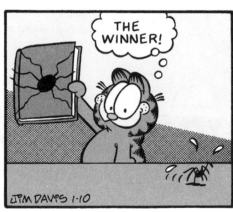

CAT BUMPER STICKERS

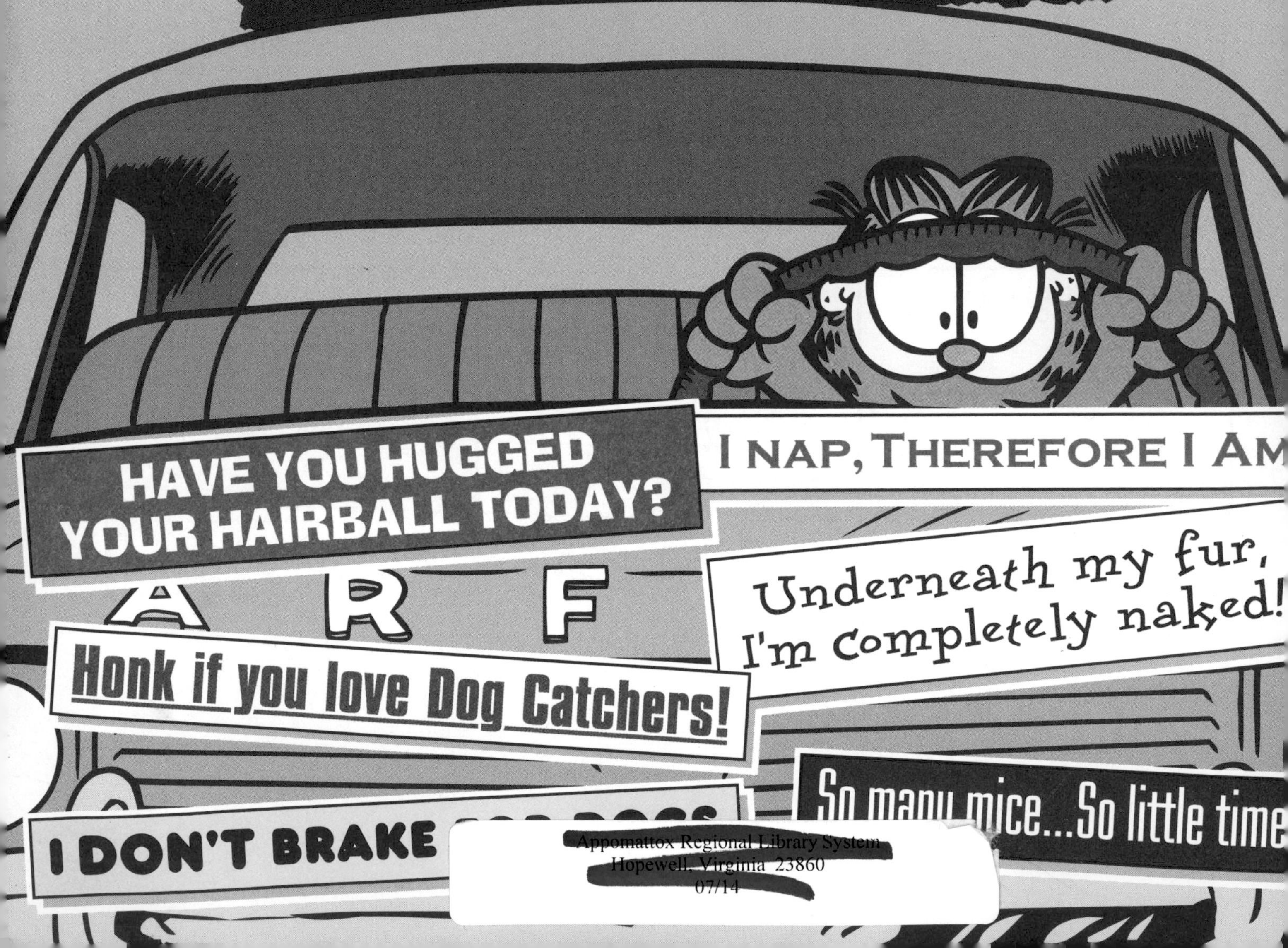
HAVE YOU HUGGED YOUR HAIRBALL TODAY?
I NAP, THEREFORE I AM
A R F
Underneath my fur, I'm completely naked!
Honk if you love Dog Catchers!
So many mice...So little time
I DON'T BRAKE